The Politics of Parliamentary Reform

The Contributors

Tony Burkett
Barbra Evans
Bruce George
David Judge
Michael Keating
Philip Norton
Michael Rush
Malcolm Shaw
Donald Shell
S.A. Walkland

The Politics of
Parliamentary Reform

Edited by DAVID JUDGE

Rutherford · Madison · Teaneck
Fairleigh Dickinson University Press

First American edition 1984

Associated University Presses
440 Forsgate Drive
Cranbury, New Jersey 08512

Library of Congress Cataloging in Publication Data

Main entry under title:
The Politics of parliamentary reform.

   Bibliography: p.
   Includes index.
   1. Great Britain. Parliament—Reform—History—
Addresses, essays, lectures. 2. Legislative bodies—
Reform—Addresses, essays, lectures. I. Judge, David.
JN521.P64   1984   328.41′09   83-25378
ISBN 0-8386-3221-1

Printed and bound in Great Britain by
Biddles Ltd, Guildford and King's Lynn

Contents

Preface

How does a book such as this come to be written? Critics may wish to add a few exclamation marks to the end of this question; but for those readers who seek merely to discover the mechanics of the production process it is as follows. The editor believes that there are notable gaps in the literature on parliamentary reform. First, although there is no shortage of reformist works there is a marked absence of discussion and analysis of the various reformist schemes. Advocates of reform tend to present their respective schemes as being self-evidently correct and feel little need therefore to engage each other in debate or to examine their own political assumptions and preconceptions. Second, reformist writing in Britain is characterised by its isolationism inasmuch as little attention is paid to the common problems and reformist schemes encountered in other legislatures. When comparison is made it is often inappropriate in that it fails to specify the different political, economic and social contexts of those legislatures under scrutiny. Third, even many 'monofocal' analyses of the British Parliament, in their concentration upon internal procedural reform, neglect the wider political, economic and social context of parliamentary reform.

This volume is designed to rectify some of these characteristic deficiencies. In particular it seeks to stimulate a more wide ranging debate on reform. To this end chapter 1 emphasises the wider determinants of parliamentary change. More importantly, the remaining chapters in Part One reflect the major strands of reformist thought in Britain. Each advocate of reform has been asked to outline his/her conception of the role and purposes of Parliament and to explain how their own therapeutic proposals would strengthen this role. Furthermore, to overcome the ethnocentrism of most British parliamentary studies, the contributors to the second part of this book have been asked to draw upon the experience of reform in three discrete legislative systems in order to detail the lessons, if any, comparative developments hold for the British discussion of reform. If there is a weakness in the overall conception and structure of the book then the fault is the editor's alone. If, however, there is a weakness in any particular chapter then the responsibility rests with the individual author. Correspondingly, praise can also be apportioned accordingly.

At the heart of this book there is disagreement, both about the nature of Parliament and the remedies for parliamentary malaise. There is however a unity which binds all of the contributors and this is the recognition that some action needs to be taken to rejuvenate Parliament. But this unity does not extend to agreement as to *what* needs to be done. The concluding chapter of this book reflects this disagreement and in turn generates further disagreement as all of the contributors would have welcomed the right to reply to the criticisms made therein. In this respect one of the objectives of this book has already been achieved in the prompting of a new phase in the discussion of reform. Each contributor wishes to clarify, elaborate and defend their own schemes in the light of the comments made in chapter 10. It remains to be seen whether this discussion takes place in or out of the law courts! But at least the debate has started.

Without the enthusiasm, commitment and diligence of the contributors this book could not have been produced. Throughout, they have revealed amazing fortitude, resilience and good humour. Moreover, they are still on speaking terms with each other and, more surprisingly, with the editor.

Without the comments of Hugh Berrington and John Foster, and those of the other contributors, chapter 1 would be even more flawed than it is. Hugh Berrington valiantly struggled through a very long early draft despite his lack of sympathy with its analytical approach; John Foster read successive drafts and offered constructive criticism and encouragement. David Judge hereby records his thanks.

Thanks are also due, once again, to Margaret Bright for her sterling secretarial skills. As a veritable human word processor she has typed and retyped successive drafts of the manuscript without complaint. She too is still speaking to the editor.

One person who is unsure if it is worth speaking to the editor is his wife, Lorraine. After yet another protracted period when her husband joined that strange academic trappist order, with its vows of silence and solitary confinement in the 'study', she may welcome his public declaration, here, of his willingness to re-enter negotiations upon the decoration of the front room.

David Judge
Lochwinnoch
June 1983

Contributors

(*In order of contribution*)
David Judge is a Lecturer in Politics, Paisley College. He is author of *Backbench Specialisation in the House of Commons*, and articles in *Public Administration*, *Parliamentary Affairs* and *Public Administration Bulletin*, etc.

S.A Walkland is holder of a Personal Chair in the Department of Political Theory and Institutions, University of Sheffield. He is author of *The Legislative Process in Great Britain*; and editor, joint-editor or contributor to numerous books including *The House of Commons in the 20th Century*, *Parliament and Economic Affairs*, *The Commons Today*. He is ex-chairman and founder-member of the Study of Parliament Group; vice-chairman of the Committee of Co-operation for European Parliamentary Studies.

Philip Norton is Senior Lecturer in Politics, University of Hull. He is author of *The Constitution in Flux*, *The Commons in Perspective*, *Dissension in the House of Commons 1974–9*, *Conservative Dissidents*, *Dissension in the House of Commons 1945–74*; and co-author of *Conservatives and Conservatism*; a contributor to *The House of Commons in the 20th Century*, and *Liberal Party Politics*. He has published articles in *Public Law*, *Parliamentary Affairs*, *The Parliamentarian*, *Legislative Studies Quarterly*, etc.

Bruce George MP (Member for Walsall, South) was formerly Senior Lecturer in Politics, Birmingham Polytechnic. He is a member of the Select Committee on Defence; presenter of numerous academic papers to international political science conferences and co-author of articles in *International Security Review*.

Barbra Evans is a radio journalist with Mercia Sound, and was a Parliamentary Assistant whilst a postgraduate student at Newcastle University. She was also research assistant for Bruce George MP.

Donald R. Shell is a Lecturer in Politics, University of Bristol. He is author of a number of articles, most particularly the regular contributions on the developments in the British Constitution in *Parliamentary Affairs*.

Michael Keating is Lecturer in Administration, University of Strathclyde. He is co-author of *Labour and Scottish Nationalism, The Government of Scotland*, and co-editor of *Regional Government in England*; and author of articles in *Local Government Studies, Public Administration, Legislative Studies Quarterly, Government and Opposition, Journal of Area Studies, Australian Journal of Politics and History*, etc.

Malcolm Shaw is Head of the Politics Department, University of Exeter. He is author of *Anglo-American Democracy*, co-author of *The House of Commons: Services and Facilities* and co-editor of *Committees in Legislatures*. Author of articles in *Parliamentary Affairs*, etc.

Michael Rush is Senior Lecturer in Politics, University of Exeter. He is author of *The Selection of Parliamentary Candidates, Parliament and the Public, Parliamentary Government in Britain* and co-author of *The Member of Parliament and his Information, An Introduction to Political Sociology* and *The House of Commons: Services and Facilities*. He is a contributor to the *House of Commons in the 20th Century, The Commons Today*, and *Committees in Legislatures*. Author of articles in *Parliamentary Affairs, The Parliamentarian, Journal of Commonwealth and Comparative Politics*, etc.

Tony Burkett is Head of the Department of European Studies, University of Loughborough. He is author of *Parties and Elections in West Germany*, a contributor to *Political Parties in the European Community*. Author of articles in *Parliamentary Affairs, New Europe, The Parliamentarian, Zeitschrift fur Parlamentsfragen*, etc.

Introduction

David Judge

Knowing what is wrong with Parliament is the key to its reform. On such profound statements as this are academic reputations built! Yet hidden within this simple statement is the full complexity of the issue of parliamentary reform; for there is little agreement on what, if anything, is wrong with Parliament, let alone what, if anything, can be done about it. Even when there is agreement both that something is wrong and that there is a common root cause for this malaise the chances are that there will still be disagreement about why this is the case and what is to be done about it. Consensus is not a marked feature of the debate on parliamentary reform.

There is nothing new about criticism of Parliament nor of demands for its reform. Indeed, calls for the reform of the British Parliament are as old as Parliament itself. Since its establishment in the 13th century few epochs have passed when this institution has not been attacked for its failure to meet the needs and aspirations of its people. Dissatisfaction appears to be endemic within the parliamentary condition. Thus, almost by definition, a book dealing with parliamentary reform can hardly claim to be novel. The mainstays of the reformist agenda – electoral reform, committee organisation, devolution, the upper chamber and the assertion of backbench independence – are indeed featured in Part One of this book. But where this work breaks new ground is in the critical examination of these schemes of reform. The advocates of particular reforms have been asked to consider the merits and demerits of the other reformist proposals. For too long reformers have talked past each other, rarely engaging each other in debate, rarely questioning the political premises of contending proposals and, in return, rarely being called upon to explain and justify their own assumptions about the role and performance of parliamentary institutions. Only when advocacy so blatantly outruns academic analysis, as with schemes for specialised committees in the 1960s, does a lively debate ensue. The collective professorial naïvety of Crick, Mackintosh,

Hanson and Wiseman has become an easy analytical target for successive generations of reformers. But as a general rule all reformist schemas – and those represented in this book are no exception – subordinate analysis to advocacy. Simple solutions, of necessity, require partial understandings of the parliamentary process for their credibility. This partiality takes the form of being 'partisan' or 'incomplete' and usually the two together.

One obvious way in which British analysis of parliamentary government is traditionally 'incomplete' is in the absence of cross-national comparison of legislatures. British students of Parliament remain rigidly xenophobic. In an era when there is widespread concern over the 'decline', 'disorder' and 'crisis' of most western legislatures it is surprising that relatively few academics or parliamentarians have looked beyond the shores of Britain for elucidation upon common legislative problems and remedies. Even when comparisons are made the tendency is either to overstate or to underplay the systemic differences between national assemblies. On the one side, the advocates of particular reforms tend to play down social and political environmental differences in support of their judicious choice of comparison. On the other side, their opponents normally point to the uniqueness of each legislature and deny the usefulness of such comparisons. Yet this latter contention can easily be stood on its head to argue that an understanding of the different political contexts within which legislatures operate helps to explain divergent structures and the varying implementation of reform. The differential dynamic of reform in diverse national settings can be revealed through examination of such political variables as the nature of executive-legislative relations; party competition; state interventions; and periphery-centre relations. If for no other reason such analysis is of importance in highlighting the simple, but frequently neglected, point that the process of reform has to be set within the political and social networks within which legislatures operate. The second part of this book therefore is of significance for its examination of the dynamic of reform in three major legislative systems: the congressional system of the United States, and the diverse parliamentary systems of Canada and West Germany. Why these three systems were selected will be explained on page 128. In the meantime, the value of comparative study is affirmed here in defiance of the isolationism of most British analyses of reform.

These bold words lead on to still bolder statements; for another way in which British parliamentary analysis is 'partial' is that the conception of the parliamentary process is itself 'biased' or 'partisan'. Now this is not to besmirch the integrity of the advocates of reform generally, nor specifically those whose views are presented in Part One. Instead, it is simply to make the point that *all* schemes of reform have implicit within them a specific conception of Parliament and its role within the wider political, economic and social systems. The ideological perspective adopted by a reformer will determine his/her view of Parliament and in turn colour proposals for reform. In this sense all reformist schemes are 'biased'.

The orthodoxy of 'liberal-democratic' analysis provides no exception to this stipulation. Its prevailing view of an essentially parliamentary-centric political system has dominated British academic study and has been adopted by liberals, conservatives and social democrats alike. In this system a sovereign Parliament (albeit with a dominant executive therein) has the formal competence to regulate society and the economy. Parliament is supreme within the state. A state moreover which is viewed as a neutral, autonomous complex of institutions which does not encompass the whole of social existence. Whilst society and the economy have some independent existence they are capable, never-theless, of being guided and moulded by the superordinate state. In fact, given this interlinkage, and given Parliament's claim to sovereignty, the legislature can hardly escape responsibility for economic and social policy failures. But the exact degree of parliamentary culpability for these wider failures is an issue which divides liberal-democratic analysts. One group hold that Parliament has been trapped by the constitutional precept of parliamentary sovereignty into accepting responsiblity for economic and social dislocations beyond its control. By implication therefore parliamentary reform in itself would have but a limited effect upon such disorders. Another group however trace the root causes of Britain's economic and social malaise back to the shortcomings of the parliamentary system. For them the key to successful economic and societal rejuvenation is to be found in the reform of Parliament.

With either group, nonetheless, the search for parliamentary re-invigoration invariably starts, and in many instances finishes, within the House of Commons. When the other two partners in the consti-tutional triumvirate of the 'Queen in Parliament' – the monarchy and the House of Lords – are considered, their roles are normally related directly to the House of Commons as the dominant partner. Hence, the focus of Donald Shell's chapter in this book on the House of Lords is on the relationship between the two chambers.

As parliamentary reform has come essentially to mean reform of the House of Commons it is incumbent upon reformers to clearly specify their conceptions of this chamber. Often, however, there is a reticence to state explicitly whether they see the House as a corporate representative whole, or divided along party lines into government and opposition, or split further by legislative function into ministers and backbenchers. Such reluctance in the past to make these statements has led to procedural changes suited only for a corporate body being pressed, ineffectually, within a bifurcated House. Yet the manifest reality of the modern House of Commons is that it is internally divided by the mutually reinforcing fissures of party allegiances and tenure of executive office. In this respect Lord Hailsham's (1978) charge of 'elective dictatorship' is not wide of the mark. It is undeniable that the centre of gravity has moved decisively towards the government side of the House given the cohesion and strength of party. Moreover, on that side power has been clasped into the hands of the government itself. Recognition of this single fact has prompted a wide-ranging search for the catalyst to break this 'dictatorship'. Although the point of departure is the same the routes followed and the destinations arrived at in this search have been many and varied. That this should be so is a reflection of the diversity of views on the purposes of parliamentary government as well as the different modes of political analysis utilised by reformers.

Underpinning many modern schemes of reform is a functional analysis of the House of Commons. Drawing upon the framework provided by Walter Bagehot (1867) many reformers take his catalogue of functions as a shibbolith of parliamentary study. Many, indeed, concur with Bernard Crick's (1970: 33) opinion that for a conceptual framework there is little need to go beyond Bagehot's own work. In so doing there has been a tendency to list and relist his original catalogue of the elective, expressive, teaching, informing and legislating functions in order to chronicle the Commons' diminished effectiveness in the performance of these tasks since the middle of the 19th century. Few reformers have bothered to ask whether in the political circumstances of the 20th century (see Johnson 1977: 44–5) this exercise has become vacuous. To understand Bagehot's predisposition towards limited government, including the limitation of executive actions by the Commons, then the limited scope of governmental activity, the consensual nature of the parliamentary elite and the weakness of party allegiances at the time need to be borne in mind. To say therefore that the function of the House is to control the government requires in itself some understanding of the political environment within which that government operates. Nonetheless, just as Crick believed that there was little need to look beyond Bagehot so many advocates of reform now believe that there is little need to look beyond Crick. Hence, Bruce George and Barbra Evans in chapter 4 draw upon the Crickian tradition to advance the case for more detailed and professional parliamentary control of the executive through the entrenchment and development of recent procedural and structural changes within the Commons. Their focus is upon internal reform, and particularly the creation of a committee system capable of ensuring greater scrutiny of the executive and publicity of its actions to the wider electorate. Through greater parliamentary control they hope to see a revitalisation of the role of backbenchers within the House as well as the reforging of popular consent for parliamentary, and hence, governmental actions. Yet there is a recognition by George and Evans that procedural reform alone is insufficient to secure enhanced parliamentary power. What is required also is an attitudinal change on the part of most backbenchers towards the performance of their legislative duties. On this point there is concord (one of the few within this book!) between George and Evans and the views expressed by Philip Norton in chapter 3.

Norton's objective is to enhance consent for the political system without undermining the effectiveness of government. The conundrum he sets himself is situated firmly within the functional tradition of parliamentary analysis, namely, how the Commons can perform its ascribed collective functions in an era of active and dominant government. His answer is a reformulation of Crick's (1968) notion that strong government requires strong opposition. Unlike Crick, however, he maintains that increased parliamentary scrutiny and influence has to be developed within the context of party. Thus, whereas Crick (1968: 80) argued that the phrase 'parliamentary control' 'should not mislead anyone into asking for a situation in which governments can have their legislation changed or defeated', Norton advances the reverse proposition. The shift in executive-legislative relations, he believes, will result from the sanction of the defeat of the government in the division lobbies. Indeed, Norton proceeds to argue that a failure of backbench 'will' and an unwillingness to use this sanction has obscured the potential of parliamentary structures to secure sustained scrutiny and influence over the executive. The prerequisite for successful parliamentary reform for Norton is attitudinal change on the part of MPs within Westminster.

The functional analysis and internal perspective of chapters 3 and 4 is counterpoised by Michael Keating in chapter 6. His 'territorial' analysis of parliamentary politics challenges the orthodoxy of functional analysis and leads him to seek the dynamic of reform not within Westminster but externally within the peripheral regions and nations of the United Kingdom. Keating's basic thesis is that the principle of parliamentary sovereignty and the myth of a unitary Parliament have distorted the play of territorial politics in the UK. This unitary structure has failed to recognise adequately the territorial differentiation and the diverse problems generated within the peripheral areas of the UK. Bluntly stated, Westminster ill-serves its regions and nations. From this attack on the failure of Parliament stems the proposals that elected assemblies for these nations and regions, and for the European Communities (while-ever the UK is a member), are essential for securing better government. Importantly, Keating realises that such changes will not be brought about by consensual and academic debate: when change comes it will be brought about by political action within the periphery.

Stuart Walkland also starts his search for parliamentary revitalisation beyond the precincts of Westminster. He looks to the party system for the redress of the imbalance between the government and the House, and sees a transformation of party relationships as a precondition for successful procedural reform within the Commons. The political foundations of 'elective dictatorship' – the dysfunctions of the party system and the institutionalisation of adversary conflict in the House – thus have to be undermined. Fundamental political reorientation in Britain, rather than mere institutional tinkering, is the key to the reassertion of *parliamentary* government. Electoral reform is therefore proposed by Walkland to re-establish parliamentary control and, more generally, to reforge the legitimacy of the parliamentary system itself. The effects of this reform are expected to extend beyond the political sphere into the economic and social realms themselves; for, in Walkland's opinion, past political failures have contributed significantly to Britain's economic and social malaise. Thus, far from being peripheral to the problems of the economy, the inability of parliamentary government in Britain to ensure policy continuity and legitimisation of the economic process has been of crucial importance. Political change is the precursor of economic and social change. In this respect Walkland's contribution is clearly within the 'liberal' tradition of parliamentary study, though some might argue that this tradition has been remoulded into a still more 'partisan' perspective.

Indeed, it is but a short step from Walkland's analysis to the overtly partisan arguments of those Conservative and Liberal lawyers in Britain who favour the enactment of a new Bill of Rights. Although these arguments are considered only tangentially in this book it is useful to consider their political premises here. In particular the case advanced by Lord Hailsham (1976) is worthy of examination for its transparent ideological and 'partisan' preconceptions of the legitimate role of Parliament.

'Elective dictatorship' is the point of departure for Hailsham's argument. His fear is that the very supremacy of Parliament, or more accurately government, and its persistent introduction of collectivist legislation, is now a challenge to the individualistic capitalist society. His avowed aim therefore is the reversal of the contemporary trend of British government towards greater state intervention. In the pursuit of this objective Hailsham's argument rapidly intertwines his general political predisposition towards limited government with his partisan predisposition against the Labour party. In particular, he states that the activities of Labour governments, in their attempts to extend public ownership in industry and public welfare provision, have infringed not only the rights of individual citizens but also have generated national economic crises. His fear is that future Labour governments will cause even greater social and economic dislocation in their drive towards a socialist state. This fear has been heightened as his earlier hope of the 1950s, that the Labour party under Hugh Gaitskell would become an 'electoral party' rinsed of its socialist ideology and competing with the Conservatives on the centre ground of consensus politics, was smashed in the 1970s as the party headed 'more and more irrevocably down the dark alleyways of irreversible and revolutionary change based on its original ideological commitment and class war' (Hailsham 1978: 19). By Hailsham's logic, if the Labour party was beyond redemption, and if its internal resolution for socialist change was strengthening, then attention had to be redirected away from the party itself towards the constitutional instruments which would enable that strength to be realised. 'Elective dictatorship' might have been acceptable when it was 'benign' and offered unquestioning succour to the established capitalist order but it was patently unacceptable by the late 1970s under the 'malevolent' direction of Labour governments. In which case the very power entrusted to the executive in Parliament now called for the need of citizens 'to be protected from our representatives no less than from our former masters' (Hailsham 1978: 13). A Bill of Rights would thus provide this protection by prescribing limits beyond which government and Parliament must not go, and by providing legal means of redress to compel executives to observe these limits. The theory of limited government, for Lord Hailsham, should thus be institutionalised in a written constitution.

Similar linkages between 'partisan' and ideological precepts and the advocacy of parliamentary reform can just as easily be cited (and will be, see pp. 192–5) on the left of the British political spectrum (see Benn 1980, 1982a). However, the point has already been made sufficiently in this introduction that all reform proposals have implicit within them ideas, not necessarily party political ones, about the structure and meaning of parliamentary government within the wider state system. Indeed, it is these different conceptions which give rise to the diversity of therapeutic proposals for Parliament. As the title of this book acknowledges 'politics' cannot be abstracted from the consideration of parliamentary reform.

However, before unleashing the proponents of reform to advance their respective cases (in Part One) and before chronicling the areas of dispute and disagreement amongst them (in chapter 10) there is another political dimension of reform to be considered. If this book is essentially concerned with the question of 'why, and what type of reform, is needed?' then it is worth considering, in preface, the related question of 'when and under what conditions is reform enacted?'. As the history of parliamentary reform reveals it is one thing to argue that reform is necessary but it is another matter to see that change is implemented. The first chapter of this book therefore traces the enactment of parliamentary reforms since 1832 and highlights the political determinants of reform. It is not written by a trained historian, as historians may find painfully evident, neither is it meant to be an authoritative historical tract. Instead, as with the other chapters in Part One, it is concerned to illuminate the purposes and nature of parliamentary government and is consciously written so as to be 'partial', 'incomplete' and disputatious. Its 'neo-Marxist' framework is one more challenge to the orthodoxy of British parliamentary analysis; in that sense it is not accepted by the other contributors, nor is it meant to guide their own contributions to this book. Indeed, so established is the 'liberal-democratic' orthodoxy within British academic study of Parliament that the inclusion of a 'neo-Marxist' perspective at all will undoubtedly be questioned by traditionalist students. But as a legitimate contribution to the debate on parliamentary government it is included. Moreover, given the unorthodoxy (some would say heresy) of its inclusion the editor has decided to get his 'retaliation in first' in the discussion to come. So let the debate begin.

PART ONE   The Why and How of Reform in Britain

1   Why Reform? Parliamentary Reform Since 1832: An Interpretation
David Judge

The history of parliamentary reform is littered with good intentions left unfulfilled, democratic arguments conceded on undemocratic grounds and undemocratic practices justified by recourse to democratic principles. In examining the apparent capriciousness of reform therefore the important questions to raise are: why is it that 'arguments which are pressed ineffectually at one moment become politically viable the next?' (Canon 1972: xiii), and under what conditions are specific reforms enacted? The purpose of this chapter is to provide some answers. However, anyone looking for simple answers should stop reading now. In particular, those traditionalist scholars who are accustomed to analysing Parliament in splendid institutional isolation might care to skip this chapter. Though they, more than anyone else, need to consider its argument that only when parliamentary institutions are fitted into their economic and social setting; and, moreover, only when the complex interrelationships between changes in the economy, its attendant society and the form of the state are analysed, can the questions above be fully addressed. In short, the contention of this chapter is that the crux of parliamentary reform in any era is the politics of the state.

In linking the fortunes of Parliament to those of the state in this manner, then how Parliament and the prospects for its rejuvenation are seen will be related directly to how the state itself is conceptualised. Indeed, as it was noted in the Introduction to this book, the orthodox view within most British parliamentary studies is of a parliamentary-centric state which is autonomous of the economy and society. A sovereign Parliament, albeit with a dominant executive therein, has the formal capacity to regulate these latter spheres. And, even though there are sharp disagreements amongst liberals, conservatives and social democrats as to how much state intervention in the economy and society is either desirable or permissable, they all assume, nevertheless, that the level of state involvement is ultimately a matter of political choice. However, whereas 'liberal-democratic' analyses see the state as having some independent existence of society and the economy, the premise of this chapter is that the British state, and hence the role of Parliament, can best be understood by reference to the nature of the economic process of production and the social relationships founded thereupon. In this way the reform of Parliament becomes inextricably linked to the development of the capitalist state and its attempts to regulate the heterogeneous relationships of the market economy and society.

If this sounds Marxist then it does so because it is meant to be. Having said that, however, it should be made clear from the outset that it is not part of the following discussion to argue that the capitalist state is a simple tool or instrument of the ruling class whose executive acts as 'a committee for managing the common affairs of the whole bourgeoisie' (Marx and Engels 1848: 82). Nor is it argued here that the 'real essence of bourgeois parliamentarianism [is] to decide once every five years which member of the ruling class is to repress and crush its people through parliament' (Lenin 1917: 46). Nor for that matter does this chapter depend for its argument upon the fruitful, but less than convincing, theories offered by such modern Marxists as Nicos Poulantzas (1968; 1975; 1976), Ian Gough (1979) and Ralph Miliband (1969; 1977; 1982).

So what is left after this distancing from the mainstreams of Marxist thought? What remains is the need to clarify exactly how the form of the state and Parliament are structured by, and linked to, the nature of the economic mode of production and its attendant society. For this purpose the recent work of John Urry (1981), which is grounded in the Marxist tradition but which extends beyond, and ultimately challenges, Marxist fundamentalism is utilised here. At best Marxist critics would claim such an approach is 'neo-Marxist' and at worst simply constitutes a form of 'bounded pluralism'. Nonetheless, its value for present purposes is that it provides a plausible explanation of the interconnections between the state's form (particularly the nature of parliamentarianism), capitalist relations of production and 'civil society'. In addition, Urry's analysis is also of importance because it does what so few British students of Parliament have been willing to do – it theorises the role of Parliament in the state system. This does not mean that his analysis is presented simply out of devilment – to rub the noses of practical politicians and the academic chroniclers of parliamentary practice in abstruse theory – far from it. Urry's analysis is used here to provide a coherent framework within which to structure the historical analysis of parliamentary reform in Britain.

The starting point of Urry's theory as outlined in *The Anatomy of Capitalist Societies* (1981) is an acceptance that the capitalist state 'possesses a form which is given by its attempt to sustain the overall conditions under which profitable accumulation can take place' (1981: 101). This 'derivation' is immediately limited however in the acknowledgement that the state also 'embodies a set of social relations which are distinct from the process of production itself'. Interposed between the realm of production and the state are the heterogeneous relations which comprise civil society. Hence, the key to understanding and theorising the capitalist state rests, for Urry, in the recognition that this state, in its attempt to guarantee profitable private accumulation has 'to organise, legislate and orchestrate the diverse relations of civil society'.

The existence of civil society is itself based upon two spheres of activity: those of 'circulation' and of 'production'. The sphere of circulation is one of individual exchange founded on freedom and equality and is required so that commodities, particularly labour-power, can be bought and sold. Yet the monetary return on land or capital is only generated with the extraction of surplus-value in the sphere of production. At this level capitalism is a social relation – an antagonistic relationship between capital and wage-labour (1981: 36–7). But, whilst this fundamental antagonism exists, its actual form is 'profoundly structured by the centrality to the relationship of the commodity of labour-power' (1981: 118). Or in plain English, both capital and labour have an interest in the continuance of labour-power. Workers obviously have an interest in maintaining their capacity to work, but so too does 'capital-in-general' in ensuring that sufficient quantities of workers with the requisite skills are available. Yet, given the anarchic nature of capitalism, labourers still have to struggle to defend their material conditions of life. Hence the paradox of capitalist production is that the class struggle generated by this process 'is essential for the reproduction of labour-power without which capitalist production cannot continue' (1981: 113).

Unlike Marxist fundamentalists, however, Urry does not believe that there are 'pure classes determined economically'. Classes only exist within *civil society*. Whilst the dominant relationship remains that within the economy – between capital and wage-labour – he conceives of other forms of struggle which are not directly structured by the social relations of capitalist production. In addition to class struggle Urry, therefore, incorporates 'classes in struggle' and 'popular democratic struggle' into civil society.

'Classes in struggle' still have a common relationship to the means of production but this relationship does not lead to antagonism with other social classes, for example the so-called 'new' middle class. 'Popular democratic struggle' on the other hand involves the organisation of ' "the people" based on non-class forms of interpellation, of gender, generation, race, region and nation' (1981: 67). Indeed, class struggle itself takes place within the organisation of 'the people' in an 'already structured civil society' (1981: 67). Civil society is thus the sphere of struggle not only of antagonistic social classes but also of other social groupings (see also Jessop 1982: 247–252).

At its simplest Urry's contention is that a particular form of the state is the product of the relationship between the economy and civil society: 'the former sets its demands, the latter provides the context within which it struggles to resolve them' (1981: 123). Thus the relative significance of the sphere of circulation *vis-à-vis* that of production in the economy affects the nature of 'struggle' in civil society and this in turn is of crucial importance in the determination of the state. Indeed, the concept of struggle as utilised by Urry provides an answer to the paradox of why there is widespread working class commitment to representative democracy and social reformism in a state which seeks to guarantee the exploitation of the labour-power of the bulk of the population. In Britain this commitment stems from the fact that the present form of parliamentarianism is in a real sense the result of popular struggles to 'enlarge, strengthen and democratise the state against capital' (1981: 145). Parliamentary democracy is not therefore merely illusory, nor simply a *bourgeois* system of government, nor a reflection of some dominant ideology. This point is of particular importance in the study of the extensions of the franchise (see pp. 14–18) as it removes the necessity of arguing that this process represented a fundamental adaptation of the political system by an omniscient ruling class. Moreover, Urry is able to argue (against Jessop most particularly: see Jessop 1978) that, precisely because of the developments in the accumulation process, it is increasingly the case (to use Lenin's dictum) that democracy is the best political shell for capitalism. This is so, not because of the illusory power of Parliament as specified by Lenin, but rather the reverse: because parliamentary democracy actually allows the representatives of labour, and other popular social forces, significant influence over the form and nature of the state and its policies. In this sense the state is no longer conceived as an instrument of a single class, but instead now reflects the interests of a variety of classes and social groupings. Moreover, in an increasingly diversified and resilient civil society 'class and popular elements within it have no way of controlling and moderating capitalist relations except through the state, since it is *the* alternative to capital' (1981: 153).

The corollary of developments within civil society is, therefore, an enlarged, bureaucratised and strengthened state required to cope with the demands for the greater regulation of the economy and provision of welfare services. But this does not imply that the state can be used by the working class to overturn the capitalist mode of production. First, because the proletariat has an 'irredeemable interest in the structuring of "its" capital' (1981: 151) and, second, because all reforms and changes produced by popular pressure 'are transmuted into something less acceptable to those popular forces' (1981: 147). By the same argument, even though the capitalist state is able to change the substance of popular demands, still it is unable to satisfy fully the demands of capitalists. The end result of state intervention is thus unintended by any major social element.

Naturally, Urry's analysis does have its defects, not the least of which is the failure to explain how the process of systematic transmutation operates in practice. Moreover, in his sophisticated analysis much of Marxist orthodoxy is discarded, including the notions that social class has some essential economic character and that a single bourgeois class is both politically and ideologically dominant. Instead, state policies and their outcomes are the product of a variety of social forces. 'No one class or social force is able to implement exactly what it wants' (1981: 122) yet these forces operate within, and indeed the state's form is given by, the 'constraints of action' of the existing form of capital accumulation.

Parliamentary Reform since 1832

Urry's analysis is of value for the study of parliamentary reform in that it provides an explanation of the development of representative democracy in Britain which links the form of the state to the overall conditions of capital accumulation, but which does not entail the automatic reaction of the former to the latter nor the dominance of the state by a single unified capitalist class. Moreover, the paradox of capitalism is clearly identified in that labour is forced to organise and defend its position to stay alive, yet through the process of 'struggle' develops a direct interest in maintaining 'its' capital. The ground upon which this fight is conducted increasingly becomes the state itself as labour seeks to control capital (and vice-versa) through state institutions, laws and apparatuses. Ultimately, however, neither labour nor capital is satisfied by the state's outputs as these cannot eliminate the contradictions of capitalism. The problem remains that the state both seeks to moderate conflict yet is itself simultaneously split by the very same conflict. A constant dynamic for change, for the restructuring of the state and its democratic institutions, is thus generated out of this changing balance of class and popular forces. But change does not come automatically. Reform, in this case parliamentary reform, has to be fought for and when conceded is a reflection of the unsteady balance of class and social forces at that time. Nowhere is this point better illustrated than in the case of electoral reform throughout the last century.

Electoral Reform

If the dynamic of parliamentary reform derives from the complex development and interconnection of the economy, civil society and the state, then without unnecessarily looking for complications, it is as well at the outset to dispose of some of the simplest, and often beguiling, explanations of the extension of the franchise. Out goes, therefore, C.B. Macpherson's (1966: 9) contention that there was an inherent logic within liberalism leading to equal political (via voting) rights. Indeed, by his own admission Macpherson recognises both that major 19th century liberal theorists were only too willing to compromise democratic rights in defence of property rights (1977) and also that the working class had to fight for the franchise (1966). Similarly, some of the cruder Marxist explanations of this process are unconvincing. In particular, the idea that electoral reform was somehow functional to the requirements of capitalism and was granted therefore by an intelligent, unified ruling class cannot explain the manifest divisions within the dominant classes, nor account for the protracted popular agitation required to secure the franchise. At the same time working class struggle, though important, should not be taken as the single explanatory variable; as with the other factors it is but one element within a complex equation. Hence, a satisfactory explanation of franchise reform needs to take into consideration a multiplex of variables including: the historical legacy of the 17th century; the potency of industrialisation and its impact upon British society – in the need to incorporate new industrial wealth within existing qualifications for political rights; working class agitation; and the fragmentation of the established governing classes.

The first stage in the extension of the franchise was, of course, the 1832 Reform Act. From the perspective of the 1980s this piece of legislation, like the commemorative plinth of any great battle, appears but a tiny mark on the landscape of history. As with any past battle the plinth remains observable but it is the ground around it that saw the action. Indeed, the political ground of importance to the understanding of the 1832 Act stretches back to the 17th century – to the civil war and the settlement of 1688. This period witnessed the construction of the frame within which the Act could be conceived and implemented. For 1688 heralded a balanced constitution where the power of the monarch was delimited and shared with the titled aristocracy in the Lords and a landed gentry of 'rural capitalists' (Moore 1966: 19–24) in the Commons. The assertion of Parliament in the political sphere in turn mirrored the overturn of the economic principle of production for use by the principle of individual profit accumulated through the market mechanism. 'The most important long-term result of the English civil war', as Gamble (1981: 70) notes, was therefore a 'clear separation between the state and an independent sphere of private interests and exchange, and the subordination of the former to the latter'. The connection between the state and its policies, and the needs and movement of civil society was made in this creation of a parliamentary order founded upon, and responsible to, propertied interest. The important legacy of the 17th century was thus a strengthened and flexible representative assembly which reflected the interests of the dominant commercially-minded landed upper classes.

Within the political frame constructed in the 17th century the interests of property and wealth generated by the new industrial processes of the 19th century could eventually be accommodated. The new industrial bourgeoisie was able to build upon the extant capitalist order established by the landed and commercial bourgeoisie. And, equally importantly, the new propertied class was able to couch its social and political demands in the vocabulary of the prevailing order. The same language was thus spoken between landed, commercial and industrial capital – even if with different accents. Yet, when the developing proletariat sought to use the same vocabulary in their demands for representation within the parliamentary state, such words in their mouths sounded like a threat in the ears of the politically established bourgeoisie. Indeed, the inextricable connection between the new industrial classes (bourgeoisie and proletariat) meant that there could be no quiet conversation between the various forms of capital on the subject of franchise reform, as the landed aristocracy could always hear the murmur of the urban working class in the background. A fear of the 'noisy classes' was to remain a constant feature of the opposition to electoral reform. Consequently, the industrial bourgeoisie had to shout above, as well as occasionally in unison with, working class clamour for political reform (Hobsbawn 1968; Thompson 1968).

When, indeed, the Representation of the People Act was passed in 1832 the chorus of the propertyless was a significant contributory factor to the success of the industrial propertied classes in having their case heard. A central objective of the Act was precisely to disengage the propertied middle classes from an alliance with the lower class. The conservative nature of this measure (see Gash 1953: 88; Birch 1964: 52) demonstrates that it did not, and was not intended to, admit the expanding urban working class into the franchise. Thus, for all that working class unrest was of crucial importance in the period 1828–32 in galvanising the Whigs into action, it did not, in its incipient organisational form, constitute a fundamental threat to the established order – as long as middle class radical leadership could be wrested from the mass. Moreover, the crucial factor that gained the new middle classes admission into the parliamentary realm was their property; for through their property they became respectable in the eyes of the governing classes.

Yet, the 'problem' of the working class still remained after the 'shopocrat' franchise came into existence in 1832 (Thompson 1968: 909). The initial response of sections of the working class was to turn to syndicalist ideas and the creation of a 'parliament of the industrious classes' (Thompson 1968: 912–13). Such ideas were shortlived. Gradually, there was a general return (via the Chartist movement) to the focus of the franchise and the demand for a competitive place within the existing political order. Indeed, the open repression of Chartist agitation, and the rapid evaporation of the movement's political legacy, is of importance in showing the considerable limitations of mass action to impose reform upon a reluctant political order. Only when that order was willing to admit the working class into parliamentary competition on something more like its own terms was the franchise extended. This is not to deny that popular agitation was of significance in applying pressure to the turnstile of electoral reforms, but simply to recognise that admission through that gate was regulated ultimately by the governing classes. Selective admission was eventually gained as the working classes demonstrated their 'responsibility' in terms of acceptance of established propertied relationships and relative social quiescence. Thus when the franchise was next extended, in 1867, it came as one indication that 'the social peace and comparatively orderly behaviour of the working classes in [the preceding] years had demonstrated to the satisfaction of many of "their betters" that there was no danger and some advantage to be gained by including in the electorate a top skimming of the workers' (McCord 1967: 383). A more dramatic illustration of this point is provided by the 1918 Representation of the People Act, which finally conceded universal male suffrage and limited female suffrage. Voting rights for women came not as a direct result of the suffragette campaign of 1906–14 but through their economic 'emancipation' in the first world war (Hills 1981: 9–10). Indeed, the contribution of women (in munitions, transport and agriculture), along with that of unskilled working class males (as soldiers), to the war effort did much to convince parliamentarians of their 'responsibility' and of their integration into the economic and ideological system of capitalism (see Therborn 1977: 23; Close 1977: 898).

But proletarian deference to property and parliamentarianism was not in itself a sufficient condition for admission to the franchise. The momentum of electoral reform was increased, to return to the turnstile analogy, by the fact that several different feet, representing the different interests of various fractions of capital, pressed the control pedal at different times. At various stages throughout the 19th century sections of the capitalist class sought to ally themselves to sections of the new industrial and urban proletariat. Economic and political competition between the different fractions of capital therefore needs to be included in the explanatory equation of electoral reform. Even before 1832 splits within the landed aristocracy, and between landed and manufacturing interests, had become apparent over the issues of Ireland (Catholic Emancipation) and agricultural protectionism (Corn Laws). Parliamentary reform in the period 1827–32 served as a wedge to widen these fissures still further. Naturally, this internal disunity and competition came to be reflected in the parliamentary parties; so that in the promotion of parliamentary reform the Whigs not only had a genuine belief that the admission of the new industrial bourgeoisie into the franchise would restore the balance of the constitution (Gash 1953: 14–15; McCord 1967: 379), but also were aware of the party advantage to be gained (Cannon 1972: 243). Similarly, the Acts of 1867 and 1884 reflect a mixture of political motives – of a search for cross-class alliances by competing fractions of capital coupled with exigent drives for partisan and personal political advantage within the Commons.

In 1867, Disraeli, as head of the Conservative party, with little interest in reform as such, saw electoral reform as a means both to consolidate his own leading position within the party as well as to outdo his Liberal rivals (Blake 1966; Wright 1970; Therborn 1977; Norton and Aughey 1981). Moreover, there was an element of 'cold political calculation' (Wright 1970: 13) on the part of Gladstone in 1884 in his attempt to placate radical discontent with the performance of his government through the introduction of another franchise Bill. At a more fundamental level, however, these Acts reflected the competition within the capitalist class to secure working class support. Thus the 1867 Act can be seen to be an attempt to forge an alliance between skilled workers and the Conservative aristocratic base against commercial and industrial capital. Furthermore, the fear of just such an alliance galvanised those sections of industrial and commercial capital represented in the Liberal party, to 'concede' the 1884 Act in order to challenge further the aristocratic monopoly of power (Tholfsen 1973: 186) and to bind deferent and 'respectable' workers more closely into the parliamentary state. Both results were required if the interests of the working class were to be represented and contained within the bounds of parliamentary action and reformist legislation rather than extra-parliamentary agitation and industrial action.

The important point of this analytical sketch of the extension of the franchise is a simple one: that reform is not produced by the force of ideas alone. Developments within the economy and the changing balance of class forces within 19th century civil society are of crucial significance in explaining the pace of electoral reform. That this point should need to be made at all arises, however, from a tendency on the part of many British political scientists to sanitise the realm of ideas from considerations of political and eonomic power (see, for example, Birch 1964). Without denying that ideas do frame the manner in which discourse is conducted in any period, the argument here is that the outcome of such deliberation is essentially a reflection of the balance of economic and social forces within civil society. This is true not only in the case of electoral reform but also in other fields of parliamentary reform.

Procedural change and the emergence of a strong executive

> The historic order of business of the House of Commons was never affected, either as a whole or in its separate parts, by juristic speculation or political theory. Its origins and growth . . . sprang from practical wants, expressed the *actual facts of political power and of historic constitutional relations.*
>
> (Redlich 1908: xxix, added emphasis)

Writing in 1908 Redlich made a direct connection between political and social change and parliamentary reform which many present-day advocates of reform would do well to remember. In fact, Redlich should be mandatory reading for anyone seriously concerned with parliamentary reform. His linkage of internal procedural reform in the House with the wider development of the British state makes him of special relevance to the present study. He demonstrates, for example, how the procedural conservatism of the Commons between 1688 and the early 19th century was a reflection of the consensual and limited character of government in that period. At this time the constitutional concessions of the preceding era – the principles of legal opposition and the rights of the minority – became firmly entrenched in the House; as did a corporate spirit and corporate manners stemming from the internal cohesion of its members. Throughout the 18th century individual MPs, as part of a corporate representative whole of landed and commercial interests, promoted these interests persistently, if piecemeal, through the medium of private legislation. In this manner the infrastructure required for emergent industrialisation was effectively established through specific enactments dealing with individual land-enclosures, or the development of private transportation services or some limited service provision by a local authority. Legislative initiative was thus located firmly in the hands of the private member, whilst government and its 'public policies' was confined to external and defence matters, or taxation and administrative law at home. In this division between 'private' and 'public' legislation the 'despatch of business [in the Chamber] went on smoothly and easily' (Redlich 1908: 66).

However, the potent force of industrialisation, once unleashed in the 19th century, generated tensions and requirements which could no longer be resolved by individual and restricted legislative enactments. Instead, general and inclusive Acts of Parliament were necessary to deal with the plethora of social and economic demands thrown up in the wake of rapid industrial and urban development. As the 19th century progressed the paradox of the liberal state became ever more apparent as the state was required to intervene in those areas of economic and social life from which it was precluded by classical liberal theory. In fact, as Parris (1960: 34) observes 'state intervention may not have been the policy but it was the growing reality'. The Public General Act became the primary legislative vehicle adopted by governments to effect this reality (see Walkland 1968: 15). But, in order to secure the passage of this public legislation, governments needed both the time and the support of Parliament.

Support was secured in the House of Commons by the development of party government. Party *government* as distinct from the party *system* emerged in the 1830s. From this time onwards two parties were equally identified with government *and* opposition (see Clark 1980: 296–7). Admittedly, the fickleness of this arrangement was revealed in times of confused party alignments, as between 1846 and 1867; but, even then, the surface fluidity of party politics concealed a basic stability. Very few amendments to government legislation were carried against the government whips, and parties continued to deal with each other as 'members of a uniform body, as organic parts of a socially homogeneous representation of the people . . . in spite of numerous violent struggles between individual party leaders and their followers' (Redlich 1908: 132). This stable consensus was far from undermined even by the extensions of the franchise. The restructuring of the Conservative and Liberal parties after 1867 to form mass-membership organisations, to increase partisan 'brand loyalty' amongst the new political consumers, and to ensure a corresponding adherence on the part of their elected representatives, did little to increase 'product differentiation' between the parties. Party programmes were still constructed within the prevailing consensus, and although there were differences of interest amongst the fractions of capital there was no chasm of opposed class conflict between the parties. In one respect therefore the party in power was 'simply an agency for introducing agreed policies' (Berrington 1968: 367). In these circumstances mobilisation of Commons' support for the government was virtually guaranteed. Mobilisation of opposition, on the other hand, was more problematic and it was not until the closing years of the century that party opposition became a structural feature of British parliamentary government. But, the significant point for present purposes is that from 1867 onwards, if not before, governments could depend upon consistent support within the House for the passage of legislation.

The second requirement of governments in addition to the support of the House was, of course, time. On this issue, however, constitutional theory and parliamentary procedure had enormous difficulty in reconciling themselves to the political practice of the 19th century. In constitutional theory the House was conceived of as 'the grand inquest of the nation', a view enshrined, for example, in the hearing of grievances before supply. More particularly, the procedure of the House was still based upon the 'procedure of an opposition' (Redlich 1908: 57) which stemmed from the 17th century antagonism between the Crown and Parliament. Out of this antagonism issued many features of parliamentary procedure, such as the corporate privileges and the principle of equality of membership within the House, now regarded as the essence of parliamentary government but which in fact arose out of the historical need to ensure that ministers of the *Crown* received neither precedence nor obtained greater rights than any other member of the House. But the 19th century requirements of capital accumulation, combined with the extension of the franchise and the development of party government, meant that it was 'both logical and essential that the Government should once again lead the House in its legislative activity' (Butt 1969: 83). In these changed circumstances the 'hard necessity of political requirements' (Redlich 1908: 206) was for procedural rules based upon co-operative rather than conflictual principles.

Without going into the details of the incremental extension of governmental control over parliamentary proceedings in the first three-quarters of the 19th century, a close correlation can be drawn between this process and the increased scope of governmental activity generated by the changed relationships within civil society and the economy. Starting in 1806 the capacity of backbenchers to obstruct government business was whittled away. In that year the privilege of individual members to claim a hearing at any time by motion made without previous notice was questioned in the ruling that at least 24 hours' notice of such motions should be given (Redlich 1908: 70). In 1811 'order days' were instituted. Henceforth, governments had the right to propose that the orders of the day should take precedence over notices of motions. It was not until the 1830s, however, that these days were appropriated exclusively for government orders, or to give government business a special immunity from the incursions of private members (Fraser 1960: 447). Governments also waged a ten year battle, starting in 1832, to remove the harassing power conferred upon private members by petitioning procedure. The outcome was a series of standing orders in 1842 which made the presentation of petitions a formal proceeding incapable, except in rare cases, of giving rise to debate. In these rules the requirements of efficient government, executive dominance and, indeed, the mediated representation of the electorate through parties, prevailed over the rights of backbenchers to raise issues in precedence to government business and the direct injection of individual and group demands into Parliament.

Overall, therefore, the first half of the 19th century marked a significant turning point in executive-legislative relations in Britain. Henceforth, 'ministerial measures were given a frank priority' (Fraser 1960: 451). Correspondingly, the cabinet's task of deciding the principles of new legislation became routinised and the importance of standing counsel of the departments of state (in the Treasury, Home and Colonial Offices) increased as they were called upon ever more to draft legislation (see Fraser 1960: 454; Mackintosh 1968a: 147). Not surprisingly, this period also witnessed the entrenchment of the conventions of collective and individual ministerial responsibility (see Mackintosh 1968a: 54–5, 519). The embryonic form of modern parliamentary government was by now clearly visible.

Accelerated industrialisation was to nourish this embryo throughout the second half of the 19th century. Governments, in their attempts to sustain the conditions for profitable private accumulation required the certainty that the necessary legislative proposals would be processed rapidly and predictably by the Commons. Predictability accompanied the growth of party government whilst rapidity was secured by the procedural reforms introduced between 1882 and 1907. In 1882 a total of sixteen procedural resolutions, which resulted in changes to ten standing orders, passed the House (Redlich 1908: 170–5; Mackenzie 1950: 138–140). The most important of which were 'the closure' to curtail debate, restrictions upon the rights of backbenchers to raise adjournment debates on matters of urgency, and the strengthening of the Speaker's power to discontinue irrelevant or tediously repetitious speeches. In addition, two experimental standing committees were established to expedite the legislative process still further. Undoubtedly, the immediate stimulus for these drastic reforms was the obstruction of Irish Members, but the long-term causation was the 'alteration in the nature of the British government itself' (Redlich 1908: 207). Indeed, this change and the attendant need to expedite government business was felt by both political parties. Hence, although the 1882 reforms were introduced by a Liberal government in the face of strong Conservative resistance; by 1888 a Conservative government (after further Irish obstruction) willingly systematised these changes in a new set of standing orders. Moreover, it was the Conservative administration of Arthur Balfour that introduced the 'parliamentary railway timetable' of 1902. Most aspects of procedure were affected by the twenty-four resolutions laid before the House in that year. Their cumulative effect was to guarantee that henceforth government business had overwhelming preference in the Commons (for details see

Redlich 1908: 194–203). The Liberal government of 1906 thus inherited a procedural framework moulded to the needs of 'strong government', and subsequently introduced only relatively minor refinements to the hours of sittings, length of divisions and standing committees in the 1906 Parliament. The new standing orders relating to standing committees were, however, of significance in their own right as they made reference of Bills 'upstairs' the normal rather than the exceptional legislative practice. In addition, their number was increased to four and their chairmen were given the powers of 'closure' in view of the controversial subjects now to be sent 'upstairs'. Furthermore, the form adopted by the legislative committees in 1907 mirrored the wider structural principles of the House in that they were partisan, executive dominated and non-specialised. From the outset, standing committees were institutional manifestations of the strength of the executive and the grip of party control in the Commons.

The fact that by the first decade of the 20th century the procedural mould was so cast and then used positively by government has to be seen as part of a single process. For the dynamic of capitalist development led the state increasingly to intervene in the spheres of the economy and civil society. On the one hand, national capital, in the face of heightened industrial competition from abroad in the late 1890s onwards, called insistently for greater state support (Hobsbawn 1968: 108). On the other hand, labour pressed governments for the amelioration of its position in the market order. The susceptibility of governments to this pressure increased markedly after 1884 when, with the working class constituting a majority of the electorate for the first time, a prerequisite for electoral success was the support of labour. Both parties, at the level of ideas and party programmes, increased their competition for the allegiance of the lower class. However, the Liberals, in their adoption of a programme of significant welfare provision and taxation measures in the first years of the 20th century, initially demonstrated their greater ability on this new terrain. But the ground upon which the parties had to compete was ever extended by the agitation and organisation of the working class itself. The growth of trade unionism and the emergence of a distinct political organisation of labour in the Labour Representation Committee in 1900 (later to become the Labour party in 1906) pressed for the acknowledgement of the corporate rights of the working class. The protection of trade union rights in the 1906 Trades Disputes Act and the improvement of the material condition of the working class through the social reforms of 1908–11 were the consequence of this industrial and political pressure. But, not only are these reforms of significance in themselves they are also of importance because they represent the crucial fact that 'the structure of power as well as the pattern of policy was developing along collectivist lines' (Beer 1969: 61). The irony of parliamentary government in Britain is that at the very time when the House of Commons had so organised its own internal affairs to match the logic of interventionism and collectivism the seeds of corporatist representation in the trade unions were germinating *outside* of the Commons. For, as will be argued shortly, the rise of the Labour party and its development as a 'national' rather than a sectional trade union party – whilst fitted to the hegemony of the liberal theory of representation – precluded the development of functional representation *within* the House. Indeed, the problem of the functional representation of labour has never been surmounted in the British state. This problem in turn reflects not only the 'general contradictions' of the capitalist order but also the specific features of the British parliamentary state. However, before setting foot firmly in the 20th century in pursuit of this argument two areas of reform so far neglected in the chapter – the second chamber and devolution – need some attention.

The House of Lords
Increased state intervention was accompanied by a shift from the general principles of the rule of law towards particularistic regulation in favour of key sectional groups in society – whether fractions of capital or organised groups of workers. As a result, the task of successive governments came to be the presentation of the advancement of specific interests in terms of their integral connection to the promotion of the 'general interest'. Indeed, after the extension of the franchise governments increasingly sought to legitimise their definition of the national interest through recourse to the 'electoral mandate' and the support of a majority in the Commons. In normal times this definitional capacity proved sufficiently authoritative to override most opposition in the House of Commons. Yet one major obstacle to the interventionist legislation of radical governments, and their concomitant definition of the 'general interest', was the ability of the House of Lords to advance an alternative definition of this interest (but one still founded, in turn, upon other sectional and partisan interests). This conflict of interest was to become of special importance in the 1906 Parliament.

A detailed exposition of the events leading up to the 1911 Parliament Act – the mutilation and rejection of a series of bills promoted by the Liberal government – is not the primary concern here. Rather, the importance of these events is they reveal that, although the battle-lines between the Liberal government and its Conservative opponents (both inside and outside of the Lords) were dug around competing conceptions of the political principles of the 'electoral mandate' and the 'general interest', the fundamental dispute was over contrasting economic and social principles. In the opinion of Tory Peers the defence of the 'national interest' was synonymous with the defence of the sectional interests represented within the Conservative party. Thus underlying the constitutional duty of the Lords to prevent the 'hasty and ill-considered offspring of one passionate election' (Balfour, quoted in Le May 1979: 190) was the partisan duty to question the parentage of Liberal governments' legislation. Those progeny which questioned most directly Conservative partisan interests, whether through the abolition of plural voting, or through challenges to the 'party at prayer' in the religious provisions of the 1906 Education Bill, were harshly treated by the Lords. But the Lords' capacity to conflate the protection of sectional interests with the defence of the 'national interest' was most vividly illustrated in their rejection of the 1909 Finance Bill.

The 1909 Budget was controversial not because of the necessity to raise more revenue to meet the costs of the new old age pensions introduced by the Liberal government (as well as for increased expenditure on the Navy) but because of the manner in which this revenue was to be raised. It would be incorrect, therefore, to see the Lords' rejection of this budget as a simple opposition to interventionist legislation. In fact, by the early 20th century the Conservative party generally recognised the need for, and the advantages to be derived from, greater state intervention. However, this was an acceptance within narrower bounds than that of a Liberal party pressured by its labour supporters. The battle between the two parties was not, therefore, about intervention *per se*, but about its level and the terms upon which it was to be based. In particular, Conservatives were concerned with the financial base upon which social policies were founded and were opposed to their costs, in the form of taxation, falling directly upon the productive sector. Simple regulation and amelioration of the social and industrial environment was one thing, but in Conservative eyes it was totally another matter when the costs of such amelioration were to accrue to property or to challenge property rights themselves. Not suprisingly, the provisions of the 1909 Budget for taxation upon 'unearned increment' derived from land, for a graduated supertax and increased death duties were perceived as a threat, and moreover a double one, by Tory Lords. On the one hand, owners of property were manifestly to be penalised under these provisions; on the other, and more sinisterly, the state now appeared to be claiming a positive right to utilise and redistribute private economic resources. Hence the Budget was condemned as 'socialistic' and the 'beginning of the end of all rights of property' by Conservatives (see Jenkins 1954: 76). As such it was resisted in the Commons and rejected in the Lords. This rejection gave rise to the constitutional crisis of 1909–11 and the Parliament Act of 1911. The question of parliamentary reform, in this case the curtailment of the powers of the House of Lords, clearly was linked to the wider political questions of the interventionist state. Indeed, as Harold Laski (1938: 128) noted the 'question of the reform of the House of Lords is one of those issues of constitutional structure the roots of which go down into the economic foundations of the state. That has been the case on every occasion of serious conflict between the two Houses'.

Devolution

The dynamic of devolution throughout the second half of the 19th century was primarily the changes wrought in the state by uneven economic and social development in the Irish periphery and the attendant nationalist upsurge in that part of civil society. This is not to advance a simple 'determinist' explanation of nationalism in terms of uneven economic development, though arguably such considerations are of vital importance in accounting for the rise of nationalism within the United Kingdom. Rather, it is to acknowledge, as Urry (1981) does, that there are a variety of social bases upon which individuals may be mobilised within society – class being the major but not the only one. All forms of 'structuration', however, essentially relate to the attempts of individuals to maintain or improve their material conditions of life within the overall conditions of the capitalist economy. Yet, as Urry (1981: 70) proceeds to argue 'although capitalist relations are dominant it does not follow that class relations (i.e. class struggle) are primary'. The form that classes take and the extent to which class struggle is predominant is given not only by the current pattern of capital accumulation but also by the differentiation of civil society within which class forces operate. In particular the national framework of capitalism – in the organisation and maintenance of nation-states – helps people to frame and interpret events. Indeed, it is the very fact that historical, cultural and economic remnants of pre-existing Irish, Welsh and Scottish states continued to overlay and influence class relations within the peripheries of the United Kingdom that enabled resistance to the cent..alising tendencies of UK capitalism to be mounted and sustained.

To return to the initial statement – the 'Irish Question' was never far from the surface of British parliamentary politics in the late 19th century. Throughout the century a host of extra-parliamentary organisations pressed the cause of Irish nationalism in Ireland and on the British mainland: often through violent and direct action. Less violently, but still importantly, the extension of the franchise granted equal political rights to the electorate in Ireland, and this opportunity was increasingly utilised to return candidates committed to Irish Home Rule. Indeed, under the leadership of Charles Stewart Parnell, a strong nationalist presence came to dominate Irish representation at

Westminster. It was the obstruction and disruption of parliamentary proceedings by this disciplined group of Irish Members that provided the immediate stimulus for the procedural reforms outlined on page 21 above. The clear message was that Britain would not be allowed to govern herself until Ireland was granted self-government. In these circumstances, the territorial demands of Ireland posed a direct challenge to the British state. A threat that was magnified at a time when the centripetal pressures of economic and social development heightened the requirement of the executive in Parliament to intervene more directly and consistently in the regulation and administration of the effects of industrial capitalism. In order to defuse the Irish challenge, in the face of failure of state repression to do so, the political solution of devolution was countenanced. Schemes were floated, consequently, for an Irish Parliament with responsibility for domestic Irish affairs, but which was to be subordinate to an imperial Parliament at Westminster. This retention of the link between Britain and Ireland was to remain the continuous thread running throughout the succession of Home Rule Bills produced by Liberal governments between 1886 and 1914. In these plans the unity of the United Kingdom was to be maintained through an acknowledgement of diversity.

Whilst detailed analyses of these Bills, and the complex reasons behind the failure to enact them, lie beyond the immediate scope of this chapter the point of importance is that they were proposed as exigent solutions to specific developments in the Irish economy and society. By extension of this argument, the fact that Scotland (and Wales) did not experience the same social and economic disjunctions from English civil society and its underpinning economy at this time helps to explain why none of the thirteen proposals for Scottish home rule introduced in the Commons from 1890 to 1914 reached the committee stage. For as Bogdanor (1979: 91) rightly points out, the frequency of the appearance of these Bills did not correspond to any great popular feeling on the issue in Scotland. They were, in part, ritual gestures on the part of Scottish MPs to show that Scotland h; : equal claims to self-government as Ireland. In reality the imperative demand came from Ireland; home rule for Scotland and Wales simply rounded the corners of a federalist solution to the Irish problem. This point was vividly illustrated when the passage of the Government of Ireland Act 1920, with its proposed Parliaments in Dublin and Belfast along with a joint Council of Ireland, gouged out the heart of the Speaker's Conference on devolution which reported that year (Fair 1980: 224–43). The sense of immediacy and urgency evaporated from the conference with the extraction of the Irish issue, and, subsequently, its report provoked almost no interest in the House of Commons. In contrast, events in Ireland sparked with uncertainty and apprehension. Nationalists in the south rejected the 1920 settlement and secured instead dominion status in 1922. This left the six counties in the north to accept home rule alone. The ultimate irony of this episode, therefore, is that the only part of the UK to have had practical experience of devolution (1921–72) gained its devolved powers for reasons entirely at variance to the centrifugal principles of devolution. In fact, devolution in Northern Ireland was accepted:

> not to provide for different legislation from the rest of the country, but to ensure that she was governed on the same terms as the rest of the country ... Thus the pressures which led to devolution in Northern Ireland were ... 'centripetal' and therefore likely to minimize friction between the subordinate authority and Westminster.
>
> (Bogdanor 1979: 47–8)

The 20th century

In comparison with the fundamental reforms of the 19th century parliamentary reform this century has been minor, hesitant and inward looking. In fact, the most exhaustive study of procedural change up to 1979 (see Walkland 1979a) is but a monument to the essential conservatism of the House. If anything, the most significant changes throughout this period have centred around the development of select committees, with the highspot coming in the creation of a system of departmental committees as part of the 1979 package of reforms. But even then their introduction – heralded as one of 'the most important parliamentary reforms of the century' (St John-Stevas, HC Debates 1979, vol 969: 35) – reveals as much about the dearth of other reforms as it does about the significance of the new committees.

Explanation is required, therefore, of why the parliamentary system has remained structurally unaltered throughout the 20th century. Orthodox explanations tend to point the finger at the political executive and the major political parties. Obviously, it has been in the interest of government this century 'to sustain a type of parliamentary proceedings in which its political control has not been threatened, and to discourage developments which might undermine its monopoly of policy' (Walkland 1979a: 4). Correspondingly, the major political parties, as the main beneficiaries of this monopoly, have had little motivation to change this position. Moreover, ambitious backbenchers have willingly accepted the norms of an executive-centric House and have been reluctant to press for reforms which would blunt the perquisites of office (Judge 1981a). Only relatively recently have backbenchers begun to demonstrate, through their actions in the House, more overt dissatisfaction with their traditional role (see Norton 1978a; 1980).

Yet dissatisfaction with the role of the House of Commons has been a recurring feature of political debate in the 20th century. Cyclical calls for parliamentary reform have accompanied cyclical downturns in the economy: the worse the economic crisis the louder have been the demands for reform. Indeed, the deeper the economic malaise the more reform of the parliamentary *system*, rather than of parliamentary *procedure*, has been canvassed. Thus contemporary demands for, variously, electoral reform, devolution, functional representation, and a systematisation of the Commons' committees echo similar reform proposals made in the early 1930s (see H.C. 161, 1931; Butt 1969: 129–46; Johnson 1979: 443–4; Norton 1981a: 201–2). But the reason why these reforms have not been enacted, as of yet, is to be found in the politics of the interventionist state. To recapitulate: the constitutional framework erected in the second half of the 19th century reflected the needs of the state to intervene increasingly in civil society to maintain the conditions for profitable accumulation and, equally importantly, to legitimise the production process. The fact that 20th century developments in the economy – long-term relative decline, the weak competitive position of national capital in the world economy, the organisation of labour and industrial militancy – have forced governments to intervene still further, has led modern executives to maximise the utility of the existent procedural weapons in order to process necessary policies and legislation. The blueprint provided by Gladstone and Balfour foresaw remarkably accurately the universal trend of capitalist countries towards strong executives and weak parliaments. In this sense there was little need for fundamental alteration of the parliamentary structure as political executives had the formal capacity (if not always the prescience nor the ability) to perform their essential legislative functions. The centralisation and concentration of formal political power in the cabinet within Westminster was well-suited for the collectivist age.

At the apex of both the parliamentary and administrative systems, the cabinet has proved to be pivotal in the inexorable transfer of decision-making away from Westminster to the state bureaucracy in Whitehall and beyond to strategically-located sectional groups. So much so, that over the last few decades British government has been characterised by the proliferation of tripartite bodies comprising the executive, industry (CBI) and organised labour (TUC). But the origins of this system stretch back to the Lloyd George era of 1906–20 when the leaders of industry and the unions were drawn into policy-making in the hope of tying both capital and labour into agreed solutions to the massive social and political unrest of that period (see Booth 1982). Yet it has been the more recent extension of the tripartite system, through pay boards; councils for prices, productivity and incomes; national economic development councils; advisory, conciliation and arbitration services, etc; which has stimulated the debate over the extent and effects of corporatism in Britain (see, for example, Winkler 1976; Grant and Marsh 1977; Cawson 1978; Schmitter and Lehmbruch 1979; Newman 1981). Whilst the intricacies of this debate are beyond the immediate scope of this chapter, the point of importance of the new system of interest representation, whether in a tripartite or corporatist guise, is that it greatly reduces the power allotted to Parliament.

Functional Representation

A recurring solution proposed to defuse this challenge has been the introduction of a functional element of representation into Parliament itself (See Beer 1969: 71–9; Smith 1979: 3–20; Coombes 1982: 128–47). By such logic, if Parliament is by-passed in the process of tripartite deliberation then it should respond by re-routing this discussion through the chamber at Westminster or some advisory 'sub-parliament'. The problem here, however, is that if tripartism has emerged as a particularly appropriate form of representation for the interventionist state (Jessop 1978: 44), it has done so because of the centralisation and concentration of power in the *executive* of the state. Executive departments have thus been able to provide an underlying consistency and certainty of policy-formulation, even to the extent of minimising the distance between successive governments' 'adversarial' policies, within which both sides of industry could seek to maximise their own sectional benefits in the negotiation of 'consensual' economic strategies.

This does not mean that any partner in this tripartite relationship can fully achieve their own goals, nor that the agreements reached in this process provide feasible and long-lasting economic solutions. Indeed, in Marxist analysis they cannot do so because corporatist/tripartite structures operate within the frame of advanced capitalist society and as such are subject to the domination of capital, class conflict and the general contradictions of that society (Panitch 1980). Yet, in periods of *national* economic difficulty tripartism has appeared to offer all three partners specific benefits. On the one side, industry and the executive have secured the incorporation and compliance of the trade union leadership into a process designed to promote policies (particularly on pay) which detrimentally affect the income and working conditions of average trade union members (see Panitch 1979: 61; Newman 1981: 115–16; Booth 1982: 205). In this respect industry has gained directly in times of economic and financial difficulty from closer access to government. On the other side, the national leaderships of the trade unions have also gained, albeit temporarily, from the power afforded to them in the centralisation and regulation of shop-floor demands in this process. More importantly perhaps, trade union leaders have believed that the result of tripartite planning would ultimately be better employment prospects for their memberships in the long-term; and they have also witnessed sufficient short-term advantages in social and industrial legislation to tie them to conservative economic policies (see Coates 1979: 53–85; Panitch 1979: 62–8).

The significance of this for Parliament is that it cannot offer such benefits to the industrial partners, as it is neither the forum for decision nor does its territorial principles of representation allow for the unmediated reflection of the sectional interests of labour and capital. The prevailing theories of representation still emphasise individualistic conceptions and portray the electorate as atomised individuals whose 'interests' are defined by reference to individual preferences or territory (whether delimited by the boundaries of 'constituency' or 'nation') rather than by economic function or class. From the outset therefore members of the newly enfranchised working class were expected by the logic of these theories, and encouraged by 'their' parliamentary representatives, to see their interests in individualistic terms rather than in class or functional terms. These latter interests were deemed to warrant representation in the industrial or economic realms of activity rather than to be intermeshed with political organisation and representation. Even when these links were forged, in the Labour party after 1906, the leadership of the PLP and the trade unions were anxious to maintain a fairly clear differentiation between the 'political' and 'industrial' wings of the labour movement. One consequence of this fairly rigid demarcation has been the impossibility of developing a formal channel of functional representation within the Commons without reforging the links between the 'economic' and 'political' realms in the consciousness of the working class. In other words, the mythology of liberal-democracy requires Parliament to represent the 'general interest', to perform general integrative functions, and to provide a general framework of law and legitimisation. Yet, tripartism on the other hand is based upon the representation of the specific 'class' interests of capital and organised labour, and involves the maximisation of sectional interests within the complex process of bargaining and negotiation to establish some form of economic 'consensus'. The very paradox of this form of representation is that it is difficult to justify in terms of established representative practices and theories, yet it is apparently ever more essential to sustain the appropriate conditions for capital accumulation. Moreover, the fact that the tripartite/corporatist system in Britain is at best intermittent and unstable in the crucial area of the management of the economy simply points to the unresolved (and unresolvable?) problem of the accommodation of labour within the capitalist order. Ultimately, the overriding paradox remains that the very indeterminancy of the tripartite system in Britain points to the need for a more stable form of functional representation, but this need in itself highlights the past failing of Parliament, and its inherent future inability, to encompass functional representation.

Electoral Reform

Just as there has been no realistic 'constituency' within civil society for the reform of Parliament along functional lines, so, until very recently, powerful backers for electoral reform have been missing. Neither capital nor organised labour has seen any great advantage to be derived from electoral reform, nor has the pattern of state intervention in the economy warranted such a change, *as long as* the post-war social democratic consensus pertained. To understand this point it is necessary to retrace our steps back into the 19th century. After 1832, it will be recalled, the danger of electoral reform was seen by its opponents to be the handing of state power over to the proletariat to use for the promotion of their own class interests. The threat to the accumulation process of a politicised working class and a radical proletarian party has haunted the governing classes ever since. But the important point is that this threat has been defused within the context of the British parliamentary system itself. Working class admission into the franchise was sought, and granted, within the accepted tenets of the liberal theory of parliamentary democracy – in terms of individualistic conceptions of representation, the independence of parliamentarians and parliamentary sovereignty. Moreover, the constitutional conformism of successive PLP leaderships served to integrate labour more firmly into the established representative order. Indeed, in common with their European social democratic counterparts, they have continued to believe that Parliament is a neutral instrument capable of being used by any political force to advance its own interests. In which case the working class in gaining a parliamentary majority would be able to embark upon an active legislative programme to remove the class differentials of capitalist society. This anticipation that the Labour party as the representative of the 'interests of labour' would enact ameliorative legislation when in office, and, moreover, that it would have the ability to do so under the doctrine of parliamentary sovereignty, has contributed significantly to working class support for representative democracy in Britain. In such circumstances the working class and the PLP appeared to have nothing to gain from electoral change and the introduction of a system of proportional representation. All that was required apparently, as the experience of the 1945–50 Labour government seemingly confirmed, was a majority government in the Commons committed to a radical programme. There was no advantage to be gained from a coalition government agreed only upon the lowest common denominator of social and economic change.

However, if the system of strong party government was so attractive to Labour in the post-war era surely it must have been unattractive to industry, finance capital and the Conservative party? In theory these sections of British society had everything to lose in the promotion of collectivism under Labour administrations. In practice their losses were far outweighed by the gains of an apparent stabilisation of the accumulation process and the legitimation of the state through the expansion of welfare provision (see Gough 1979; Jessop 1980). That losses were incurred by capital, particularly at the level of ideas, should not be understated. Nor should it be forgotten that nationalisation, redistributive taxation and greater immunities for trade unions all attracted protracted opposition. But these legislative setbacks were mitigated in the longer term. At heart the social democratic reforms offered a means whereby the economic infrastructure could be moulded by the changing needs of accumulation whilst, at the same time, incorporating labour more firmly within the interstices of capitalist society. Indeed, the fears of capital could be abated while-ever Labour governments continued to espouse and promote the 'national interest' in office and were willing to accept a stipulation of that interest made by the major industrial, financial and bureaucratic groups within the state. If capital could live with social democracy so could the Conservative party. In fact, the experience of the 1940–5 wartime coalition had convinced many of the party's leaders that the welfare state posed no threat to property. Moreover, the period in opposition (1945–51) enabled the Right Progressives within the party to articulate the case for the new economic techniques of demand management along with welfare provisions as part of a new post-war settlement in which to revitalise capitalism (Gamble 1974: 63). The success of the party at the general elections of 1951, 1955 and 1959 did nothing to divert Conservatives from the welfare state consensus, nor to diminish in their eyes the attractions of 'adversary politics' and 'strong government' founded thereupon.

Electoral reform thus held no attraction for the major political parties who were the prime beneficiaries of the existent electoral system. Nor did it appeal to either side of industry as long as the interventionist consensus lasted. It is instructive to note that the most serious challenge to the plurality voting system, the Representation of the People Bill 1931, was launched during a period of minority government and party instability when the Labour party had not yet experienced the fruits of majority rule nor committed itself wholeheartedly to an interventionist economic strategy. The PLP under Macdonald's leadership had by 1929 come to regard the Liberals as not too unpalatable allies and subsequently there was little reluctance to consider the prospect of a formal coalition between the parties in the event of electoral reform. If anything, the PLP leadership was more sympathetic to the prevailing economic orthodoxies and more prepared to accept a definition of the 'national interest' in terms of 'sound money' and a 'balanced budget' than were the Liberals. In this respect industry, and the City especially, had little to fear from Labour. Yet capital retained a deeply engrained suspicion of the Macdonald government and was haunted by the prospect of future state intervention induced by a more radical future leadership. But, the major opposition came from the principal beneficiaries of the plurality system – the Conservative party. It opposed in the Commons the 1931 Bill's proposal for an alternative vote system, and eventually wrecked the Bill in the Lords. On this occasion the Upper Chamber could well argue its defence of the 'general interest' as there was remarkably little public interest in, or pressure for, electoral reform (see Bogdanor 1981: 142). The balance of party interest (until now?) was never again so favourable to electoral reform.

Devolution

A more recent failure to enact parliamentary reform after the passage of constitutional legislation through the House of Commons occurred in 1979 with the Scotland and Wales Act. The genesis, progression and ultimate demise of this legislation has been so recently and thoroughly chronicled that no useful purpose is served here in the repetition of the details of this failure. All that it is necessary to note is that parliamentary reform was countenanced seriously at a time of economic depression when partisan, class and nationalist interests appeared to converge within civil society to challenge the centralisation of the British state. Whereas academic argument and intellectual promotion of the principle of decentralisation failed to move parliamentary opinion to favour devolution, the threat posed by an apparently strong and burgeoning Scottish nationalist movement to the British state and the British parties galvanised the Labour government into action in the 1974–9 Parliament.

This is not the place to consider the causes of the Scottish National Party's (SNP) electoral upsurge in the 1970s. Indeed, analysis of the complexity of the SNP vote and the paradoxes therein has already filled numerous books (see, for example, Hechter 1975; Brand 1978; Miller 1981; Nairn 1982). At their heart, however, all explanations of Scottish nationalism recognise, with varying emphases, the importance of Scottish economic circumstances to the rise of political nationalism – whether manifested as a protest against 'relative deprivation' or as a reaction to the 'development gap' between the peripheral Scottish economy and that of England produced by the exploitation of North Sea Oil (see Nairn 1982). Set within the wider frame of the relative decline of British capitalism the economic threat articulated by a strong nationalist movement, in its ability to politicise the oil issue, let alone the possibility of appropriating oil revenues exclusively or in large part for Scotland, had to be countered by any British government. For the Labour government in 1974 the SNP not only posed a threat to the British state itself but more immediately, and to some Scottish Labour members more importantly, posed a threat to the electoral hegemony of the Labour party in Scotland. On both counts, as well as on account of other factors (see Keating and Bleiman 1979: 170), the Labour government was forced to act: the politically expedient Scotland Act was the result.

With hindsight the nationalist challenge proved to be less acute than could have been foreseen in 1974. By 1979 the international dimensions of the economic crisis were so apparent as to undermine the simplistic economic palliatives of the SNP (significantly, oil was not a major issue in 1979 – see Miller 1981). Moreover, the bulk of Scottish manual workers remained loyal to their Labour party roots. Part of this loyalty arose at least from an awareness that 'Scottish labour is part and parcel of British labour and wants to remain so, retaining national collective bargaining and fighting for common economic and social objectives' (Keating and Bleiman 1979: 198). In this sense the depth of political nationalist feeling, as distinct from a 'consciousness' of Scottishness, was overestimated by the major parties in 1974, and probably accounts for the quietude in Scotland after the 1979 Referendum result. Nevertheless, the apparent strength of a popular nationalist movement in the mid-1970s, generated out of the conditions of the peripheral Scottish economy, placed parliamentary reform firmly on the agenda of the British state. Once again the connection between the politics of the state and the timing of parliamentary reform is evident.

Conclusion

Parliamentary reform over the last 150 years has been inextricably linked to the development of the state and its attempts to regulate the heterogeneous relationships within the British capitalist economy and society. In following Urry's (1981) analysis it has been accepted that the state operates to sustain the appropriate conditions for capital accumulation and the maintenance of a healthy workforce. The form of the state is thus related to the nature of capital and its changing requirements. Yet, at the same time, it is also derived from the interactions of diverse popular and class forces within civil society. In this context Parliament is a crucial institution in the British state as it has enabled the representation of popular and working class forces alongside the interests of capital, and so has enabled the former to influence the outputs of the state to their own advantage. Indeed, as the state has been enlarged and strengthened to this end, so the allegiance of the populace to Parliament and the capitalist state has been secured. Labour, as much as capital, has a vital interest in the maintenance of its own material condition through the efficient and effective operations of the state in sustaining the process of production.

This shared interest in the regulation, ordering and amelioration of the social consequences of capitalist relationships was clearly visible by the second half of the 19th century. The strength of liberal ideology could not obscure the creeping extension of state intervention, nor could liberal theories of parliamentary representation obscure the fact that the constitutional framework had been restructured to ensure the certain and predictable passage of public legislation at the expense of the traditional rights of the individual parliamentarian. Procedural reform was thus posited upon the needs of the state and the requirements of 'strong government'. This very strength stemmed directly from the representativeness of Parliament, where the diverse interests of society could, for long periods, be articulated within the confines of a fundamental consensus over the objectives of the state and the constitutional structure itself.

Throughout the 20th century the merits of strong and centralised government have continued to be pressed by the major political parties. Moreover, modern governments have retained the international orientation of their 19th century predecessors and have sought to regulate the national economy in terms of world economic conditions. In particular, post-war governments, in their endeavours to emulate the economic growth rates of their major competitors and to modernise the infrastructure of the British economy, have passed a plethora of legislative enactments which have increased their responsibilities for economic management, industrial regulation and welfare provision. The underpinning social democratic consensus for these developments simply reflected the recognition of both capital and labour of the benefits to be derived from increased public spending in an era of economic growth.

The procedural structure of Parliament inherited from the 19th century proved well suited to the expeditious processing of the legislation required by the interventionist state. With only minor modifications, to take account of the new responsibilities of the state (e.g. the development of committees dealing with the nationalised industries, race relations, science and technology) or the increased technicality and expansion of old responsibilities (e.g. the Expenditure Committee), the House of Commons continued in its supportive and legitimising roles to a strong executive. When parliamentary reform was canvassed in the late 1950s and 1960s executive supremacy and strong single-party government were unquestionably accepted as part of the natural constitutional order. Schemes for increased parliamentary investigation, scrutiny and control of the executive were persistently launched throughout this period; a few, such as the specialised committees, partially floated and then predictably submerged in the tide of strong, single-party government. However, whilst the Commons was experimenting with toy boats in its own bath water in the chamber, the international economic sea upon which the British welfare state had been floated became ever more turbulent and hostile. Fissures within the social democratic consensus widened markedly in the 1970s as the rapid downturn in the world economy presented successive British governments with the problem of slow, and even 'negative', growth in the national economy in face of the ferocious competition on domestic and international markets. The 'strength' of British government was patently lacking in such circumstances. Both major parties therefore began to reconsider their support for the post-war welfare consensus and to look for alternative state forms for economic salvation. The Labour party developed its Alternative Economic Strategy with its proposals for extended central planning and co-ordination of a national economy severed from the world economy. The Conservative party under Mrs Thatcher on the other hand believed that British economic decline could be reversed by 'rolling back' the state, shedding the taxation and expenditure burdens of the welfare state, and resurrecting the 'rule of law' against the monoplistic activities of the trade unions in the labour market. Moreover, out of this polarisation emerged the SDP/Liberal Alliance which believed that Britain's economic crisis was rooted in the political system, and which offered its political panacea of electoral reform.

The significance of all of these strategies is their intertwining of the reconceptualisation of the state with a reconsideration of the role of Parliament. The paradox of Mrs Thatcher's electoral victory of June 1983 is that to 'roll back the state' requires a strong state to perform this task. Hence, the Conservative Manifesto's commitment to uphold parliamentary supremacy and to 'pursue sensible, carefully considered reforms where they are of practical value' undoubtedly means 'where they are of practical value to strong *government*'. Should the Thatcherite strategy fail the economy, then the clamour from the Labour party and the Alliance for alternative forms of the parliamentary state will surpass the cacophony which greeted the election result itself. One thing is certain however, reform of the parliamentary system is firmly back on the political agenda for the 1980s: that it is so is a result of changes within the economy and the restructuring of British society.

2 Parliamentary Reform, Party Realignment and Electoral Reform
S.A. Walkland

I shall reveal my hand from the start by proclaiming that it is impossible, except at the considerable risk of abstracting the subject from its determinants, to separate Parliament, or any other political institution for that matter, from the political and economic systems in which it is located, and of which, in Britain, the House of Commons is essentially their quintessence and focus. Earlier historians of Parliament seemed to know this instinctively. It has remained for a complacent generation of British political scientists and commentators to think otherwise. The American historian of the Carolingian period of English parliamentary government, Wallace Notestein (1924), was aware when he wrote his seminal essay *The Winning of the Initiative by the House of Commons* that the comprehensive procedural and internal organisational reforms of the Commons in the pre-Civil War period – the first of the only two major overhauls of the procedures in the House in the last 350 years – were a weapon devised by parliamentarians in the political struggle between the classes represented in the Commons and the Stuart monarchy. Similarly, the next great wave of constitutional and parliamentary reform, so ably chronicled by Josef Redlich (1908), was a reflection of the massive economic changes of the 19th century. Again the Commons reacted positively, if hesitantly, to the political demands of industrialisation, which has always required an accompanying measure of democracy, and to the need for centralised and representative governmental responses to the requirements of a relatively rapidly changing socio-economic system.

If earlier commentators were able so easily to recognise the political and economic determinants of reform, why then in this century, and until recently, and even now in the case of a number of students of Parliament, has there been such a reluctance to study Parliament within the wider contexts in which it operates? The answer is complex, but reveals much about the current controversy over parliamentary government and about the recent reform movement in general. One part of the answer is that students of government, and many practising parliamentarians, have been profoundly affected by an inherited 19th century liberal philosophy which has had such a marked influence, not only on the practice of 20th century British government but also on its interpretation by academics and other commentators. There is no space in this short chapter to go into the detail of the many strands of this inheritance – a strong feeling for history, often romanticised when it comes to the interpretation of the constitution; a strict conceptual division between public and private powers; an accompanying and equally strong instinct, whether amongst Marxists or liberals, to separate politics from economics, which has produced a marked dissociation of political from economic enquiry in British social science; and a tradition of limited government, limited not in the range of activities undertaken, but in a reluctance to use public power, hence the emphasis which it puts on the consensual agreement of individuals and groups as a means both of arriving at and implementing public policy. It is as a result an inheritance which elevates the political process and gives political parties an importance greater than in many other West European polities. In Britain, as Samuel Beer (1969: 88) has remarked, 'party is indeed king'. There is in Britain no other main source of political power outside the representative political process – no powerful and independent bureaucracy – a state within the state – as in France, no strong body of public law shaped and implemented by a powerful judiciary, as in West Germany. All the more reason why attention in Britain should be focused on the political parties, not merely as entities in themselves, but as the conditioning agents of British constitutional and institutional life. What is meant in Britain by the constitution is really a reflection of political practice and a description of existing institutions, which only takes on meaning within the political bond which holds them together, and which informs not only their functioning but their general character. If this is over-whelmingly true of Parliament, it also holds with other key institutions, the civil service in particular.

But given this self-evident politicisation of institutions in Britain, which goes more deeply than anywhere else outside the Anglo-Saxon tradition, how has it come about that the characteristic focus of recent British studies of government has been the institutions themselves, abstracted from the political and cultural contexts in which they have their being, and which so obviously determines their modes of operation, their internal organisation and procedures, and their general ethos? That there has been a pronounced tendency in Britain towards formalistic analyses of institutions cannot be denied by anyone with an acquaintance with the post-1945 literature of political science, and examples are hardly needed. The answer to this paradox is that in many ways the liberal tradition of politics in Britain has aided this focus, so confidently, and largely unconsciously, has a generation of political scientists and politicians taken for granted the existence of a broad political consensus which seemed, mistakenly, to underpin the operation of modern British politics, and which was so evident a factor in the late 19th century when the forms of British parliamentary government were established. Complacency about the course of British politics has been the curse of much examination of the processes and institutions of British government since 1945. As Keith Middlemas (1979) has observed, in his acute if overstated analysis of the politics and government of British industrial society, a 19th century conception of British history survived unquestioned well into the 20th century, in which it appeared that a state of political equilibrium was natural to society, which could only be lost by incompetence and mismanagement on the part of the formal institutions of the state. Questions about the actual distribution and use of political power in contemporary society were on the whole neither asked nor answered. As Middlemas (1979: 17) remarks, 'anyone interested in these matters would have had difficulty in piercing through the formal descriptive screen of Crown and Parliament, legislative, executive and judiciary'.

In the post-war period in Britain, the assumption of an inherited consensus was strengthened by what, in retrospect, were the superficial indications of a political system united on a limited degree of state control and nationalisation, on a welfare state and on Keynesian stabilisation policy, which, with its essentially liberal derivation, could be adopted by both major parties without damaging their basically opposed beliefs and doctrines. It was generally accepted that such a two-party system could ensure the goals of any polity – stability tempered by responsible change and progress, plus economic growth, full employment and a stable currency, which would, apparently, be permanent features of a state and economy so guided. In my under-graduate days such a system was assumed to enshrine so much wisdom as to be immune from questioning – it was regarded as the ultimate that frail human intelligence could devise. Then it was a model to be followed; now it is an example which other nations attempt to avoid at all costs. What was not observed was its essential dysfunctionality for positive industrial change; that it was an essentially conservative, if not reactionary, system, buttressed massively as it was, and still is, by the life-support system of peculiar electoral arrangements, and with an incapacity, especially in the case of the Labour party, to meet developing circumstances. Britain is practically unique amongst West European states in that, until the arrival of the SDP, its complete political structure was rooted in the late 19th and early 20th centuries, and carried with it an accompanying baggage of assumptions, attitudes, doctrines which had been assimilated in the same period. But nothing could upset the reasoning behind this model. Essential complacency was underwritten by the outcome of the 1939–45 war. This led in Britain to nothing in the way of a social or political revolution, despite the appearance of the first majority Labour government in British history. Parliament and most other institutions came well out of the war, and the immediate aftermath did not, in contrast with other European states whose experience had not been so fortunate, lead to any fundamental critique of the political and constitutional structures which were widely perceived to have served the country well. So far as Labour's immediate programme was concerned Parliament's traditional and received procedures proved quite adequate – public bill legislation for basic nationalisation and the founding of the health service, traditional budgetary processes for the implementation of demand management. What procedural reform occurred was mainly a gearing-up of the legislative process in the Commons to accommodate an increased work-load, to match developments in the legislative machinery of the Cabinet.

The real impetus for the modern parliamentary reform movement began in the late 1950s, after 15 years of complacency. Again it was largely economic and social in its motivation. This time, unlike the 19th century, it was the problems of a national economy in relative decline which provided the spur to action. By this time most comparative economic indices were unfavourable to Britain. The national result was a massive and generalised mood of introspection – a new generation questioned fundamentals but in a curious non-political and non-ideological manner. As has been noted, the outcome of the Second World War had not produced a social revolution of any magnitude, despite the rhetoric of the Labour party. Rather it had reinforced most social and political traditions in Britain. The British social revolution, such as it was, took place in the 1960s, guided by, to quote the 1964 Labour manifesto, the 'New Thinking', whatever this may have been. But by 1960 the conditions for a massive pragmatic and technocratic initiative were building up; a few years of Butskellism had ushered in the 'end of ideology' debate, foreshadowed by Crosland's (1956) revisionist tract *The Future of Socialism*. Convergence theory had taken hold in international relations and superficial prosperity had worn away sharp economic inequalities. A generational change in politics and society was making itself felt, in which the institutions and working of parliamentary government were not to escape criticism. The man to match this historical moment appeared in the person of Harold Wilson – always a better managerialist than a principled politician. As usual in the history of post-war reform, the characteristic reaction was widespread institutional innovation, unaccompanied by any political critique. For a time it seemed that nothing was to escape the urge for institutional reform – the planning of public expenditure, the institutions of economic management, of science and technology, of the civil service, the universities, the structure of local government and, of course, Parliament itself. It is hugely depressing in retrospect to see how little was in fact achieved by this vast and expensive movement. Either the political conditions for its success were not analysed and given sufficient weight, as in economic planning and parliamentary reform, or as the editor (Judge 1981b) has pointed out in the case of civil service reform, the political culture of central government was ignored.

Perhaps the most characteristic proponent of parliamentary reform in this period was not a political scientist but a political economist, Andrew Shonfield (1965), who in his trail-blazing work *Modern Capitalism*, urged basic and fundamental alterations in Britain's administration, industrial relations, and the organization of state industry, in line with the best practices of Continental Europe. He believed passionately in the need for economic planning and in a new relationship between Parliament and the experts – a new breed of planner-politician, on the French model, engaged in sympathetic negotiation with the processes of parliamentary politics. His last chapter in *Modern Capitalism*, which should have been devoted to analysing the political pre-conditions for the changes he wanted, is taken up with a discussion of the institutional innovations he thought were needed in the House of Commons to make planning accountable – fairly standard stuff in which he echoed some of the arguments of other parliamentary reformers of the period, notably Bernard Crick. Crick (1968) himself, in his book *The Reform of Parliament*, which provided a blueprint for a generation of reformers, was similarly somewhat mystical on the capacity of a reformed Parliament to galvanise society into new patterns of thought and behaviour – improvements in the communicative function of Parliament would lead to more sympathetic relationships between voter and the Commons, which would translate the popular will into dynamic policy. But when it came to particulars it was institutional rather than political reform which was urged. Despite the high-flown rhetoric of a Shonfield or a Crick, nothing fundamental had happened to change the essential dysfunction of two-party politics. All reforms worth having in the Labour party had died with Gaitskell, and the system continued as before, with the debacle of the National Plan and the massive alienations which followed it. I recall that as early as 1963 I made the point, in an article, that nothing, and particularly Parliament, would change unless a new political context was found (Walkland 1963). It fell at that time on deaf ears, although the argument has become more compelling with the passage of time. It is worthwhile noting that the reformers of this period of the 1960s supported the political *status quo*. They were almost to a man Labour party supporters, and even when not overtly party political, the heterogeneous group of technocrats which called reform into being were practically all vaguely left-wing, and helped to provide the impetus for the victory of Labour in the 1964 election. I have only been able to discover one writer of the period who queried fundamentally the capacity of the existing political system to deliver the sort of regeneration which was being canvassed. This was Michael Shanks (1961) (now incidentally a member of the SDP) in his polemic *The Stagnant Society*. An advocate of a positive industrial strategy and an incomes policy, he was sceptical of the ability of the existing party system to deliver this. His chapter 7 foreshadows almost exactly the arguments now current concerning the state of British politics – he forecast an early split in the Labour party after the Gaitskell revisionist debate, a realignment of moderate Labour and Liberals to provide the major vehicle for his policies, with a corresponding split in the TUC, etc. His most acute observation was that Labour, because of its doctrinal ambivalence, conveyed a 'blurred image' – a factor of considerable importance in its ability to induce confidence in economic matters. That his diagnosis was correct has been demonstrated in the 1970s, but he severely underestimated the durability of the system that he criticised, and the power of the forces, particularly the electoral system, which sustain it.

If we now take a critical look at the reforms in the Commons which have been effected since 1966, the first point which should be made was that they were essentially products of a superficial intellectual analysis on the one hand, and political opportunism on the part of governments on the other. This is not the way that lasting and significant reforms arise, except in the technical sphere. There is in fact no way that the House of Commons, by taking thought, can add substantially to its stature. Impetus to genuine reform arises from political circumstances; this is not to say that the emphasis on the investigative procedures of the House did not have some logic – it was dimly discerned that the main inherited procedures of the Commons, in particular public legislation procedures and conventional financial controls, were inadequate for situations in which more flexible intervention by government in public affairs, with policy made by consultative processes of which the Commons was only too little aware, was becoming a dominant mode of public activity. But the assumption that the House as a result of this sort of reform could exercise more political control over these activities would have needed to assume a politically more independent Commons than the two-party system provides. The movement for a strong committee system in Parliament ignored one of the most elementary findings of comparative legislative research – that the strength of a legislative committee system varies inversely with the strength of the party system in a legislature. The unyielding adversary character of the two-party system in the British Parliament could not provide a responsive host to this type of innovation, unless the agencies were concerned only with technical or basic constitutional functions of which the party system approves – the Public Accounts Committee is an example. But any major organisational changes or additions to the ways in which the Commons operates are bound to fail if they arise primarily from a process of ratiocination, and are not propelled by politics. Such a typical and permanent feature of the US Congress as its powerful committee system responds not to any conscious process of institutional innovation, but to the factors of the constitutional situation in which Congress is placed and, more importantly, to the character of the political parties which operate the constitution. What the British reformers could do was to fudge the issue – to invent committees of 'advice and scrutiny' with little or no discussion of what would happen if the advice went unheeded or the scrutiny proved ineffective. Reformers like Bernard Crick stressed the communicative function of the new agencies – a reformed Commons would mirror to the electorate the implications of government activity and reflect back the hopes and wishes of the voters, vitalising in the process the development and execution of public policy. But this role has not been enhanced by reform, and remains more deficient at present than at any time this century. If Parliament is to be likened to a two-way mirror, then it is a distorting one. Political attitudes in an essentially unrepresentative Commons are geared up to an extent which produces a caricature of political feeling in the country, and has contributed to the fall in support for the major parties which has now reached a situation where no government represents much more than one in three of the electorate, a figure which is likely to grow worse in future elections. If, despite the reformers, Britain in the last twenty years has become a more divided and embittered country, it might be asked what else could be expected of a system which consistently puts complete political control into the hands of distinct minorities?

A few things need to be repeated about the Crossman generation of reforms of the late 1960s. The process took the form of a trade-off between government and backbench MPs, in which the government, in managing to get the Finance Bill or parts of it off the floor of the House, came out as the beneficiary. Otherwise the effects of the reforms were puny; the mountains had laboured and brought forth a mouse. The few new committees which were installed depended on the fortuitous circumstance of a reformer being appointed as Leader of the House in 1966. In addition care was taken to ensure that they only operated on the periphery of politics – all the gut political areas such as the economy, defence, foreign policy, were studiously avoided. Little work of lasting value was done by these agencies, with the possible exception of the Committee on Science and Technology. But to set against this there were the clownish activities of the Committee on the Department of Education and Science. In this first experiment we see one of the major weaknesses in the conception of this type of committee. It is a misnomer to call them committees, insofar as the full House of Commons does not remit particular enquiries to them, which might be expected to have gained some prior political attention in the plenary chamber. Rather the House surrenders areas of activity to be investigated largely at the whim of committee chairmen or a small group of committee members. It is not surprising that quite often the House doubts the relevance to its political interests of some of the investigations that are decided upon in this fashion. It was also, of course, in this period, that the beginnings were seen of that potential for delay, obstruction and harassment, in minor but significant ways, with which government can always impede the work of these agencies. The truth emerged quite early, *pace* Dr Norton, that given the polarised political structure of the Commons, and the customary discipline of government supporters, the committees possessed nothing in the way of political sanction, without which they remained powerless. Under a reformed political system it could be that their reports would find a response in powerful groups of MPs to which the government would need to pay attention; all they can hope to be in the present situation is an intellectual factor in policy debates, and, largely, governments have not shown themselves keen to conduct these sort of arguments with small groups of committee members.

I must make one exception to this general criticism, and this relates to the Expenditure Committee which operated for a decade in the 1970s. It is not surprising that this should form an exception, since the Committee, and in particular its General sub-committee under the able chairmanship of Michael English, was attached closely to what has always been accepted as an important constitutional function of the Commons. But again it needs to be recognised that the Expenditure Committee came into being largely as a result of government initiative, without which the work of the Procedure Committee which adumbrated its creation would have come to nothing. It was intimately connected with the government's political aim of more effective control and management of public expenditure which had figured prominently in the Conservative manifesto of 1970. A fruitful partnership eventually emerged between government and the General sub-committee. What in fact was achieved in this decade was an overhaul of the Public Expenditure Survey Committee system, originally designed as part of the Plowden reforms aimed at more rational public resource allocation, but subtly changed in the 1970s from a method of future planning to one of effective annual control. Built-in inflationary elements were removed from expenditure planning, and a monetarist philosophy installed, with concentration on the money supply and the level of the PSBR. One might also mention the work of the Industry sub-committee, whose views on the financing of the state sector – in particular British Leyland and Chrysler – turned out eventually to be more soundly based than those of the government. It is a negative feature of the new committee system which was set up in 1979 that there is now less disciplined work than there used to be on the Supply Estimates and on the Public Expenditure White Paper.

If an interim judgement on the new generation of select committees is attempted then, although they involve half as many again MPs as the superseded structure, little in the way of increased political influence can be noted. By early 1983 the House of Commons had only debated specific committee reports on five occasions, although committee findings have been occasionally referred to in other debates and in standing committee. Sub-committees have not been allowed to proliferate, although they are on the whole too small anyway to command much authority. Despite a prodigious output of reports (209 in the first three years of operation) their aim, in the words of the former Leader of the House (St John-Stevas, HC Debates 1979, vol 969: 36), of altering the whole balance of power between Westminster and Whitehall, has come nowhere near achievement. The aim was always silly – it took no account of past experience and rested on no political analysis of the problem. There has in fact been no fundamental change – it is the mixture as before, but more of it. The few positive achievements of the committees – the repeal of the 'Sus Law', help with the settlement of a minor industrial dispute, assistance with the saving of the Scottish Symphony Orchestra – are insubstantial. One cannot but feel that the government's reaction to the very large demands made on the executive by the new agencies, as enshrined in the 'Rayner Review' of government statistical services, is justified in trying to instil in MPs as well as officials some sense of cost-consciousness. The Liaison Committee of chairmen has not as yet managed some essential co-operation; the committees operate largely as separate entities, with some needless duplication. There has, for example, yet been no sign of a Committee on Nationalised Industries formed from relevant depart-mental committees, for which provision is made in Standing Order.

But more importantly, the essential weakness in the concept of bipartisan committees attempting to operate in a parliamentary context which has seldom been so polarised, is becoming evident, as committees and their chairmen engage in what is, for some key committees, the seemingly impossible task of integrating party politicians into a common approach. Signs of tension between committee members have been many, often resulting in reports which so obviously reveal differences of party opinion that they attract little notice. In particular the Employment and Scottish Affairs Committees need to be singled out, with choices of topics for investigation informed entirely by party considerations. Strategies have been adopted by committees to achieve some sort of agreement, but the result has been to instil a feeling of fudge into many of the exercises. There has, for example, been agreement between members of committees to avoid controversial topics; or concentration, as with the Treasury Committee, on the reasoning and manner of government policy-making, thus avoiding the need for a positive critique; low-keyed chairmanship; emphasis on evidence rather than on conclusions; the acceptance of reports so bland as to be virtually useless – the strategies can be multiplied. In total they cast doubt, as was always the case, on the wisdom in present political circumstances of this sort of exercise. It is moreover clear from the history of reform of the Commons in the last twenty years that the process has been politicised. Its substance has been subordinated to party ends. For example, the alacrity with which the Conservative government adopted the recommendations of the 1977/8 Procedure Committee (HC 588 1978) owed more to a political desire to be seen to be supporting parliamentary government after the abdication of responsibility by Labour to the unions under the so-called 'social contract' than to any deep concern with the debility of Parliament. It is illustrative of the same politicisation that the recent pamphlet on parliamentary reform published by Labour's NEC, under the chairmanship of Eric Heffer, recommended changes in the structure and functioning of the Commons which are designed solely to support and to facilitate the implementation of measures initiated by any future left-wing ministers – a packet of proposals which together constituted a travesty of liberal parliamentary government.

But far too much time and space has been spent in the literature on this particular and highly limited facet of Parliament, to the detriment of wider critiques of the system as it now operates. Those few reformers who, like Bernard Crick, if one excepts the unpolitical prescriptions, put an emphasis on the prime function of Parliament as focusing the political aspirations of the electorate and in producing a constructive and rewarding relationship between Parliament and people surely got the emphasis right, even if their instrumental arguments were faulty. But it is some considerable time since such a situation can be said to have existed. The British people are now grooved through hard experience to expect failure from their system of government. As Max Beloff has pointed out, the public reaction to the Falklands war had nothing to do with bellicosity or jingoism, but that for once the country had done something efficiently and successfully, which came as a much-needed relief from a generally diffused anxiety and a pervading sense of decline. It may be the case, as Ronald Butt (1969) observed in his book *The Power of Parliament*, that '. . . the solution of particular problems is not the basic purpose of Parliament'. But it is worth examining some of Butt's reflections, written when relative economic decline had become generally discernible, in the light of what has happened in the 16 years since he first wrote. Even in the first edition of his work in 1967 he could detect a growing malaise in the British political system, which he likens to the wave of discontent with Parliament which arose in the 1920s and 1930s, and produced reactions with totalitarian overtones. But he is realistic enough to realise that although a sense of failure rubs off on institutions, '. . . it would be a diversion from the necessary political, social and economic change to assume that the impetus can come from parliamentary reform'. And again from Butt, before he swung solidly to the right and put himself behind the neo-liberals in the Conservative party,

> . . . it may not be out of place to suggest that the remedies must be generated through new social and political impulses – perhaps reflected through the structure of the political parties which use our parliamentary machinery – rather than by blueprints for parliamentary reform. For, if the right impulses are generated politically and socially, there can be little doubt that Parliament will respond, as it always has.

The dysfunction of the party system which Butt recognises, particularly for producing a consistent strategy of successful economic management, has become much more marked since he wrote. Yet the response of the major parties to failure and to a corresponding decline in electoral support (the perception of the electorate of dysfunction has always been more acute than that of the politicians) has been to retreat further into ideology and to resist hysterically movements for constitutional and consequential political reform. It is the final disservice of the governing parties that as they become less relevant they grow evermore self-protective, whatever the cost to the nation. Very few of their politicians are prepared even to examine the consequences of their decline into sectarian minorities. The chimera of total power, of perpetual zero-sum politics, persists, manifestly though it ignores pubic demand. A parliamentary system which grows unrepresentative, dominated by parties reliant to an increasing extent on dogma, is bound to fail in a number of ways. Ronald Butt, in *The Power of Parliament*, wisely concentrates on the larger functions of the system, and it is worthwhile commenting on the success of Parliament in meeting these fundamental requirements. The first that he discerns is the parliamentary task of 'preserving legitimacy in government'. But is this to be done by any House of Commons, or does the reflection of a majority electoral will have any part to play? If so, there has been no legitimate Parliament since the election of 1936. For some reason which this writer has never been able to understand, the electorate acquiesces meekly in an electoral system which always returns minority governments in terms of votes cast, which proceed to adopt public policy which the majority finds repugnant. The situation has grown worse – I would say intolerable – with the drop in support for the major parties of the last ten years or so. That this has contributed to a situation where increasingly Parliament's claim to legitimise public policy is called into question cannot be denied. Although the parties have demanded a mandate to effect radical changes in society (this is not to say that radical changes of a different sort are not needed) their control over the outcomes, and in particular over non-governmental forces in society, has declined. It is now commonplace for organised groups, which can command more support from their members than can governments, to resist by all available means intentions of which they do not approve, in the usually correct assumption that a change of party government will relieve them of the need to obey the law, or to co-operate with announced policy. Richard Rose's (1980) denial of this – his identification of what he calls a 'rolling consensus' from one administration to another, is not supported by detailed analysis of major public policies, especially in the economic field, of the last twenty years. What continuity there has been in this sector has owed more to the actions of civil servants, with their concern for a minimum degree of stability, than to the politicians. In many areas of concern a settled public intention over time is becoming impossible to devise. The system can no longer contain them, and more and more areas are becoming closed off from effective political action.

The second major function which Butt perceives is 'to maintain the freedom of the citizen under law'. But what does he make of a system which forced through Mr Foot's closed-shop legislation, written largely by the unions themselves, by a government which rested on the support of 29% of the electorate? Or the same government which could deny individual firms threatened by nationalisation their rights under hybrid bill procedure, by the expedient of using its technical majority to suspend standing orders? Or a system which produced governments which have more regularly been brought to the bar of the European Commission and Court of Human Rights in recent years than any other signatory to the Convention?

Thirdly, according to Butt, 'to ensure that the dialectic of politics never ceases'. My dictionary defines dialectic as 'the art of investigating the truth of opinions, of testing truth by discussion'. Prime Minister's Question Time? The charades which pass for debate on economic and industrial issues in the House? If the Commons on important occasions increasingly resembles a cockpit, this relates directly to Butt's fourth function: 'To channel into broad and manageable streams the ultimate choices available to the community'. There is no space here, nor is it necessary for anyone with a detailed knowledge of recent parliamentary history, to expose the relentless frustrations of the broad choices which have been put to the electorate by the parties. But more important than past failures, we have now reached a position where there is no point of contact between the parties on the key issues of defence, foreign policy, Europe, economic and industrial strategy: the parliamentary dialogue on these matters is now a dialogue of the deaf. In Butt's terms, these differences are no longer manageable within a liberal parliamentary polity. To persist with this situation would be to usher in a period, to the end of the century and beyond, of such massive uncertainty and discontinuity as to ensure the ultimate decline of Britain and to threaten democracy itself. Between the neo-Marxists and the neo-liberal populists there can be no accommodation. Nor can the parliamentary leadership of the parties, especially on the Labour side, any more be relied on to mitigate these harsh dissonances. As Samuel Beer (1982a), perhaps the most distinguished outside commentator on the British political scene, has percipiently noted, there seems little hope that either the Labour party in its present form or a neo-liberal Conservative party can produce a lasting consensus in British society which would form a new and continuing basis, largely immune from marginal swings in public support, on which consistent and long-term policy can be built. The forces of resistance to both are too powerful and deep-seated to produce a consensus sufficiently wide and durable to protect it from fundamental reversal as a result of future elections.

The truth is that individuals and groups have lost fundamental trust in the political process – as Beer (1982a: 452) remarks, 'they have lost belief in the legitimacy and effectiveness of the mechanisms of public choice'. That the system needs to be opened up and once more present the possibility of options for action embracing a wide spectrum of preferences is now obvious. The underlying situation is that British parliamentary government, and the political system which informs it, is not responding, as has happened at other critical times, to social change and evolution. It is worthwhile my again quoting Paul Rose (*The Guardian*, 12 February 1979), the Labour MP who opted out of the Commons in 1979 as a result of his recognition of the deficiences of the system to which he was contributing his support:

> Society itself is more varied and sophisticated. The concept of two monolithic classes represented by the two parties is as simplistic as applying Adam Smith's or Karl Marx's analyses of Victorian capitalism to the EEC or Comecon. To regard the present electoral system as sacrosanct and alternatives as heresy is particularly foolish in the light of multi-party

democracies which flourish in other parts of Europe and farther afield . . . I believe that our present parliamentary system stifles individuality and innovation. It is illiberal and based on the flow of power from the top downwards. It is a reflection of the ossification of institutions and attitudes which are responsible for Britain's economic decline . . .

As should be apparent from the preceding analysis, there are a number of inter-connected reasons why electoral reform is desperately needed in Britain. The inter-connections mean that, unless perhaps for the last one, there is no particular primacy in the justifications offered. First, there is the problem of the continued legitimacy of parliamentary government in Britain. Assuming that support for the Alliance party is diminished by the 'wasted vote' argument, on the results of recent by-elections and the 1983 General Election there must be upwards of 30 per cent of the electorate which feels itself effectively disenfranchised by the present system. This is intolerable in a parliamentary democracy. It seems to me incredible that the Boundary Commission can be challenged in the courts (for purely party political reasons) on the grounds that its recommendations distort the electoral process, when the first-past-the-post electoral system which it serves has hugely more inherent distorting effects. Secondly, electoral reform, especially if it replaces the present system by the Single Transferable Vote (STV), will open up to the electorate a wide variety of choice of candidates from the same party, and undermine the power of constituency activists. As it is, given the preponderance of safe seats in the British parliamentary system, the bulk of the membership of the House of Commons is currently chosen by fewer people than before the 1832 Reform Act. Thirdly, and staying with the parliamentary effects of electoral reform, the existence of a powerful centre party, which would effectively be promoted by a changed electoral system, would, since for the foreseeable future coalition politics would result, produce a Commons which would need much more attention and careful management by government than the current parliamentary situation requires, and would go a considerable way towards redressing the balance of power between Westminster and Whitehall which has always been a principal aim of parliamentary reform. As a corollary to this, a Commons so politically constructed would provide a more receptive vehicle for the operation of procedural innovations such as select committees, which might at last be able to produce a convincing bilateral critique of government. Within the present power structure of the House such reforms stand little chance of success. But to stray beyond the limits of Parliament for the fourth and fifth reasons, the permanent existence of a centre party, moderating the ideological indulgences of both Labour and Tory, would provide a new and permanent political context to which the powerful economic interest groups, especially the unions, would need to adjust. The present two-party system, especially in relation to incomes policies, has been unsuccessful in relating the unions to public purposes, and there is massive evidence of a chronic institutional and political malaise in this field. The unions are, however, realists, and ultimately would accommodate to a political framework in which the abandonment of policy for electoral gain would no longer feature so prominently, and in which the Labour party, despite the private reservations of many of its MPs, could no longer act in government as the pliable arm of the TUC. Finally, and perhaps most importantly, a realignment of political forces in both country and Parliament, which, with the introduction of PR, would be dramatic, would provide for some much-needed consistency of policy. Constitutional change is needed as the precondition for a successful economic policy. The adversary style of British two-party politics and the frequent alternations of parties in government have disrupted continuity, particularly in the development of a permanent incomes policy and economic planning institutions. A new climate for investment and for the integration of the unions into positive economic decision-making would result from constitutional change. Such a development is not merely peripheral to the problems of parliamentary government – it is central. As Norman Gash (1978) has observed, 'A successful [parliamentary] system rests on the axiom that the parties must agree on fundamentals and differ only in details'. I believe that a wide agreement on the continuance of a liberal capitalist state and economy exists in Britain, and that only the warped nature of the representative system prevents this from being self-evident. The Labour party knows this, too, hence its rooted opposition to electoral reform. As its former Secretary, Ron Hayward, put it in an ingenuous letter to *The Times* a few years ago, 'With PR would vanish all our hopes of a socialist Britain'. No better statement of the willingness of the major parties to distort democracy for ideological ends can be found.

To develop a wider and more compelling consensus on the basis of constitutional reform has been the task many times in the past. The writer would argue that such a time has come again, and that a new basis for restoring trust in British institutions is badly needed. For authority must be based on consent and trust – to counterpose the two is to fail signally to misunderstand the nature of liberal representative government. To Samuel Beer, the way forward is represented by the SDP/Liberal Alliance, and the potential support for the same basic attitudes which at present is imprisoned within the other parties. As Beer (1982a: 453) remarks, the Alliance is attempting to come to terms with the revolution in social attitudes and culture which has so weakened the other parties, and that 'thanks to these attitudes towards both policy and politics their attempt to mobilise consent runs closer to the grain of political reality than the attempts of their rivals'.

A few concluding words on the party system and the nature of consensus. Any long-term change in the political structure of Britain will result, for some time at least, in a modification of the two-party system. But the myth of this system, founded on the illusion of permanence in institutions, remains dominant, despite the cumulative evidence of its dysfunction. The percipient observer of the British party scene may note that the illusion is buttressed almost unconsciously by the Anglo-Saxon tradition, and there can be no doubt that until recently this system, enveloping a sub-system of interest groups, has served Britain, and countries nurtured in the British tradition, well. The question so far as Britain is concerned is whether it can continue to do so, and the evidence is that it cannot. Some two-party systems have shown an enviable capacity for development and self-renewal – that of the USA is a prime example. In Britain the Conservative party has shown an equally pronounced capacity for adaptation and development – its post-war conversion to the requirements of a new political settlement ensured the continued stability of the British political and social order at a critical time. Nor should one assume that its capacity for development has been arrested or reversed by the onset of neo-liberalism. The larger defects of this phase of Conservative philosophy are patent, but it would be erroneous to claim that all of its facets are valueless, or that it does not enshrine many truths that needed telling. But a longer perspective demonstrates that it is the Labour party which has occupied the central position in the post-war British political system, and, through its trade union connection, within industrial society in general, and that it has been this factor that has been critical to the recent historical development of Britain. Detailed analysis of the political economy of Britain since 1945 bears this out, and, in general, '[it is] the Labour Party that lies athwart the economic sinews of the nation in a way that the Conservative Party does not'. The Labour party's capacity to meet changed social and economic conditions has never been much in evidence – a case can be made that it has been regressive. As Henry Drucker (1979) has pointed out, it has persisted, in a way that similar European parties have not, in its basic ethos and doctrines, in the face of rapid social development, declining class-consciousness, whether due to affluence or nationalism, and the rise of other parties. The advent of the Alliance, and the possibility of electoral reform, though feared by Conservative Central Office, fortunately poses an ultimate threat to the Labour party, since it could probably only enter a coalition at the cost of a split, as in 1931. Historically the Conservatives win out in coalitions; to occupy a veto position is usually sufficient for most Tory purposes.

That the foregoing analysis was widely perceived as correct by substantial segments of the electorate was superbly illustrated by the results, in terms of votes cast, of the June 1983 General Election. It has been argued in this chapter that the issue is the survival of Britain, both economically and as a liberal polity, and that this survival has to be based on a consensus for moderation and stability – a recognition that the different world of the future, a world of weakening class loyalties and economic uncertainty, demands a different political structure to deal with it. It is against the ingrained instincts of the British people for precisely this moderation and consistency that the two-party system has been battering for too long. But constant talk of the end of consensus by the ideologues of the traditional parties flies in the face of the slow-moving mechanisms of social response and administration, mechanisms which are always subject to the inertia of tradition. But a vicious electoral system did its worst in June 1983, producing a distortion of the electoral will which authorities other than this author have called nothing less than grotesque. A pattern of voting which under PR would have produced moderate and permanent coalition was translated into overweening single-party government, free for a second parliamentary term from coherent and effective opposition. Our parliamentary system is diminished thereby; our economic prospects rendered dire; the future of the country gravely uncertain. Those who have argued, either on the grounds of political self-interest, or on the flimsiest of intellectural analyses, against a change in the electoral system, and they include some contributors to this volume, will bear considerable responsibility for the degradation of parliamentary government and continued economic decline which will, without doubt, characterise Britain for the foreseeable future.

3 'The Norton View'
Philip Norton

Parliament and parliamentary reform in Britain cannot be seen in isolation from the wider political, economic and social changes which affect society. Yet, ironically, many of those who now state this realisation with the greatest vehemence confine their analytical focus and their prescription to constitutional reform, principally reform of the electoral system.

This chapter is premised on the first assertion but rejects the narrow focus and the prescription of electoral reformers. It proceeds on the assumption that the problems with which Britain is now faced – many of which are not peculiar to Britain – are affected by and in part reflected in Parliament but that that affect is limited. Parliamentary reform is capable of having some but very limited influence upon this nation's capacity and willingness to overcome its current economic malaise.

In so far as Parliament can have some effect, it is this paper's contention that it should, given present conditions, seek to facilitate enhanced consent for the political system while not negating effective government, that is, the ability of government to raise and allocate resources to meet its commitments of public policy. Parliament can serve to provide a fine balance between effectiveness and consent, the twin pillars of political authority (Rose 1979). It is an important and necessary responsibility. But it is not one that will solve Britain's economic ills. For that one has to look to government and, just as importantly, beyond government. The concentration of electoral reformers and others on constitutional change – and the self-righteous vigour with which they advance it – generates a dangerous pursuit of myopic optimism. This chapter is informed by a more balanced assessment of the possibilities afforded by institutional change, and for its analysis and prescription draws upon hard data and an awareness of what is as the basis for what can be. We eschew pursuit of some idealistic (and not clearly articulated) role which there is little substantial evidence to suggest that Parliament could or ever will play.

The House of Commons in the political system

A legislature, according to various writers, is a functionally adaptable institution that can fulfil various tasks in a political system (see Mezey 1979: 4). Though some would question the extent to which the House of Commons, the dominant element of the constitutional triumvirate of the Queen-in-Parliament, has proved adaptable, it is nonetheless perceived as well as expected to fulfil certain functions. Foremost among these, the cornerstone of a number of other functions, is that of representation. The concept itself has rarely been subjected to close analysis (Pitkin 1967: 3) and is far from problem-free. It is beset with added complexity in the British context, given especially the role of party (Norton 1981a: 52–62). Reduced to its most simplistic, the Members of Parliament, individually and collectively, are deemed to defend and pursue the interests of those whom they are elected to represent; the latter comprise the electoral body of individual electors, divided into territorially-defined units, with each individual enjoying the right to cast one vote in any election to public office. As a representative assembly, the House of Commons is expected to fulfil the function of scrutiny and influence of government on behalf of the electoral body; at a macro-level, this takes the form of scrutiny and influence of national policy, and at a micro-level it takes the form of seeking redress by government of constituents' grievances. The legislature provides the personnel of government and legitimises both the government and its measures; by so doing, it serves as an important support of the political system. In terms of political authority, it can be seen to play a pivotal role in the maintenance of consent.

In the 1980s, the reality is that we are faced with a difficult conundrum when we contemplate the position of the House of Commons in the political process. On the one hand, it has failed to fulfil its task of scrutiny and influence of government. The dominance of the executive in Parliament was well established by the end of the nineteenth century. Since that time, government has been assured of the assent of the House of Commons. The problem has not been that the House of Commons has given its consent to government measures, but rather that it has been perceived as giving unquestioning assent to such measures without first subjecting them to sustained scrutiny. Increasingly, electors have felt alienated as their individual wishes and interests have been subordinated to the interests of party. On the other hand, any attempt to strengthen the position of the House of Commons in relation to that part of it which forms the government, helping ensure that it fulfils the role expected of it by the electoral body, would be a threat to the effectiveness of government at a time when that effectiveness is already under threat. Government is beset by problems of 'overload', of having to gain the co-operation of diverse and powerful groups which have sanctions against government which they may be willing to employ, of having to contend with an increasingly complex international environment over which it has little direct influence, and of having to manage an economy which severely restricts government's scope for action; an economy which previously allowed government to pursue policies and make commitments which raised expectations, expectations which did not subside when the economy did. For the House of Commons to act as a further counterweight to government effectiveness could undermine rather than enhance consent. As government effectiveness diminished, so consent would decline. As Anthony King has observed, 'legislative influence by no means guarantees optimal outcomes' (1981: 78). In terms of political authority, a more powerful House of Commons would not be cost free.

The difficult questions with which we are faced, I would suggest, are two in number. First, is there a means by which the House of Commons can fulfil the functions expected of it while maintaining some balance between the needs of governmental effectiveness and consent, increasing the latter without seriously undermining the former? And, second, if so, how can it be achieved? The answers to these questions can be subsumed under two headings, the 'Westminster model' in answer to the first, the 'Norton view' in response to the second. The latter is not dependent upon, nor tied inextricably to, the former, but it does provide the means for its realisation.

The Westminster Model

The Westminster model of government evolved from the experience of British government in the period from 1867 to 1914 and may be said to constitute a coalescence of constitutional precepts and institutions with a recognition of prevailing, or what were perceived to be prevailing, political realities. Reference to it, indeed attachment to it, became common, but it was rarely delineated in definitive terms. Its essential characteristics I would identify as follows.

The model is essentially a government-centred one, indeed a cabinet-centred one, with the initiative for the formulation of measures and the maintenance of the Queen's government resting with the Cabinet. The Cabinet is party-based, being formed as a consequence of a party having won a majority (or possibly a plurality) of seats at a general election. Measures formulated by the government, assisted by its permanent officials and probably on the prompting of outside groups, are submitted to Parliament; the elected element, the House of Commons, subjects those measures to sustained scrutiny and debate before legitimising them. By virtue of the concept of parliamentary sovereignty, still the cornerstone of the British constitution, the legislative outputs of Parliament are deemed to be binding and accepted as such by the courts. The election of the Commons provides the political strength for popular acceptance of parliamentary sovereignty, the legislative measures having been scrutinised and approved by Members of Parliament on behalf of those whom they were returned to represent. Hence, the House of Commons, by fulfilling the functions of scrutiny and legitimisation, serves as an important support of the political system.

This model enjoys the advantages of incorporating the role played by parties: the opposition is deemed to be the main element in Parliament which ensures that government is subject to public scrutiny; the government majority, a majority facilitated by the first-past-the-post electoral system, ensures that the measures receive assent. During a Parliament, party government is responsive to the wishes of the electorate via the House of Commons; ultimately, it is responsible to the electorate in a general election. Hence, a somewhat idealised model: government effectiveness is facilitated by government being able to ensure passage of its measures via a party majority, and consent is maintained by virtue of the fact that such measures are subject to parliamentary attention and that at the end of the day the party in government can be turned out at a general election; consent which, in turn, enhances government effectiveness.

The attractiveness of this model of government was such that it enjoyed support not only at home but also abroad; the concept of 'responsible government' (for which read 'responsible but effective government') which it embodied had an especial appeal to some American observers (Epstein 1980); to some extent, it still does (Norton 1981b). However, whatever the attraction of the model in a normative sense, it was seen increasingly to be flawed as a descriptive one. Conditions no longer appeared to fit the Westminster model of government.

In terms of the relationship between Parliament and that part of it which forms the government, this has been apparent for some time. The House of Commons failed to keep pace with developments in government and administration. The Commons itself, based on party, came to be dominated by party. A combination of loyalty to party, a belief by government supporters that a defeat of the government in the lobbies (on whatever issue) would necessitate the government resigning or requesting a dissolution, an acceptance that the government of the day 'knew best' by virtue of superior resources and information, and fear of the powers wielded by party whips and constituency associations, ensured that the government – if it enjoyed an overall party majority – was ensured of the passage of its measures. Government supporters lacked the resolve to submit their leaders to sustained investigation; opposition members lacked the facilities to do so. Control of the timetable and of a parliamentary majority facilitated the emergence of what has subsequently been dubbed an 'elective dictatorship' (Hailsham 1976).

Recognition of the hegemony of government in the relationship between government and the House of Commons is not new. It found expression in various tracts, and in evidence to the Select Committee on Procedure, in the 1930s (see especially Jennings 1934; also Hansard Society 1967); it has been more recently articulated since the early 1960s and especially in the past decade. Reformers of the 1960s, having recognised the deficiencies of the existing relationship, sought essentially to restore rather than replace the Westminster model. They argued for changes in parliamentary procedures, and for better pay and facilities for Members, in order that the House of Commons could subject government to scrutiny and, through information and debate, keep it responsive to the underlying currents and drift of public expectations; the tasks of the House were deemed to be those of influence, advice, criticism, scrutiny and publicity (Crick 1968: 80). The government was expected to govern, but 'strong government needs strong opposition' (Crick 1968: 246). In short, an attempt was made to change conditions to ensure a better fit with the normative model.

The reformers of the 1970s took a very different approach. Many of the reforms advocated by reformers of the 1960s saw the light of day through the medium of Richard Crossman as Leader of the House. By the early 1970s, it was apparent that the reforms had failed to achieve a shift in the relationship between the House and that part of it which formed the government (Norton 1981a: 205-7). Recognition of this fact, coupled with the indecisive results of two general elections in 1974 and Britain's worsening economic plight, generated calls for a new relationship between government and Parliament, indeed, in many cases, for a reformulated constitutional structure (e.g. Johnson 1977; Liberal Party 1980). The Westminster model of government served not as a useful guide but rather as a hindrance, an unnecessary encumbrance. Debate began to centre around John Mackintosh's question: 'Away from the Westminster model towards what?' (1974: 191). The agenda of political debate in Britain now includes calls for a new electoral system and, constitutionally the most radical proposal, for an entrenched Bill of Rights. The Westminster model has been allowed, indeed encouraged, to fade into the mists of history.

Given the realisation that conditions did not fit the Westminster model, and given the experience of the 1970s and the contemporary debate, the reader may be forgiven for raising an eyebrow at the advocacy in this chapter of the merits of the Westminster model. My argument is simply stated. It is not a reactionary one. I do not argue the case for a reversion to some past glories of executive-legislative relationships. Rather, my argument is that Britain has never experienced the Westminster model of government. This is not to argue that there has not been a 'golden age' of Parliament, but that is not pertinent to the argument about the Westminster model. Nor is it to question the fact that many have believed, and have been taught, that Britain has enjoyed the experience of this type of government. (Indeed, this is central to understanding the maintenance of consent). Realisation that Britain does not enjoy the Westminster model of government has not extended to the realisation that it never has done: the model was formulated at a time when conditions were changing to produce a form of government that could not be subsumed under that model. Recent decades have not witnessed a demise of the Westminster form of government; rather, Britain has experienced the extension of a form of government which has existed largely since the end of the nineteenth century. In arguing the case for the Westminster model as a normative model, I am not therefore seeking to cling to an outworn descriptive model. Rather, I would seek to turn Mackintosh's question on its head. The question should not be, 'Away from the Westminster Model towards what?' but, instead, 'Away from what exists towards the Westminster model?'.

My contention is that the Westminster model, or at least some modified Westminster model, provides a useful normative framework for positing the relationship between the House of Commons and government, one that is especially relevant within the wider context of contemporary British politics. The Tory strain in British politics which emphasises the importance of strong government remains relevant in the 1980s for reasons already touched upon; government, more so than hitherto, needs to be able to maintain its effectiveness, to be able to allocate resources to meet its policy commitments. Concomitantly, the Whig strain which in its modern manifestation favours Parliament providing the limits within which government may govern remains important, again more so perhaps than hitherto. Government is faced with ever-growing demands by external bodies, bodies which have sanctions which they can and do employ against government. A more specialised society tends to give increasing political influence to functional groups and to bureaucrats, bodies which are responsible if at all to their own members and to their own bureaucratic ethos. Government cannot ignore them, quite the reverse, but if it is to maintain the consent of the collectivity of individuals that form the electorate it must have regard also to the body which represents the electorate, and from which it itself is drawn: the House of Commons. Indeed, a House of Commons capable of subjecting government measures to sustained scrutiny and influence could serve to strengthen rather than weaken government in its relationship with functional groups and civil servants. There is thus a case for a House of Commons fulfilling the role posited by the Westminster model, and for doing so within the context of party.

In the contemporary debate on the British party system, criticism of the two-party system appears to be confused with criticism of party *qua* party. Party serves not only to aggregate and give shape to votes cast by electors, it serves also to provide a valuable counterweight to the influence of interest groups. Such groups already have the ear, and to some extent the arm, of government; to remove party would be to facilitate a factional system, as exists in the United States (Jones 1981), one in which groups potentially could dominate the parliamentary as well as the executive constituent of the political process. Party strength may weaken the effectiveness of select committees in seeking to perform the function of scrutiny of the executive, as a number of critics have observed; what is less often realised is that the *absence* of strong parties works against committees of the United States Congress fulfilling the same task. It can be contended that the fact that groups do not dominate the House of Commons is irrelevant; as long as such groups can persuade or coerce government to agree to their demands, then the Commons will concur with the government. But that serves to reinforce the case for a strengthened House of Commons, one which government cannot take for granted. A House of Commons which exerts effective scrutiny and influence of government, and is seen to be performing that function, can both serve to limit the power of non-elected groups in British society and concomitantly enhance consent for the political system. Hence the case for the Westminster model of government as a prescriptive model.

How then can one ensure that conditions change to fit the model, to ensure that the prescriptive coincides with the descriptive, in a way that it has not done before? The answer, I will argue, is to be found primarily within the House of Commons; at its root lies an attitudinal change on the part of Members of Parliament. The 'Norton view' posits a change of attitude on the part of MPs as a necessary, albeit not sufficient, condition for a change in the relationship between the House of Commons and that part of it which forms the government.

Before proceeding, though, two points should be borne in mind. The Westminster model prescribes a limited, but nonetheless important, role for the House of Commons in the political process. Given the disparate distribution of power in Britain today, no one body enjoying predominance in the making of political decisions, it would be difficult to posit more than a limited role for the House of Commons. It is and can be one of several actors on the political stage, one of several influences impinging upon government. Nonetheless, given the nature of some of the pressures brought to bear on government, all the more reason for trying to ensure that the House of Commons does play that albeit limited role. Secondly, as with most models, one cannot expect the normative model to provide a perfect fit with what actually happens. Its value is in prescribing a framework, one that gives some meaning to existing structures and relationships and provides the frame of reference for structures and relationships which one seeks to create. In positing changes for the House of Commons, we are thus working towards an ideal, one that is hardly likely to be fully realised, but one nonetheless that is worth working towards. It is one which is, at least, more realisable than other prescriptions which have been proferred in recent years.

The Norton View

The approach which has been termed the Norton View is one that seeks a shift in the relationship between the House of Commons and that part of it which forms the government through an attitudinal change on the part of Members of Parliament. It does not reject structural changes but argues rather that an attitudinal change is a prerequisite to effective structural or procedural change. It is an approach which exists independently of that which advocates the Westminster model of government; but it provides an effective means whereby the relationship posited by the Westminster model may be achieved. It may be said to be in the tradition of British politics in that it profers no radical prescription divorced from experience, seeks change which will not do violence to the existing political fabric, and draws upon recent experience in order to demonstrate that it is a viable approach. Its aim is to realise a House of Commons that can provide the limits within which government can govern, subjecting it in so doing to effective scrutiny and influence, while allowing government nonetheless to govern, to indulge in forward planning on the assumption that it is likely but not guaranteed to gain the assent of the House, knowledge that the House cannot be taken for granted providing a government more responsive to anticipated parliamentary reaction. In such a relationship, the House of Commons is able, or as able as it is likely to be, to fulfil both the macro and micro functions expected of it.

The Norton view posits no new powers for the House of Commons. Rather, it argues that the power necessary to ensure a shift in the relationship between the House and that part of it which forms the government exists already: the power to defeat the government in the division lobbies, in effect to deny legitimisation to the government and to its measures. This power is a long-standing one. What has been absent has been the willingness to utilise this power: the political will has been lacking. That this should be so is not surprising. The reasons for it we have touched upon already: Members want their party to succeed and will normally wish to vote for it; even on those occasions when they disagree with their leaders, they are constrained from voting against them by fear of the presumed constitutional consequences of a government defeat and for fear of what may happen to them at the hands of the whips and their constituency parties; they lack also alternative authoritative information to pit against the government. Acceptance of the existence of these constraints has impelled Members to vote with their party; the consequent party cohesion in the division lobbies reinforced, or at least did nothing to undermine, such presumptions. For the past century, party cohesion has been a feature of the Commons' division lobbies (Lowell 1924; Beer 1969). It is not surprising that many observers should therefore discard the threat of defeat as an effective weapon in the hands of Members. Reformers of the 1960s who sought to strengthen parliamentary scrutiny and influence emphasised the need to disseminate information to the electorate; 'parliamentary control', declared Bernard Crick (1965), 'is effective not because of the division lobbies but because debates are aimed at the electorate'.

What has not been realised has been that the assumptions underlying the constraints on Members' voting behaviour have been built largely on sand. The belief that any government defeat in the division lobbies will necessitate the government resigning or requesting a dissolution has been variously expressed (Moodie 1964: 100; Harvey and Bather 1965; 234; see Norton 1978b: 360); acceptance of it by Members of Parliament has clearly influenced their voting behaviour. Nonetheless, it may be described as a constitutional 'myth': it has no basis in any authoritative source nor in any continuous basis of practice. The constitutional convention may be simply expressed: a government is expected to submit its resignation or request a dissolution in the event only of a defeat on an explicit vote of confidence. If defeated on an issue central to its policy, it may seek subsequently a vote of confidence from the House *or* resign or request a dissolution; if defeated on a matter not central to government policy, it need concern itself only with whether to accept the defeat or to seek its *de facto* reversal at some later stage (Norton 1978b: 360–78). Few divisions are held on votes of confidence.

The presumed political constraints are similarly fallacious, albeit not quite to the same extent. The primary functions of the party whips are those of communication and management. Their disciplinary function is essentially a minor one and their presumed disciplinary sanctions akin to the Emperor's Clothes. Their essential power is that of persuasion; and to some extent their persuasion rests on the existence of the belief in the other constraints mentioned. Contrary to popular belief, the whips do not enjoy the power to withdraw the whip from dissenting Members (Norton 1978c: 409). Their other powers are of limited importance, useful perhaps but insufficient to coerce Members determined to enter a dissenting lobby; in Uwe Kitzinger's (1973: 173) words, they constitute 'the small change of political life, with which habits of conformity can be cemented, but with which no one would expect to buy great votes of principle'. One former Member put it somewhat more starkly: 'In fact there is no such thing as "the tyranny of the whips" because the whips have no sanctions whatever at their disposal' (Woodhouse 1976). The whips serve primarily to facilitate party cohesion, not to force it.

The influence of constituency parties is somewhat more potent, and generally recognised as such by Members. It remains an important – indeed, *the* most important – constraint, but not as powerful as some would believe. If a Member is well-entrenched within his constituency, the chances of him or her being denied re-adoption because of dissenting behaviour in the division lobbies are extremely slim. Beliefs to the contrary have been fuelled by a misinterpretation of the fate of the Conservative 'Suez rebels' of the 1950s, notably Nigel Nicolson in Bournemouth East. His opposition to the government's Suez adventure was a necessary but not sufficient condition in motivating his local association to choose another candidate. Since the Second World War, no Member of Parliament has been denied re-adoption by his local party solely because of deviant voting behaviour in Parliament; indeed, few cases of rejection can even be attributed to a solely political motive.

The assertion that the government has resources which cannot be fully matched by the House of Commons remains valid, although occasionally over-stated. It is also correct to assert that government remains reluctant to reveal information on which many decisions are reached. Two points should nonetheless be borne in mind. First, optimal decisions are not a consectary of superior resources; those resources may be misused, not fully utilised or may be divided within themselves. Governments, despite (possibly because of) a large body of civil servants and other facilities, can get things wrong. Information emanating from departments may be misunderstood, ignored or utilised for partisan or even personal reasons. Second, knowing the information on which a decision is based is not always necessary in order to evaluate the merits of that decision. Hence, restricted information and a claim by government to superior resources do not constitute a logical bar to the House of Commons debating, and more importantly seeking to influence, the decisions of government.

The constraints presumed to operate on Members may thus be seen to rest on tenuous foundations. One would expect Members to want to vote usually with their party, and it is necessary for the balance posited by the Westminster model that they do so, but there is no reason why on those occasions when they dissent from their leaders they should not do so; there are strong reasons why they should do so. However, contending that the assumptions on which the foregoing constraints are based rest on sand and demonstrating that point to the satisfaction of the collectivity of Members of Parliament, as well as outside observers, are not one and the same thing. Indeed, to have developed the preceding argument a decade or so ago would have had little impact; readers would have merely had to glance at the division lobbies to remain unconvinced. What has given the lie to the assumptions on which the constraints are based, and concomitantly provided a strong factual base for the view of this author, has been the parliamentary behaviour of the past ten years.

The increasing difficulty of government to maintain effectiveness in the 1960s and early 1970s precipitated various policies which created unease on the government backbenches in the House of Commons. Such policies provided a necessary but not sufficient condition for a serious increase in intra-party dissent in the Commons' division lobbies. The sufficient conditions were provided in the Parliament of 1970–74, when the manner of the leadership of Edward Heath served to transform covert dissent into public dissent in the division lobbies (Norton 1978a). In that Parliament, Conservative MPs dissented not only on more occasions and in greater numbers than hitherto (significantly so), they did so with more effect. For the first time in recent history, government backbenchers proved willing to enter a whipped opposition lobby to deny a majority to the government. They did so on six occasions, three of these defeats taking place on three-line whips; the most important was on the immigration rules in 1972 when fifty-six Conservative Members abstained or voted against the government (Norton 1976). 'These examples are especially telling because the Conservative government of 1970–74 did have a parliamentary majority at just the level of modesty once thought most likely to ensure solidarity and so its policy-making effectiveness' (Epstein 1980: 19). In addition, fifteen Conservatives proved willing to vote against their own government on a vote of confidence on the second reading of the European Communities Bill in 1972. The incidence of intra-party dissent in this Parliament is significant given later events of the decade. 'The rising intra-party dissension of the early 1970s', as Epstein (1980: 19) observed, 'makes it unlikely that the better-known dissension during the Labour government of 1974–79 could be characteristic only of circumstances in which there was either the barest party majority or none'.

The defeats of 1970–74 were reinforced by those of the two subsequent Parliaments. In the short Parliament of 1974, the Labour government was defeated on seventeen occasions, a consequence of opposition parties combining against a minority government. In the Parliament of 1974–79 the government was vulnerable to defeat as a result of its own backbenchers voting with the opposition and after April 1976, when it became a minority government, to opposition parties combining against it. The government suffered a total of forty-two defeats, twenty-three of them attributable to Labour backbenchers entering the opposition lobby and the other nineteen attributable to the combination of opposition parties in the 'No' lobby. Various of the defeats suffered at the hands of backbench dissenters were the result of a significant number of Labour Members entering the opposition lobby; on occasion the government went down to defeat with majorities of fifty or more against it (Norton 1980: 459). Disunity within the ranks of the parliamentary Labour party was such that to find a similar period when 'party votes' dipped below the proportion of ninety per cent of divisions one has to go back to the sessions of 1906 and 1908 (Beer 1982b; Norton 1980: 440). The defeats themselves were on important issues, increasingly so – the government's devolution legislation, taxation, the Dock Work Regulation Bill, Expenditure White Papers, the European Green Pound and the policy of imposing sanctions against firms breaking the five per cent pay limit, for instance, culminating in the defeat on a vote of confidence on 28th March 1979. The defeats suffered in the division lobbies were the tip of an iceberg. Over one-hundred defeats were incurred in standing committees.

In the seven years between April 1972 and April 1979, a total of sixty-five government defeats were imposed in the Commons' division lobbies. To find a similar number of defeats one has to go back to the period from 1863 to 1869 inclusive (Norton 1980: 442). These defeats were clearly important in themselves, affecting both the policies and behaviour of the government. They had also a much wider significance. They served to dispel the assumptions underlying the constraints presumed to operate on MPs and to generate a change of attitude on the part of Members as to what they could achieve in their relationship with government.

The experience of the 1970s was sufficient to dispel the various assumptions underlying the constraints presumed to operate. In response to the various defeats in the lobbies, the government of the day responded in line with precedent; the popular view that there was a deviation from previous practice (Jordan 1979: 38; Schwarz 1980) is incorrect. What changed was not the basis of the government's response but the number of defeats. When defeated on a vote of confidence, the government requested a dissolution. When defeated on issues central to its basic policies, it sought a vote of confidence. When defeated in votes on matters not at the heart of government policy, it contented itself with accepting them (which usually it did) or seeking their *de facto* reversal at some later stage. The experience, once its lessons were learned, had significant implications for both back-benchers and the government. A majority of the House could force the government to think again without necessarily raising any wider constitutional implications. The House may have its way on a particular issue; the government remains in office. 'Thus, awareness of the difference between types of government defeats in the lobbies can help ensure some element of stability in government, the government only being required to resign if defeated on a vote of confidence, while permitting Members a degree of freedom in voting behaviour which previously many felt that they did not have' (Norton 1978b: 378). The whips were shown to be 'not so much whips as feather dusters' (King 1974: 59). They took no disciplinary action, covert or overt, against persistent dissenters; they had neither the powers nor the wish to do so (see Norton 1978a: 163–75). Constituency associations proved less willing than might have been expected to take action against dissenting Members. The only Conservative Members to run into trouble with their local parties because of their parliamentary voting behaviour were a minority of those who voted against the government on the vote of confidence in 1972 and persisted in their opposition to the European Communities Bill; none was denied re-adoption (Norton 1978a: 177–91). No persistent Labour dissenter in the period of Labour government fell foul of his constituency party; on occasion, dissent gained the plaudit rather than the opprobrium of party activists. Of Labour Members denied re-adoption in recent years, none has been denied because of deviant voting behaviour. Even those who have run into trouble with party activists because of apparent political disagreement, influences other than a political divide can be seen to have been at work. A well entrenched Member is difficult to dislodge, for whatever reason.

Encouraged doubtless by the revelations of the Crossman *Diaries* (1975; 1976; 1977) and the experience of government economic policy, MPs have become increasingly doubtful about the government's claim that it 'knows best'. Members have proved willing to question more the assertions of government, on occasion turning to alternative sources of information (Norton 1978d: 235). Some individual Members have been seen, or considered by other Members, to have shown more foresight than government on various issues: Peter Tapsell on economic and energy policy in 1970–74, for example, and Keith Speed on defence policy in 1982. Such instances, however sporadic and exceptional, serve to reinforce the growing unwillingness to take for granted what the government puts forward. It serves to encourage a greater willingness to utilise select committees and the use of specialist advisers.

As the number of defeats built up in the 1970s and the constraints presumed to operate to be flimsy edifices, so Members began to realise that they had opportunities to influence government of which they had not been previously aware. As the decade progressed, a change of attitude on the part of Members of Parliament, or at least a plurality of them, became perceptible. This change was noted and commented upon by George Cunningham (1980: 192–3) the Member responsible for engineering a number of government defeats:

> Just as a habit of blind obedience can grow, so can a habit of thinking and voting for oneself on occasions. . . . The interesting thing is that, as the period advanced, it became easier to approach colleagues asking them to look at an argument and consider supporting a move against a specific Government proposal. Slowly, enough Members came to take a mild degree of voting independence for granted. They ceased to believe that the Government in the end must know best and they enjoyed the use of the power the electorate had given them.

Members began to realise the potential afforded by their willingness to combine on occasion against the government. It provided the basis on which they could generate the structures necessary to facilitate sustained scrutiny of administration and executive policy. Select committees were perceived as the most suitable vehicles for such scrutiny and for enabling backbenchers to realise their new 'participant' rather than 'deferential' attitude towards government (Beer 1982b). The willingness of Members to force their will on government produced a debate on the recommendations of the Select Committee on Procedure (HC 588 1978) in February 1979 and extracted from the Leader of the House, Michael Foot, the opportunity to vote on the recommendations (HC Debates 1979, vol. 963: 383–4). The 1979 general election then intervened. A combination of back-bench pressure and a reforming Leader of the House, Norman St John-Stevas, resulted in the proposals going through an unconvinced and generally hostile Cabinet (Norton 1981a: 232), being approved by the House of Commons by 248 votes to 12 (HC Debates 1979, vol. 969: 247–50). As much as anything, the new select committee structure could be characterised as being the product of the initiative and the wishes of the House of Commons and not that part of it which forms the government.

The experience of the past decade thus provides empirical credence for the Norton view. If the House of Commons is to fulfil the role of scrutiny and influence of government it can do so only if the political will exists among Members of Parliament. Once Members have that will, it is possible to provide the limits within which government can govern and create structures that will facilitate sustained scrutiny and influence of government. An attitudinal change is a prerequisite to effective structural change. It is a change which will and to some extent has taken place within the context of party. Party remains central to Members' beliefs and behaviour. It is important that it remain so. Party gives some coherence to Members' attitudes and behaviour. What has changed has been the presumptions which forced almost unthinking cohesion. Hence, a party government can assume a supportive majority in the House of Commons, but not an unquestioningly loyal majority.

If the House of Commons is to fulfil effective scrutiny and influence of government, there is still a long road to tread: the events of the past few years have realised the beginning of moves in the right direction, not the arrival at the point of destination. Members must develop further the willingness to question and to call to account the government and to subject it to sustained scrutiny and influence. The select committees must be developed further and a more effective linkage established between their activities and the floor of the House. There must be more extensive use of bodies such as the Special Standing Committees which have the power to examine witnesses. There must be better and more effective machinery for the scrutiny of government estimates. There also needs to be better facilities for Members to fulfil their functions, not only at the macro but also the micro level. Both the House of Commons Commission and the Liaison Select Committee need to be developed in order to help achieve some of these aims.

There is thus still a long way to go. The events of the 1970s show the way to go. The experience of the 1979–83 Parliament was not disappointing. The government suffered one significant defeat, on the immigration rules in December 1982. On at least ten occasions, the government withdrew or modified measures under threat of defeat. More importantly, a number of proposals did not see the light of day because of anticipated parliamentary reactions. (The more the number of 'non-decisions' the greater the apparent influence of the House, though the less easy it becomes to detect). The select committees have also begun, albeit sporadically, to realise the aims of Members. Testimony to the influence of the committees is to be found not only in the positive attitudes expressed towards them by backbenchers but, more tellingly, by the increasingly negative attitude taken toward them by ministers and officials.

Whether or not the House of Commons moves forward remains to be seen. It will be difficult to revert to pre-1970 practices. As various Members have conceded 'the old days of party discipline are dead and buried' (Heffer 1978; see also Beer 1982b); the old assumptions have been dispelled. However, there is no guarantee that the House will attain the role expected of it. If it is to do so, then the view of this author stresses that its realisation can be achieved through Members of

Parliament willing it and being prepared to use their basic power: the vote. As the British government discovered in 1982 in the dispute over the Falkland Islands, negotiation is most effective when undertaken from a position of strength. It is a lesson which MPs themselves would do well to learn. 'The vote is the teeth of democracy in parliament', declared Dr. David Owen (1981: 161). 'Take away the ability to put issues to the vote and there is no power'. The House of Commons needs its gunboats and the resolve to use them when it deems necessary.

Conclusion

The Norton view posits the means by which re-alignment in the relationship between the House of Commons and the executive can be achieved, one in which the House subjects government to effective scrutiny and influence. The role is one that is basically limited but one that can contribute to the maintenance of consent for the political system. The Norton view posits no more than this. For greater government effectiveness, for the resolution of Britain's social and economic problems, one must look elsewhere. Systemic change can have only a very limited effect upon the country's fundamental problems. The limitations of systemic change should have been learnt as a result of systemic change elsewhere, for example, in local government and the National Health Service.

This approach, then, stipulates the way in which a balance in political authority, as existed in the eighteenth century and before and which was assumed to exist under the presumed operation of the Westminster form of government, may be achieved. It seeks to do so in order to contribute to a stable polity. It draws on a model of government which I would suggest enjoys support, as a normative model, at both the elite and the mass level. The contribution can be a modest one. Prevailing political conditions ensure that it can be no more than that. Those same conditions highlight the need for that modest contribution to be made.

4 Parliamentary Reform – The Internal View
Bruce George and Barbra Evans

> The net result of ten years of institutional tinkering in the House of Commons is plain to see. No changes have taken place which have altered significantly the manner in which the House operates nor the influence which it can exert. Perhaps the only development which potentially may gradually change the character of the place is the very proliferation of committees.
>
> (Johnson 1977: 57)

Whilst over the last twenty years we have seen changes in almost every walk of life, in governmental institutions and politics in Britain the structure and procedures of Parliament have remained largely intact. In fact, the most important traditions, such as the examination of government policy on the floor of the House rather than in committee, stretch back hundreds of years. Top hats, beards and gaslights aside, the Palace of Westminster in the 1980s bears a strong resemblance to the one described in the Victorian novels of Trollope and Disraeli. We have now reached the stage where even the exterior of the building is crumbling away, demonstrating most vividly that the superstructure of Parliament has not weathered the elements and the years as well as the internal fabric of parliamentary democracy.

Nevil Johnson was right to say that 'institutional tinkering' had achieved little. The executive has, in the past, swung the pendulum to ease its control of the legislature and there is little to challenge its total domination, aided by the strong two-party system, of Parliament. However, the flickers of reform have been kept alive by various individuals and committees in the House of Commons and although, for reformers, the pace has been painfully slow, the Parliament elected in May 1979 was ablaze with reform when compared to previous ones. It is the reforms introduced since 1979 which we will focus upon: their genesis, their practical operation and their potential for future development.

Terms of Reference

We have based this chapter, as an MP and a researcher, and both political scientists, on our experience of working in and around the House of Commons. We have adopted a polemical approach, which has been forced upon us as 'reformists' in the Palace of Westminster. But this does not mean that we fail to recognise that 'not all change is for the better'; for example, some reformers would be happy to see government power itself increased whilst others on the extreme left propose changes which would result in the abolition of the Houses of Parliament altogether. Moreover, we should point out from the outset that we employ a liberal definition of the term 'procedural reform'. Thus, we have looked beyond Erskine May's (1976: 205) definition of procedure as 'the rules and arrangements made by . . . [the] House for discharging its constitutional functions' and accept that any new role for the Commons is dependent also on attitudinal change amongst politicians. But in preface to our review of procedural reforms in recent years, and in order to assess their weight and likely consequences, we need to ask one fundamental question: what are the objectives of parliamentary reform?

Basically how reform is conceived depends upon one's view of Parliament's role in the wider political system. Stated starkly: we believe that the legislature should aim to control the executive more firmly along the lines defined by Crick (1968: 80): 'Control means *influence*, not direct power; *advice*, not command; *criticism*, not obstruction; *scrutiny*, not initiation; and *publicity*, not secrecy.'

What concerns us most is that the House of Commons hardly fulfils even the limited functions of control and influence, so succinctly described by Crick. In this respect the reforms of the 1979 Parliament have our support. If parliamentary control is to be effective it must be detailed and professional; and its principal instrument must be the committees of the House. Additionally, we want to see Parliament not only scrutinising the executive effectively, but also performing the educating and informing functions as ascribed to it by Bagehot (1867: 150–3).

Yet we cannot but recognise that our objectives are not shared by all Members. In fact many MPs are very happy with the structure and procedures of the House as they are now. Traditionalists and 'floor-men', like Michael Foot, believe that all MPs must have the opportunity to intervene in as many aspects of parliamentary business as they wish on the floor of the House and are reluctant therefore to see further extensions of committee powers. Other MPs reject the recent changes as they see Parliament's important functions to be the provision of government personnel, and the sustaining of governments and are content to accept the role of the House as a rubber stamp for executive decisions. Others still, such as members of the Labour Co-ordinating Committee (1982: 3) distrust Parliament and do not give it a central position for the achievement of their aims. The point is that although an MP might arrive at Westminster filled with reformist zeal, the House is not exactly packed with Members keen to increase the legislature's powers. Far too many MPs are far too content with the institution they have grown to know and love. Nevertheless, we believe that there is evidence to suggest that we may be on the verge of a significant breakthrough in view of some of the essential groundwork completed in the 1979 Parliament.

But reformists also have to be realists. They have to understand the mechanics of reform and know where the opposition as well as the impetus for its implementation comes from. Reformists need infinite patience and that is running out at Westminster.

The Mechanics of Reform

The normal practice of the House is for any significant changes in procedure to be proposed on the basis of Government Motions following previous consideration by a Select Committee on Procedure.

(J. Biffen, HC Debates 1982, vol. 22: 276)

Undoubtedly when it comes to the actual implementation of reforms, the government has a virtual monopoly. This is not to suggest that it is not susceptible to pressure from both within and without the House, but in the final analysis the government of the day selects which reforms it wishes to introduce. In its selection it tends to choose 'changes' which will facilitate the process of getting government business through the House. What tends to be ignored are 'reforms' designed to make the House's scrutinising role more effective. An important actor in this process of selection is the Leader of the House. Richard Crossman and Norman St John-Stevas in this office were both crucial in the imple-mentation of major committee reforms. Both were willing to concede the main thrust of our argument here that greater scrutiny by back-benchers leads to better, more effective legislation and policy at the end of the day.

When the government introduces motions for reform they are then debated and usually voted upon. In theory it would be possible for backbenchers to unite across party lines on such occasions and out-vote the front benches, but in reality this happens infrequently. Another source of authority in the machinery of reform is the Speaker. Erskine May (1976: 211) draws a parallel between the rulings of the Speaker and the decisions of judges in courts in that rulings are made on challenges to points of order according to the Speaker's interpretation of past decisions. The last Speaker, George Thomas, was of importance in making rulings which effected not only parliamentary 'change' but also 'reform' (see HC Debates 1980, vol. 986: 301, on making more information available to MPs on EEC documents).

Essentially therefore governments might introduce procedural 'changes' but are unlikely to put forward 'reforms' which favour backbenchers unless their hand is forced. So we need to know where the impetus for reform comes from.

Impetus for Reform

Pressure for reform comes from many points on the political compass. A handful of zealous individual MPs carry the banner of reform in the House. Although the banner is carried by the few, rather than the many, the staff bearers are some venerable Members. Included in their number in the 1979 House were George Cunningham (SDP), Edward du Cann, Terence Higgins, Norman St John-Stevas (Conservative), Michael English, Joel Barnett and John Garrett (Labour). These were the people who, if not serving on Procedure Committees, were to be found writing books, broadcasting, speaking in the House or submitting memoranda and letters proposing ideas on reform.

Apart from individual MPs a wide variety of different groups get caught in the reformists' net; amongst others, local authority associations, clerks of the House, the Study of Parliament Group, and the political parties themselves all advance their own plans with their own particular objectives in mind. Yet if we look for a common thread running through periods of reform over the last twenty years, i.e. the Crossman reforms in the mid-1960s, the introduction of the Expenditure Committee in 1971, the new select committee system of 1979; we find that the vast majority arose out of the reports of the Select Committees on Procedure. This is not to deny that the history of recent Procedure Committees reveals that relatively little has been achieved as a result of their outpourings (the period 1956–76 saw 44 reports, most of which resulted in minor changes; see Proctor 1979: 15). But occasionally political circumstances combine to endow a Procedure Committee's report with true significance. This happened with the 1977/8 Procedure Committee's report (HC 588 1978). Six significant forces, each important in its own right, combined together in an intoxicating mix. First, the committee had a wide remit and undertook its task diligently and systematically. Second, its membership covered the traditionalist-reformist spectrum; so that any agreed suggestions had a good chance of gaining wide acceptance among MPs in general. Third, the Conservatives on the committee found themselves supporting proposals partly because Michael Foot, then Leader of the House, was so opposed to them (which shows that political personalities can have a positive influence for the most negative of reasons). Fourth, experience in the 'hung' Parliament after 1976 convinced backbenchers that they should not let such an opportunity for reform slip through their grasp. Ironically, it was not until the Tories were returned with a large majority that the reforms actually went through. Fifth, the timing of the report was crucial; towards the end of the Labour government yet sufficiently close to the Conservative government to maintain the momentum between the two parliaments. One final impetus, connected to this latter point, was the commitment of the major political parties to reform in their manifestos in the intervening election. The Conservatives followed their election promise almost to the comma:

> We sympathise with the approach of the all party parliamentary committees which put forward proposals last year for improving the way the House of Commons legislates and scrutinises public spending and the work of government departments. We will give the new House of Commons an early chance of coming to a decision on these proposals (Conservative Central Office 1979: 21).

So by the summer of 1979 the tremendous determination of the Procedure Committee paid off by forcing the government and the House to realise that there was a case to be answered. Nearly four years on we are in a position to review what happened to the committee's 76 recommendations.

Reforms: Action and Delay
It is always a difficult task to determine the fate of committee recommendations, mainly because those recommendations vary enormously in the type of action called for. Fourteen of the 76 recommendations required no further action, as for example No. 35 which said: 'The Public Accounts Committee should continue in its present form'. The report was divided into six main sections on: public bill procedure, delegated legislation, European legislation, the select committee structure, financial control, and the organisation of sessions and sittings. Each of these are assessed in the sections below and, by analysing what happened in each one, we can see where progress has been achieved.

No progress has been made on delegated legislation and very little on public bill procedure. The only change to be adopted in the organisation of sittings was the recommendation which proposed morning sittings on Fridays. The recommendations on financial control, as we will see, have in effect been superseded by the Reports from the PAC, the Treasury Select Committee, the Procedure Committee (Supply) and the government reactions to those reports.

One recommendation we wish particularly to highlight, and one which has been partially implemented, is No. 55: 'Members should be able to call on personal research assistance, paid centrally by the House, and in addition to, and separate from, the provision of secretarial assistance' (HC 588 1978: cxxvii).

As we stated at the beginning our attitude to reform is not a narrow one restricted solely to procedure and we consider attitudes towards staffing, for example, to be extremely important. In fact if we had to choose one single reform, which would have the greatest effect in professionalising our legislature and increasing accountability it would be an increase in staff. Our definition of staff encompasses personal staff (research and secretarial), committee staff and advisers, and research staff attached to the library. When Bruce George came into Parliament in February 1974, the secretarial allowance was a meagre £1,000; by early 1983 it stood at £8,820. Secretarial salaries in the House still compare unfavourably with those outside. Moreover, this figure is supposed to include research assistance, which hardly permits Members to hire the research skills of the Brookings Institute or Chatham House.

The *Daily Telegraph* (5th March 1982) recently ran an editorial comment indicting MPs' research assistants, commenting that: 'Beyond the primitive requirements of a good secretary and a telephone, an MP has need only of his initiative and integrity'. The *Telegraph* leader writer shows little appreciation of just how much work a full-time MP gets through. Speaking in the chamber, serving on standing and perhaps select committees, working on party committees and meeting outside interest groups make up only half of the load; there is also the constituency to look after. The danger is that if Parliament refuses to pay for adequate assistance, other groups will step in. Take, for example, Tristran Garel Jones, MP, who formerly had an assistant paid for by Mothercare.

Facilities are improving gradually; the new committees do have access to more researchers, the government has announced plans to provide more facilities on Bridge Street just across the road from Westminster Palace and the library has purchased a computer to improve indexing. But it is a campaign which should not be relaxed.

Ultimately, however, the Procedure Committee's main claim to fame is in having recommended the new select committee structure, but even here we see that only 15 out of the 34 related proposals were adopted as recommended. The fact that three were still rejected, even though they had reached the floor of the House, demonstrates that storming one beachhead does not win the war. Some MPs, having agreed to the fundamental reorganisation of the select committee system, probably felt that was enough to be getting on with. The House rejected the proposal to make eight days in the chamber available for the debate of select committee reports. Also rejected was the motion to give committees the powers to call for persons, papers and records, with certain powers of redress to take precedence over public business if a refusal had been met with. However, it is important to note that these recommendations were not backed by the government and they were voted on as amendments put by Willie Hamilton (HC Debates 1979, vol. 969: 2436).

The New Select Committee Structure

Select committees are part of the history of Westminster, but what is new is the structure. The Procedure Committee described the then existing system as 'unstructured', 'unplanned', 'piecemeal' and 'patchy' and pointed out that: 'The unsystematic character of the present system has arisen largely because the House has at no point taken a clear decision about the form of specialisation to be adopted' (HC 588 1978: lii).

The departmental structure gives the new committees a new status, particularly as they are now committees in their own right as opposed to sub-committees of the Expenditure Committee. Their remits are much wider than ever before and each committee is 'charged with the examination of all aspects of expenditure, administration and policy' within the department it monitors. The test to show that these new committees are perceived as more important than their predecessors is to examine how enthusiastic Members are to serve on them. To do this we have taken a close look at the levels of attendance and turnover for the new committees. Table 4.1 shows the number of Members serving on each committee and the number of meetings each committee held on average over the three sessions 1979–82. Ann Robinson (1978: 54–89) did a similar analysis of the Expenditure Committee and, whilst not strictly comparable, reference to her findings highlight some promising traits in the new committees.

The average attendance for all 14 departmental and 3 'legal' sub-committees is 75 per cent, Robinson's (1978: 70) recorded average attendance for the six Expenditure Committees over the sessions 1974–6 was 71 per cent. Considering the increase in both the number of committees and members this figure shows an increase in involvement on the part of the membership. Similarly, the number of meetings has increased. Take, for example, the old Defence and External Affairs Committee, which was supposed to cover both defence and some areas of foreign affairs; in 1975/6 it met 25 times. In 1980/1 the two new committees covering these subjects held between them 78 meetings. This suggests that both the workload and the member's commitment has increased, with a subsequent rise in the status of the committees.

With the exception of the Environment Committee there is no particular correlation between high turnover and low attendance,

Table 4.1 The new select committees: average attendances, turnover, meetings
(Parliamentary sessions: 1979–82)

Committee/Sub Committee	No. of Members	Average Turnover Dec. 1979–Oct. 1982 %	Average attendance Dec. 1979–Oct. 1982 %	Average No. meetings per session Dec. 1979–Oct. 1982 %
Agriculture	9	15	80	27
Defence	11	12	73	41
Education, Science & Arts	9	4	70	47
Employment	9	15	71	32
Energy	11	9	64	38
Environment	11	33	69	29
Foreign Affairs	11	12	78	39
s.c. Overseas Development	5	25	68	29
Home Affairs	11	6	84	30
s.c. Race-Relations & Immigration	5	7	88	30
Industry and Trade	11	6	79	33
Scottish Affairs	13	23	79	35
Social Services	9	15	70	36
Transport	11	6	72	36
Treasury and Civil Service	11	25	88	39
s.c. Treasury and Civil Service	7	14	70	20
Welsh Affairs	11	10	77	33
Total average		14	75	34

which suggests that Members leave to move on to other tasks rather than through boredom. John Golding, for example, chairman of the Employment Committee claimed that his committee was a springboard for promotion with both Giles Radice and Oonagh Macdonald moving on to the Labour front bench. And from the Defence Committee, former chairman Cranley Onslow became a junior minister in the Foreign Office.

Working Methods

It is often said that MPs at Westminster work in 635 different ways. Put these together in permutations of nine or eleven and you begin to get an idea of the pattern of work adopted by the new committees. Suffice it to say that no two committees work in an identical manner. Nevertheless we can review the experiences of 1979–83 and begin to pick out the merits and demerits of committee operations.

Proctor (1979: 30) points out that since 1960 there has been a steady increase in the number of Members involved in select committees, as in the number of meetings and reports made to the House. Similarly, there has been more freedom to travel to gather information, more money to appoint specialist advisers, more frequent use of the practice of taking evidence in public and of the right to call ministers and their civil servants to answer questions on matters of policy and administration. In all these aspects the new committees have continued the trend towards increased activity (see tables 4.2 and 4.3).

The terms of reference of the new committees are sufficiently wide to enable each committee to determine its own work pattern. Their official remit is to 'examine the expenditure, administration and policy of the principal government departments . . . and associated bodies'. The means to fulfil this function is to make an enquiry, to call witnesses and take evidence (usually in public) and then to report to the House. In this task the Procedure Committee 1977/8 proffered some advice to the new committees on working methods. It recommended that they should look at expenditure and the policy objectives underlying the departmental estimates; it did not expect to see too many long royal commission type enquiries; it hoped they would be able to respond speedily to current problems and new proposals; and it hoped they would become the eyes and ears of the House by providing advice and informed comment on matters worthy of further political consideration.

The type of enquiries undertaken by the new committees has varied in accordance with the time available, the subject and the enthusiasm of Members. Committees have had to decide whether to go for short or long enquiries and also, whether to avoid political 'hot potatoes'. But a common desire of all committees has been to bring a greater transparency to the government decision-making process. Reports have thus

Table 4.2   The new select committees: Average number of meetings; formal evidence sessions; pages of evidence; reports printed and number of reports, sessions 1979–1982

Committee/Sub committee	No. of meetings	Formal evidence sessions	Pages of evidence printed	Pages of reports printed	No. of reports
Agriculture	27	15	441	49	3
Defence	41	23	657	49	5
Education	47	29	971	171	6
Employment	32	23	594	43	6
Energy	38	21	1114	68	7
Environment	29	9	368	63	4
Foreign Affairs	39	19	490	130	6
– sub committee	29	11	416	—	—
Home Affairs	30	14	379	113	6
– sub committee	30	18	721	—	—
Industry and Trade	33	20	685	61	8
Scottish Affairs	35	17	664	93	8
Social Services	36	14	1288	168	4
Transport	36	22	745	121	4
Treasury and Civil Service	39	19	629	116	6
– sub committee	20	12	474	—	8
Welsh Affairs	33	24	711	66	2
Total average	32.5	18.2	667	71	4.2

Note: Figures are *averages* for the first three parliamentary sessions in which the committees have been in operation.

Source: B. George, HC Debates 1982, vol 32: 173–7.

Table 4.3 The new select committees: Number of memoranda, number of witnesses appearing before the committees, sessions 1979–1982

	Average No. of memos per session (1979–82)	No. of Cabinet Mins*		Other ministers*		Open structure* civil service		No. of all witnesses* from central govt.	
		no. of witnesses	no. of appearances	no. of witnesses	no. of appearances	no. of witnesses	no. of appearances	no. of witnesses	no. of appearances
Agriculture	12	2	2	0	0	14	16	54	63
Defence	27	3	6	2	2	49	74	145	184
Education	27	8	15	10	16	38	56	102	133
Employment	4	4	11	7	8	24	32	28	36
Energy	15	5	5	2	2	6	14	41	50
Environment	6	2	2	4	4	11	16	36	49
Foreign Affairs	51	5	8	8	14	46	88	50	66
– sub committee	30	0	0	3	3	20	30	43	62
Home Affairs	9	3	3	3	3	13	17	39	46
– sub committee	16	4	4	4	7	13	17	69	82
Industry and Trade	51	5	8	7	10	23	26	68	78
Scottish Affairs	16	3	5	8	9	25	19	62	82
Social Services	16	4	7	6	6	18	32	55	92
Transport	13	4	4	2	2	20	38	43	63
Treasury & Civil Service	49**	4	10	1	2	54	114	69	135
– sub-committee		4	4	2	2	52	59	70	80
Welsh Affairs	7	4	6	2	2	26	48	70	98
Average	22	3.8	5.9	4.2	5.4	27	41	61	82

* Total numbers 1979–82.
** Including sub committee.

Source: R. George, HC Debates 1982, vol 22, 265–8.

attempted to focus the attention of not only the government and the House on particular problems but also to provide the media, interest groups and the wider public with information about government policies and possible alternatives. In these respects there have been successes and failures in all categories. An examination of some long enquiries as well as shorter reports reveals that there are still many lessons to be learned.

Long Enquiries

The length of enquiries can vary dramatically, from one short evidence session to upwards of a year. Similarly, reports can vary from a few paragraphs to tomes. Some committees immediately delved into contentious subjects, others, for example, the Foreign Affairs Committee began with an enquiry into the organisation and policy of the Foreign and Commonwealth Office. This provided them with an invaluable grounding in just how the Foreign Office thinks and operates. One aim of select committees should be to build up a bank of expertise for future reference. Furthermore, long reports can also deal with 'hot' issues, as did the Treasury Committee's (HC 163 1981) report on 'monetary policy' which offered a mid-term indictment of the government. Despite the controversial nature of this report the Treasury Committee still managed to achieve unanimity. Such consensus was, however, noticeably absent from the Defence Committee's enquiry (HC 36 1981) into a replacement for Polaris. It was evident that there would be no agreement across party lines. Indeed, the Labour members managed formally to submit an alternative draft report which once voted on had to be printed in the Proceedings of the Committee, thus circumventing the rule that divided committees cannot present a minority dissenting report. Nevertheless, the enquiry was worthwhile because it brought out into the open the arguments underlying the government's nuclear strategy. In addition, it will provide a useful reference guide for any future reappraisal of that strategy.

The experience of the Environment Committee should serve as a salutory lesson for other committees. Up to October 1982 it had only produced 6 reports, though it held its own by keeping up with the average number of published pages of reports. This indicates that it has fallen into the trap of going for long Royal Commission type enquiries. The reports on Council House Sales (HC 366 1981) and the Private Rented Housing Sector (HC 40 1982) illustrate this tendency. Indeed, we would suggest that its relatively high membership turnover and low attendance is because the committee has become so bogged down in long enquiries that it has lost its momentum and political sex appeal.

Short Enquiries

Short enquiries do not necessarily lead to short reports, the length of the report is more likely to be dependent on the complexity of the problem, the amount of written evidence submitted, the quality of the specialist advisers to the committee as well as the time available and the interests of Members. For example, the Foreign Affairs Committee spent only four sessions examining the problems of the repatriation of the Canadian Constitution in 1980 and yet produced a three volume report. The report (HC 42 1980) challenged the government's proposal to repatriate the constitution because at the time the Canadian prime minister, Mr Trudeau, had reached agreement with only two of the ten provincial governments in Canada. The Foreign Affairs Committee thus played a very significant role in compelling Trudeau's federal government to reach an accommodation with the provinces. In so doing it struck a hefty blow on behalf of the Commons at the Foreign Office, which had traditionally seen policy-making as its own private domain.

Despite being short, reports aimed at particular policies need to be thorough, but they also need to be well-timed. The Education Committee appears to have developed the art of putting out a report after just one evidence session and timing it to get maximum publicity. In 1980 the committee helped to save the Proms; and in the summer of 1981 it helped to save the Theatre Museum by issuing a 15 paragraph report rejecting the arguments of the Rayner Scrutiny Committee for closing the museum. Chris Price, the chairman, said that timing was all important and if, for example, a cabinet committee was to discuss the British Library on a Wednesday, then his committee would go for maximum impact by trying to publish a report on the Tuesday.

The division between long and short enquiries is partly a bogus one because most committees will follow up their reports, whatever the original length. Foreign Affairs produced two more reports on the Canadian constitution. Social Services used its specialist advisers to monitor the success of its two big reports on perinatal mortality and medical education. Committees may indeed decide to monitor the progress of their recommendations by inviting officials to explain the departmental response and the fate of those recommendations. The Defence Committee, for example, held a review of what happened to all of its reports and recommendations. All of these activities are part of the exercise to increase Parliament's knowledge of the internal workings of government departments and to keep the committees well in the forefront of their respective department's consciousness.

As for future progress we would recommend, along with some other MPs, a 'two track' system of enquiries with committees meeting twice a week. They can then take on one lengthy enquiry per session and two or three shorter reports which would be reactive to government decisions, plus of course a review of the estimates for the expenditure plans. The Defence Committee came close to this pattern of work in 1980. Alongside the investigation into nuclear weapons it ran shorter enquiries into RAF Pilot Training and the 'D Notice' system. It also managed a report on the Defence Estimates. The two smaller enquiries were operated by 'subterfuge' committees. These were in effect sub-committees, even though the Defence Committee is not allowed to have these. However, the result was complaints among the membership about too much work, and the committee has subsequently relaxed its workload.

If we have complaints it is that some of the members of select committees do not put in enough work and that there is a lack of collective diligence on the part of committees in some areas. Nowhere is this failing more apparent than in the lack of scrutiny of departmental estimates. Apart from some lack of enthusiasm to put in sometimes tedious and protracted work, it is also a structural problem in that the committees have no functional role in relation to government expend-iture plans. Only when this is changed will the committees really hold the key to controlling the executive.

Table 4.2 shows the comparative work rates of all the committees. If we take the averages for pages of evidence and published pages of reports in the parliamentary sessions 1979–82, then we can assess which committees were pulling their weight. We leave readers to draw their own conclusions, but we would point out that some committees, such as Environment and Agriculture, fell consistently below the average, whereas Social Services was obviously keen to 'publish and be damned' (see Lowe 1981; George and Pieragastini 1981).

Two more points about the membership of a committee are worth noting. MPs have been fairly keen to get on to committees, recently there were more than 80 applicants for two vacancies on the Defence Committee. What is equally important is that in principle at least appointment to the committees has been removed from the direct influence of the whips. Instead, Members are appointed by a Commit-tee of Selection so that, in theory anyway, an MP is judged on his or her own merits, rather than by his standing with the party whips. Secondly, it is generally recognised amongst Members on the committees that the quality of the chairman in holding the team together is of crucial impor-tance. In addition to controlling proceedings, he maintains close liaison with the Committee Clerk, and influences the selection of staff and advisers as well as the manner in which reports are drafted and agreed to. In the 1979 Parliament the style of the chairman varied widely from the forceful and authoritative like Edward Du Cann of the Treasury and Civil Service Committee, to the more softly, softly 'primus inter pares' approach, like the first and third chairman of the Defence Committee, Sir John Langford-Holt and Sir Timothy Kitson (see Davies 1980).

As regards staffing, the new committees were given unlimited power to appoint specialist advisers. In July 1980 the 17 committees and sub-committees had a total of 70 specialist advisers on their books, by November 1982 this figure had doubled to 150. This was an average of 9 per committee, but the number per committee ranged from 28 (Treasury and Civil Service) to 4 (Transport). In the 1981/2 session, advisers, who are paid on a per diem basis, worked a total of 1,717 days at a cost of £104,136, which works out at an average of £61 per day. However, this £61 is not a straight payment and includes the adviser's expenses. Fears that these advisers will form a 'counter bureaucracy', taking over from MPs, are obviously unfounded. In the session 1981/2, each adviser worked on average 11½ days, which made him or her strictly part-time. Whilst the use of advisers has increased and committees now keep names on their books so that they can be called on at any time, Members should, however, try to push for more technical advice, otherwise their scrutiny of Whitehall departments runs the risk of degenerating into ill-informed comment. We would also recommend the use of specialists in management to help with the scrutiny of the estimates.

The select committees also have access to Temporary Assistants who are recruited specifically to work full-time on two-year contracts. In early 1983 there were six of these assistants (two with the Treasury Committee, and one each with the Education, Environment, Transport and Social Services Committees) working under the supervision of the Committee Clerk. The clerks, however, remain the backbone of the structure, providing routine administrative support, drafting skills and some specialist advice. The new committees are luckier than their predecessors as each has as a minimum one clerk, an assistant clerk, and a secretary. Sub-committees are also entitled to a clerk and half a secretary.

Relations with the Government and the House

Working methods are important to the quality of the committees' reports, but to measure the impact of their work we need to look at the effect of those reports on the government and on the House. We do not wish to go over the arguments about whether one-party governments will ever take notice of all-party committee reports. Suffice it to say that the new committees are striving to be useful and they do afford the opportunity to make ministers and civil servants more accountable. Indeed, as can be seen in table 4.3 the new committees have been less hesitant to call ministers to give evidence than their predecessors. During the entire 1970–74 Parliament there were only 7 ministerial appearances before the six sub-committees of the Expenditure Committee (Robinson 1978: 103), whereas in the single session 1981/2

62 ministers made a total of 89 appearances before the new select committees. Ministers are, of course, not always the most helpful of witnesses, but a 2½ hour appearance before a committee does at least give MPs a chance to pursue a particular line of questioning, which they cannot do at question time in the chamber where MPs are only allowed the luxury of one supplementary question. Question time is sometimes a farce, and, as one former junior minister described it, 'bloody easy' for government ministers.

The new committees also set a good pace for taking evidence from civil servants and for requesting written memoranda from central government departments. For example, in the 1981/2 session 163 open structure civil servants made 255 appearances. By comparing each committee's figures with the average we can assess how much effort each one put in to bring department officials to account. However, Committees have to be wary of too close a contact which could transform them into a public relations aid to the department they were originally supposed to scrutinise. There is little evidence to suggest this happened, and certainly on the Defence Committee the relationship remained a healthy, adversarial one.

Committee recommendations take various forms and require different types of response. The best method is for the committee to list its main recommendations at the end of the report, then it is easier for the committee to assess whether they have been accepted, rejected or if the government has adopted the delaying tactic of 'keeping the recommendation under review'. How seriously the government treats the committee is, however, reflected in the speed of its replies to committee reports. The Procedure Committee's recommendation, that the government should be required to respond within two months, was not adopted, but the average length of the lapse was about four months, which was an improvement on the mid-seventies. Robinson (1978: 132) records 'In 1976 there were complaints from committee members that replies to some reports were two years outstanding. The more normal lapse of time is about six months'. The longest the government took to reply in the 1979–83 Parliament was 65 weeks, to the Environment Committee's report on Council House Sales.

The government's response is important to the impact of a committee's work, but the report is formally made to the House. The Procedure Committee recommended that eight Mondays be set aside for debating committee reports, with the form of the motion being decided on by the committee. This recommendation was rejected. Yet many see such a formal link between the committees and the House as of vital importance. Norton (1980: 481) has argued that 'the threat of action on the floor of the House in consequence of a committee's recommendations or findings is the way to ensure an effective government response'. By November 1982, the only reports which had been the subject of specific motions debated in the House were the reports on 'Race Relations and the "Sus" Law', on 'Perinatal and Neonatal Mortality' and on 'Medical Education'; which represents under two per cent of reports produced.

Nine other reports were listed on the Order Paper and others were often referred to in debates. The Defence Committee was quite lucky, in that defence was debated in the House at regular intervals. Indeed, the committee appeared to have won the right to comment on the Expenditure White Paper before it was debated in the House. Its report on 'Strategic Nuclear Weapons' (HC 36: 1981), however, met with less success. It was rumoured that the government was so concerned about the possible impact of the 'minority' report, that the Defence Secretary rescheduled the major announcement of his defence review findings to coincide with the report's date of publication in an attempt to divert attention from it.

In general, the new departmental structure and the higher activity rates of the committees allows us to conclude that the new committees are working to the House's advantage. However, not until they are given a more functional role in relation to government legislation and expenditure will they exert the real influence which some reformers hoped (Davies 1980: 1). A number of studies are being undertaken to evaluate the performance of each committee and the committees as a whole. In the meantime polar prejudices guide the assessment of their work. On the one side parliamentarians such as Norman St John-Stevas and Speaker Thomas believe that the 'setting up of these committees has proved to be a giant step forward in bringing back to the Commons a power and authority it had lost' (Thomas 1982: 349). On the other side many original sceptics remain; to them backbenchers have been diverted into relatively harmless directions, or have wasted parliamentary and executive time. Perhaps the answer lies between these polar views, but in the opinion of the authors, an impressive start has been made and the power of the House has been increased with a potential for further advance awaiting the committees in the new Parliament.

In the 1977/8 Procedure Committee, Michael English moved an amendment recommending that all bills be sent to select committees, either the departmental ones or *ad hoc* ones, but it was rejected (HC 588 1978: 63). Instead it was decided to give standing committees four investigative sittings, before moving on to their normal line by line scrutiny. These have been adopted on an experimental basis and are reviewed below. First, we will take a brief look at one select committee which does have a slightly more functional remit than the new select committees.

The Select Committee on European Legislation

The relationship between the House of Commons and the European legislative machinery has always been an uneasy one, basically because the House is wary of any authority which can be seen to usurp its own sovereignty. The Select Committee on European Legislation arose out of recommendations made by the Foster Committee (HC 463 1973) which dealt with the likely problems of Britain's accession to the EEC. The committee was appointed in July 1979 for the life of the Parliament and had a membership of sixteen. Its remit was to consider draft proposals from the Commission for legislation and other documents submitted to the European Council of Ministers, and to report, with its reasons, on whether they raised questions of legal or political importance as well as to make recommendations for further consideration by the House. The committee did not debate the merits of proposals, but judged which 'instruments should be brought to the attention of the House, with or without a recommendation for debate'.

In the session 1980/1 the committee met on 32 occasions, reported on 745 instruments of which 208 were deemed to raise questions of legal or political importance, and 81 were recommended for debate. At the start of the next session 61 remained undebated, 81 instruments were added and 20 recommendations for debate withdrawn; during the session 66 instruments were debated on the floor (in 22 debates, mostly late at night) and 7 were debated in the Standing Committee on European Documents (under SO 73B).

The committee's main authority is vested in the requirement that ministers should not, except in very exceptional circumstances, consent in the Council of Ministers to the adoption of any legislative proposal which has been recommended for debate, before that debate has taken place. This government undertaking was enshrined in a resolution of the House on 30 October 1980 (HC Debates 1980, vol. 991: 729, 837–44). The chairman, Sir John Eden, considered that the committee performed tasks of a 'relatively routine and unglamorous nature' with 'relative success'. We would argue, however, that if the committee was better staffed (though it is relatively well off with a clerk, an assistant, four clerk advisers and a legal adviser) and had more influence over the time-tabling of debates in the House, then its detailed scrutiny of the vast mountains of EEC documentation could be more effective.

Special Standing Committees

Normal standing committees have been used increasingly since the Second World War to examine bills on a line by line basis after the Second Reading debate, thus saving time on the floor of the House and nominally performing the function of scrutinising legislative proposals (see Griffith 1974; 1981). Standing committees reflect the strengths of the parties in the House as a whole, members are whipped and proceedings are dominated by adversary party political tactics. In this setting scrutiny appears to be of secondary importance. In his evidence to the Procedure Committee, John Peyton, then Shadow Leader of the House described standing committees as 'the most horrible blot' and went on '. . . it has never been my good fortune to serve on any standing committee which has not been a disgraceful operation and time wasting without any other virtue at all' (HC 588 1978: 17–18). The Procedure Committee recommended that 'Standing Committees on bills should in future be permitted to have up to three days sitting in select committee form for the purpose of taking evidence in public; bills would automatically stand committed to committees with this power unless the House otherwise ordered' (HC 588 1978: cxxii). Unfortunately the recommendation was adopted only as an experiment, which means that the role of the Leader of the House, in persuading colleagues to subject their bills to the new procedure, becomes a vital one. Under St John-Stevas three bills in the 1980/1 session were committed to Special Standing Committees. These were the Criminal Attempts Bill, the Education Bill and the Deep Sea Mining (Temporary Provisions) Bill (Lords).

The Criminal Attempts Bill provides a particularly noteworthy example of the potential usefulness of these committees. The committee had one deliberative sitting to determine how to conduct its enquiry and which witnesses to call. The late Sir Graham Page, chairman of the Conservative backbench legal committee, chaired the investigative sessions, then David Watkins (Labour) took over as a member of the Chairman's Panel for the standing committee stage. In addition there were nine Conservative, seven Labour and one Social Democrat, making a total membership of eighteen at any one time.

The committee then held three evidence sessions in public and examined 27 witnesses in all. Included amongst these was Patrick Mayhew, Minister of State at the Home Office, and the minister responsible for guiding the bill through the committee stage and as such, also a member of the committee. The witnesses included representatives from the Home Office, the judiciary, the National Council for Civil Liberties, the police and the Law Society. Most interesting of all were the views of Professor Smith from Nottingham University.

The bill was designed to repeal the 'Sus' laws, but also to introduce the concept of committing non-crimes. Thus a person in the future could be convicted of attempting to steal, even though the pocket he picked was empty. The government draft did not follow the Law Commission's suggestion, instead it tried to encapsulate Professor

Smith's ideas. But when Smith appeared before the Special Standing Committee, he said that, although he sympathised with the objective of the bill, 'I have come to abandon it when we attempt to put it into legislation, because I think that it is quite impossible to define in general terms in a statute' (SSC Debate 3 February 1981: 89).

This volte face meant that the government was forced to table an amendment replacing the whole of clause 1. Introducing the amendment at the beginning of the normal standing committee phase, Patrick Mayhew announced:

> In the light of the evidence submitted to the committee, the Government concluded after very careful consideration, that the clause will not do as it stands, in that it does not achieve the Government's purpose. We have been advised that it is not possible to draft a provision that would give clear, readily comprehensible, and unambiguous effect to the Government's policy.
>
> (SSC Debate 3 February 1981: 216)

Whether the government would have been made aware of its error without those evidence sessions must remain an open question. What is clear is that the sessions provided an opportunity for both the government and committee members to focus their attention on the issues before them.

In the 1980/1 session we sent a questionnaire to each member of the three committees and our findings suggest that as an experiment it worked very well. Our response rate among 52 non-ministerial Members was a very respectable 87 per cent. The results gave a resounding vote of confidence for Special Standing Committees. 22 out of 37 respondents said they would like to see all committees use an investigatory phase and a further 10 said they would like it employed for bills which did not involve too much party conflict. When asked for a judgement on the utility of the experiment 28 said it has been 'very worthwhile', 8 said 'fairly worthwhile' and only one said it made no difference.

If members with Special Standing Committee experience were able to decide on the future of these committees then clearly they would be safe. But their experimental status makes them dependent for their future on the Leader of the House. In the session 1981/2 only one bill, the Mental Health (Amendment) Bill (Lords), was sent to such a committee. In this period Francis Pym replaced Norman St John-Stevas, and then with the Falklands reshuffle John Biffen replaced Mr Pym as Leader of the House. Although Mr Biffen has introduced some reforms of the supply procedure (see below), his reformist colours have yet to be revealed.

Clive Bennet (1982: 4–5), the Clerk to the Mental Health Committee, has written a useful summary of the proceedings, in which he concluded, 'All that can be said with any certainty is that the

Committee was a fascinating one, that the degree of co-operation and compromise achieved was remarkable, and that the bill has been thoroughly scrutinised in every clause and line and is a very different creature from the one which went into committee.'

The scrutiny is the important point. The committee held eighteen sittings in standing committee, in addition to the four preliminary investigative sessions. The bill was heavily amended with thirteen new clauses and eighty amendments, which included six defeats for the government. In interview in July 1982 Terry Davis, who led for the opposition on the Mental Health Committee, said the most useful point to come out of the investigatory section was the opportunity it afforded members to get to know each other. Most valuable of all was an informal tour of Broadmoor which some members went on. This act of 'building bridges' between the parties was more important than the evidence itself. However, he thought the exercise was only useful because it gave the opposition more influence, which could only work on a very technical bill; if political principles were involved, and if he were in government, he said he would rather see the bill go through without any amendments at committee stage.

MPs who answered our questionnaire did not agree fully with Davis. The vast majority said that the evidence sessions had provided useful material. Of 37 respondents, 27 said they used the information from the investigatory phase for speeches made in committee, and 19 did likewise for speeches in the chamber. Seven said the evidence had changed their views and a further ten said it had influenced them.

As for how the standing committee system should operate overall; two felt it was satisfactory now; eleven would like to see Special Standing Committees for 'certain' types of bills ranging from 'technical, complicated' bills to 'non-political, simple' bills; fifteen said all committees should have an investigative phase, and a further two said this should be given a trial run; finally, seven said that it should be up to the committees to decide how to proceed. As to how Special Standing Committees should operate: some ,anted more investigative sittings; some thought two chairmen for the two different sections were unnecessary; some even wanted pre-legislative committees, with MPs, ministers and civil servants all participating in drafting bills.

A consensus opinion, and one to which we would subscribe, would allow each committee to decide on its own course of action once the committee had been formed. The 'experimental phase' has now completed two sessions and four bills have successfully passed through a Special Standing Committee. The time has come for the government to admit the experiment has been successful.

Financial Reform

The way in which we fail to examine expenditure in my opinion is a disgrace in a modern Parliament.

(Rt. Hon. Edward Du Cann, MP)

The present position, whereby huge sums of money are granted to the Government virtually without debate, is quite intolerable in a democratically elected Parliament.

(Rt. Hon. Joel Barnett, MP)

From all the quotes indicating the House's failure to control finances, it seemed most appropriate to use those of two chairmen of the Public Accounts Committee, one a Conservative and one Labour (HC 118 1981). Parliament's lack of control over the purse strings has been well documented elsewhere (Garrett 1980: Robinson 1981: Flegmann 1980). Here we propose only to look briefly at the potential for reform based on current developments.

The Public Accounts Committee was set up by Gladstone in 1861 to ensure financial regularity within government departments. Five years later the office of the Comptroller and Auditor General was established to assist the PAC. The statutory framework under which this state audit operates has altered little in 120 years, in fact, 'these arrangements have been held to be one of the glories of our constitution and the means by which an elected Parliament effectively controls the spending of the government bureaucracy' (Garrett 1980: 173).

The modern reality of parliamentary financial control, however, is that it does not work. Indeed, since the mid-1960s pressure for financial reform has mounted both inside and outside Westminster. Attention has come to be focused around two particular demands, both of which the government has resisted thus far (Cmnd 8323 1981). First, there is a strong feeling that the House of Commons should have the right to audit the books and records of all public bodies in receipt of public money including public companies, nationalised industries and local authorities (HC 535 1977: 153–60). Only half of British public expenditure is covered by the CAG (Garrett 1980: 175). Second, the CAG is more subject to executive control than any other western state auditor (Normanton 1966: 273). Demands have been voiced therefore that the CAG should became an officer of the House, rather than acting on behalf of the Treasury, so giving the House the right of appointment and to order particular enquiries. Following the rejection of these demands (Cmnd 8323 1981), some 300 MPs signed an Early Day Motion tabled in December 1981, calling upon the government to reconsider its views and 'to introduce legislation to allow proper accountability [of the CAG] to the House of Commons' (Notices of Questions and Motions 10th December 1981: 1341). On 28th January

1983 Norman St John-Stevas introduced a Private Members Bill to this effect (see pp. 94–5).

Both of the above demands are important to re-establish the right of the House to examine public expenditure. Gradual progress is being made, one further example of which is the concession by the government, made in the passage of the Local Government Finance Bill which allows the CAG to examine local authority expenditure in general. But in reality such reform only constitutes 'tinkering'. What is needed is a systematic review of the House's financial procedures.

In 1978 the Select Committee on Procedure (HC 588 1978) recommended just such a review. In pursuit of this recommendation the House voted to establish a Select Committee on Procedure (Supply) to examine 'the House's present procedures for considering and voting on the Government's requests for Supply and to make recommendations' (HC 118 1981: i). This committee was constrained, however, both in its term of appointment, for a single session only; and in its terms of reference, to supply procedure only. Nonetheless, it did recommend the appointment of another select committee with wider terms of reference, this one to encompass all aspects of financial procedure. In January 1982 the Select Committee on Procedure (Finance) was subsequently established and is due to report before the end of 1983. Moreover, the Select Committee on Procedure (Supply) made a series of other proposals by which more effective scrutiny could be re-established. Foremost amongst these were: (i) that the departmental select committees should devote some time each year to the examination of the relevant departmental estimates; (ii) that eight estimates days should be set aside when the estimates could be debated and voted upon; and (iii) that 19 days per session should be available when opposition business would be discussed (these would replace the established 29 Supply days).

The Supply Committee's recommendations were initially debated in the House on the 15th February 1982, and in the light of this debate the government later framed motions to give force to these recommendations. Five months later, on the 19th July, these motions were debated and voted upon. The House, on a free vote, leaned more towards the government's interpretation of the report and one that differed markedly in some respects from the Committee's original recommendations. Hence, for example, the proposal for eight estimates days was whittled down to three, and the recommendation that a new Estimates Business Committee should select which estimates should be debated was rejected and the task was given to the Liaison Committee of select committee chairmen. The House further approved a government proposal for the method of voting on the estimates, and the House can, if it so desires, vote to reduce the estimates.

The estimates days can be taken at any time in the session, the exact dates to be determined by the whips. The Liaison Committee, however, will have a difficult task in choosing, in the face of many conflicting requests from individual Members and select committees, which estimates should be debated. The current standing orders of the House are designed to ensure that the government gets its supply each year to a set timetable. Three guillotines therefore operate on or before the 6th February (normally votes on Winter supplementary estimates), 18th March (normally the Spring supplementaries), and the 5th August (normally the main estimates). At the time of writing it is not known how the new system will operate or how and when the subjects and dates will be chosen. If these debates are chosen to link select committee investigations into the estimates a significant step forward will have been taken. But it must be hoped that further reforms will follow the Procedure Committee (Finance) report. This committee in session 1982/3 looked at a wide range of questions such as parliamentary control of government borrowing; budgetary reform to integrate revenue and expenditure proposals; a 'Green' Budget; scrutiny of long-term expenditure projects; and parliamentary control and examination of local authorities and nationalised industries.

The House of Commons Commission
A reform of considerable potential, which has largely escaped attention, was the establishment, on the 1st January 1979, of the House of Commons Commission under the House of Commons (Administration) Act, 1978. For the first time the House has control over its internal affairs, including: staffing, pensions, remuneration, expenditure (over £14 million in 1981/2). The Commission consists of the Speaker, the Leader of the House, one MP nominated by the Leader of the Opposition, and three other non-ministerial MPs. Each year the Commission prepares and lays before the House an estimate of the expenses for each of the House's departments. The House of Commons (Administration) Vote (Class No. XIII A) is not subject to any formal cash limits, but the Commission (HC 385 1981) takes the view 'that, subject to the continuing need for the House to exercise its primary function of controlling the Executive, it should observe the same financial restraints as operate in the public service generally'.

The Commission has proved that it has the authority to make changes, for example, by establishing a new Refreshment Department. It is accountable to the House through a nominated spokesman in the House, who also answers parliamentary questions; and it is potentially influential as it approves the funds, requested by the Liaison Committee (consisting of the 22 committee chairmen) for staffing, travel and other expenses incurred by the committees. Yet the crucial point is that the House of Commons Commission is well placed to co-ordinate the campaigns for reform. It is not dependent on the Treasury for funds, and as such should be seen as a powerful independent force. This potential should be realised by giving the Commission tasks such as the appointment of the Comptroller and Auditor General, and the responsibility of recommending to the House the membership and powers of select committees. It is time for the House to demand to control its own reform and not for it to be dependent on occasional magnanimous gestures from an executive, which still has almost total control over the division lobbies.

Internal Reform – A realistic approach

We began this chapter by conceding that up until 1979 'institutional tinkering' had achieved very little. However, we now believe that having stormed the beachhead, the army of reformers in the House of Commons is well placed to advance the campaign. The major problem is to identify the best route to march along. We have shown that there are many different views on reform, but also, out of the chaos, Procedure Committees can, if the environment is favourable, plan programmes for procedural reform which are acceptable to all, even a reluctant government. There is evidence to suggest that there is more prospect for parliamentary reform in the next few years, than for a long, long time. We agree that attitudes are important, and Norton's work (1978a; 1980) on dissent and rebellion among backbenchers has been important to show that MPs are independent enough to think for themselves; but equally important is that reforms build up a cumulative effect: as more MPs become exposed to them, more become aware of their own potential power as backbenchers and therefore interest in reform increases. That is why we argue that the only realistic way forward is through internal reform; internal pressures are built up by reports from Procedure Committees, the Public Accounts Committee, and now the new select committees. More backbenchers thus become aware that after all they are of consequence, and as a result the government will be forced to move.

One important test for our argument, that through past experience more backbenchers have become aware of their own reformist potential, came in the last Parliament. In May 1983 backbench pressure from all parties helped to secure the passage of the National Audit Act, which began life as Norman St John-Stevas' Parliamentary Control of Expenditure (Reform) Bill. With one important exception, the main features of the bill survived, but virtually every clause was rewritten, largely by the government, during the committee stage. The Act provides, as did the bill, for the CAG to be an officer of the House appointed on the initiative of the Commons and after consultation with the chairman of the Public Accounts Committee, and for the establishment of a Public Accounts Commission to control the work of an independent National Audit Office. This Office is empowered to conduct 'economy, efficiency and effectiveness examinations of government departments and other public bodies', but, significantly, these powers do not extend to the Nationalised Industries. The government, which at best was lukewarm in its attitude to the bill, made it clear that the bill would be killed at the report stage unless a compromise was reached in standing committee on the Nationalised Industries. After protracted government pressure, Mr St John-Stevas and his supporters agreed to the compromise on the Nationalised Industries and the bill raced through its final stages – accelerated by the announcement of the election. But the very fact that the National Audit Act reached the statute book indicates just how far the reformist movement in the Commons had developed in the 1979 Parliament.

We have admitted to taking a polemical approach to reform, in that we believe the reasons for it need to be expressed in as strong terms as possible, but this does not detract from our argument that the best way forward is through internal reform. We have shown that reform is a haphazard business, but so is the nature of politics. Indeed, under present conditions, internal reform is the only option, and barring the emergence of a coalition government after the next general election in 1988, which might introduce electoral reform, it will remain the only workable option.

The modernisation and democratisation of parliamentary institutions must continue, indeed the pace must quicken. To demand further reforms of the venerable House of Commons is not made out of self-interest nor is it a naive yearning for a restoration of a bygone age. The Commons has not so much had its powers usurped, they have been given away with hardly a fight. We have argued, nevertheless, that a significant change was wrought towards the restoration of the power of the House in the 1979 Parliament, precisely through the means of internal reform. These gains must be consolidated. Will the new Parliament of 1983 see even more significant changes? We hope so!

5   The House of Lords
Donald Shell

The House of Lords is anomalous. Any attempt to pretend otherwise is doomed to failure. A House of Parliament which consists of almost 1200 members, two-thirds of whom are there because they have inherited this right, is manifestly at variance with the values of a modern democratic society. That the House may be harmless and that many of its members may be absentees does not alter the substance of this anomaly, though such facts may help to explain its continued existence. But the continued existence of the House, though anomalous, is by no means irrelevant to an understanding of the British parliamentary system. And before we consider the many proposals currently advanced for reform or replacement of the Lords, we do well to reflect on what its continued existence has to tell us about the nature of the constitution and society of which it is a part.

Britain has an unwritten constitution. This means that no attempt has ever been made systematically to determine the shape and form the major institutions of government should take in relation to the needs of the whole society. The British temperament would be disinclined to trust such an exercise, and in its place prefers a pattern of institutions shaped by forces of the past, whose justification therefore lies not in the reasoning of any single generation, but in the circumstances of national history.

This ensures that the form of our central institutions remains similar from one generation to the next: the dignified facade (Bagehot's phrase, used by Lord Hailsham) is unchanged, whatever may have happened behind that facade. To Lord Hailsham this provides the constitution with one 'advantage of priceless value: its immemorial antiquity' (Hailsham 1976), and many would agree that institutions hallowed by the passage of time provide a firmer basis for the exercise of government authority than would newly created bodies.

But this can only be so if behind that facade institutions do adjust and are adapted so that their relationship to modern values is not too tenuous.

It is the very capacity gradually to change, and cumulatively to change in quite fundamental ways, which has ensured the survival of the institutions concerned. Parliament as a whole illustrates this fact; as a legislative body Parliament consists of three parts – Monarch, Lords and Commons. The most junior historically speaking is the Commons, yet it is the Commons which has now become dominant, indeed so dominant that for many the term Parliament is regarded as synonymous with the Commons. The monarchy continues because it has surrendered its effective powers elsewhere, though some discretionary powers of considerable importance remain personally with the monarch, notably the power to dissolve Parliament and the power to invite someone to form a government. That conventions tightly define the exercise of these powers is true, but the conventions which clearly exist do not (and cannot) cover all possible circumstances which may confront a monarch.

The Lords has likewise lost most of its effective powers, and some constitutional conventions have now arisen to restrain those powers which remain, though such conventions lack the precision of those which circumscribe the role of the monarch. But the House remains recognisably still a House of Lords, with Lords Spiritual and Lords Temporal, the latter sub-divided into five ranks of peerage. Except in special circumstances bills must pass both Houses, either of which may make amendments, before they can be enacted as Acts of Parliament. The government is answerable in both Houses, and ministers may be drawn from either House. In these important senses Parliament remains bicameral and the Lords remains recognisably the same House as has existed for centuries.

Yet behind the facade there have been great changes. The franchise reforms of the nineteenth century confirmed the supremacy of the elected House. When that was threatened by the Lords the struggle between the two Houses culminated in the decisive adjustment effected by the 1911 Parliament Act. After this the Lords could no longer veto legislation; the power it retained was only the power to delay. This was a fundamental change, even if it took the House as a whole some years to recognise the fact. More recently its composition has changed, notably following the passage of the 1958 Life Peerage Act. When that measure was first introduced Bagehot's prediction of a century before – that atrophy rather than abolition was the greater danger to the House – seemed near to fulfilment. The main opposition party in the House had almost ceased to exist as an organised force and the average daily attendance of all peers was below 100. The advent of life peers did facilitate a considerable broadening of the field of recruitment to the House, with the main direct beneficiary of the Act being the Labour party whose strength in the House has grown steadily since, as has the non-party element. It is not so much that life peers dominate proceedings in the House (that is only true on the Labour benches) but that their presence has been a catalyst to the whole House, which has become a much more active place in the last twenty-five years.

The importance of the House, its role within the political system, as well as its active membership, have all changed in very significant ways. There have been some decisive happenings in this process, but it has been a process rather than a single sudden event. Yet despite this change it is still meaningful to talk about a single House of Lords. The fact that Britain has an unwritten constitution is both a cause and a consequence of this continuity of institutional development which has been illustrated. But the question arises, does the absence of a written constitution mean that there is no limit to the change and adaptation which may take place? Can the constitution ever be broken? Most commentators would emphatically answer that it can; the mere fact that it is unwritten does not mean that many central features of the constitution are not clear enough, and if these are breached, then they are breached. But this raises the further question as to what safeguards are available to ensure that basic principles of the constitution are observed. The corollary to an unwritten constitution is the doctrine of parliamentary sovereignty. The notion of sovereignty may practically speaking be perpetually ambiguous, but this doctrine does indicate something important about the British constitution. Parliament alone can alter by ordinary legislative procedure statutes which are basic to the constitution. If the Lords withholds its assent to a bill, that bill may nonetheless be passed through the use of the Parliament Act. But the Parliament Act itself specifically excepts any bill to extend the life of a Parliament, and here the Lords still has an absolute veto. Thus the postponement of a general election beyond a five-year interval could always be forestalled by the Lords. If the Lords were removed it would be desirable to introduce some similar constitutional safeguard; if this were not done the monarch would potentially at least carry a heavier constitutional responsibility than at present. Similarly, the removal of a judge requires approval by both Houses of Parliament; if the Lords were abolished the independence of the judiciary might become harder to sustain if judges could be removed by simple majority in one House. The need for constitutional safeguards is a point admitted on the whole by abolitionists, and it is one to which we will return.

The fact that the whole British constitution was never consciously designed, but instead has gradually developed, also means that its component parts have come to relate to each other in all sorts of subtle ways not immediately obvious. As much is probably true of any political system which has persisted over time. To remove or replace one part may have surprising repercussions elsewhere. 'Were it not for the Lords the Commons would be a much more ancient assembly', suggested Ian Gilmour (1969: 301) making the point that some MPs who might otherwise have remained in the Commons have been prepared to move to semi-retirement in the Lords. Another element of flexibility in the political system which abolition would diminish concerns the field of recruitment to ministerial office; at present a Prime Minister can bring into government as ministers a sprinkling of non-MPs by creating such life peers. This has not been done widely, nor could it be, but it has been done regularly.

This gradual adaptation of major institutions within the framework of an unwritten constitution nevertheless may still have left the British constitution essentially undemocratic. The evolution from pre-democratic hierarchic forms of government to democratic forms has been gradual, remains partial and is incomplete. The continued existence of the House of Lords illustrates the point. Even the principle of one man one vote one value – basic to liberal democracy – remains unrealised in relation to the centre-piece of the British constitution. Parliament is a tripartite body, two parts of which – Lords and Monarch – can make no claim to democratic legitimacy. The reasons why Parliament has taken this form are easy enough to see when we consider its origins. The House of Lords pre-dated the Commons in that the practice of summoning notables preceded that of summoning representatives of the lesser aristocracy in the lower House. It was the rise of democratic feeling which brought the lower House to the fore; but Liberal as well as Conservative thought of the 19th century was profoundly distrustful of democracy and in particular of popular elections. A means of placing some restraint upon the elected House was widely thought to be essential, and the House of Lords was conveniently available. This suited the interests of the propertied classes which remained of great importance. From being justified in its own right – as an assembly of powerful magnates whose support the monarch must maintain – the House derived a new justification as a brake upon the Commons. But this century has seen the widespread acceptance of democratic values, and has therefore rendered less plausible the justification of the unelected Lords imposing a restraint upon the elected Commons. And the whole concept of an hereditary right to sit in the legislature can only be said to be deeply alien to modern values. Furthermore, if peers by succession make the House unacceptable to democratic values, peers by creation can hardly be said to clothe it with the mantle of legitimacy. The continued existence of the House of Lords as the second chamber of Parliament is symbolic of Britain's incomplete acceptance of democratic values.

But does such an argument mean that no justification exists for a second chamber of any kind? This century has seen a modest trend towards unicameralism elsewhere in the world, with New Zealand (1951), Denmark (1953) and Sweden (1971) all abolishing their second chambers. More striking is the general retention of bicameralism. In some countries a federal structure provides an obvious reason for retaining a second chamber. But even in unitary states, or where the second chamber is unrelated to any federal structure which exists, it has been customary to offer justification in terms of the value of retaining a body which provides for a 'second look' at legislative proposals. It is noticeable too that those countries which have abolished second chambers, or introduced new constitutions making no provision for a second chamber, have tended to be relatively small (the above three) or unable to sustain even the claim to be democratic that Britain can (for example, Kenya, Syria). In principle bicameralism does provide for more points of access to government, and a second chamber can provide for representation of the people in a way supplemental to the first. These complementary points are both of some significance in a large complex society where the value of a second chamber is arguably greater than in a small homogeneous society. Bicameralism which originated in a pre-democratic age, may be said in the modern period to have found new justifications. But the persuasiveness of such justifications depend in part upon an underlying model of the role of Parliament. If the purpose of Parliament is simply to make government easier, to enable a party with a majority to carry its policies through, to translate its ideas into action with as little hindrance as possible, then better to have a unicameral Parliament. Failing that, then better to keep the second chamber weak, lacking credibility and intimidated into quiescence. There is probably something of this attitude in all British party leaders, illustrated by the reluctance of governments to introduce reforms that strengthen Parliament. If, however, the purpose of Parliament is to constrain governments, to subject them to scrutiny and criticism and in so doing not only to influence but to some extent to circumscribe and control their activity, then justifications for a second chamber may more readily be found. Furthermore, the apologist for this latter model of Parliament would also argue that it is precisely through such activity that Parliament can actually serve to strengthen government *vis-à-vis* the whole society it attempts to regulate; it is through obliging governments to meet criticisms of their policies, and to adjust their proposals so as to win consent from a Parliament representative of all major interests in a society that support for government is positively mobilised.

If this latter model of Parliament is accepted then the justification or otherwise for a second chamber can be argued on the basis of how adequately the first chamber performs, and what supplementary role the second chamber is capable of performing. It is, of course, commonplace for abolitionists to argue that fundamental reform of the Commons must be introduced concomitantly with the removal of the Lords. So it is desirable when considering the existing work of the Lords also to assess the possibility of transferring this work elsewhere. The most important existing function of the Lords is the revision of bills. The quality of legislation is a matter of serious concern for any legislature, and it is certainly a matter of concern for the British Parliament. Much legislation leaves the Commons in a form unfit to be let loose upon the public. Reform of Commons' procedure – for example the introduction of a select committee stage additional to the present stages – may help improve some bills. But while abolition of the second chamber may create the opportunity for a radical overhaul of Commons' procedure, whether it would result in changed attitudes among MPs, such as to make much effective difference to the scrutiny of legislation, is much more doubtful. Any revised Commons' procedure would come under the same pressures; 'guillotines' would still be used. To resort more to general bills, which set a framework within which ministers could take decisions introduced as statutory instruments, would diminish the opportunities for effective scrutiny of legislation.

Even without such procedural changes, it is arguable that having a second chamber to do what the Commons has already done but from a different point of view is valuable. At present the Lords does provide a different kind of environment to the Commons; it is less partisan, rather more professionally expert and more detached from government. There is a different character to Lords' debates; no guillotine exists so parliamentary consideration can be given to those parts of bills which have been guillotined in the Commons. The fact that the committee stage of bills is taken on the floor of the House means that the whips never quite know who might turn up and sometimes peers with considerable reputations in particular fields make surprising interventions, unwelcome to frontbenchers. A considerable amount of detailed amendment does take place, particularly on bills which are less important in a party political sense, including especially bills first introduced in the Lords. A study of legislation introduced by private members indicates that the Lords plays a useful role, which cannot be measured simply in terms of the number of Lords' bills which reach the statute book but must also reckon with those Commons bills which have had their predecessors debated and given some precise formulation in the Lords.

In assessing the degree to which the two Houses operate in a complementary manner it is not, therefore, the matter of parliamentary time alone which needs to be considered but also inclination. The scrutiny of European Community instruments further emphasises this point. So long as Britain is a member of the European Community it is obviously desirable that EC legislative instruments should receive scrutiny from the British Parliament. The Lords took to this task a good deal more readily than the Commons, and as a result provides a far more thorough scrutiny of draft instruments, and the context within which they are framed, than the Commons. The House has made use of select committees in a number of other areas, notably in 1979 establishing a Science and Technology Committee when the Commons abolished its committee in this area. It is easy to criticise the role of select committees, and hard to give convincing answers to searching questions about their effectiveness, but the point can be made that the Lords has through such committees mobilised considerable expertise at virtually no expense to investigate and report on subjects which have been of some parliamentary and public concern. The same general point can be made about debates in the Lords. On a range of issues some peers can be found who speak with considerable authority and are prepared to use the opportunity which the House provides to engage the government.

The purpose of delineating in this summary fashion something of the activities of the present House is not so much to establish how useful or otherwise it is, (that would be a much lengthier exercise) but to indicate the value a second chamber may have. In itself the House of Lords is a hangover from a pre-democratic age. But bicameralism is neither a democratic nor an undemocratic feature of a constitution. And there is no reason in principle why a second chamber should not enhance the democratic quality of parliamentary government in Britain. Providing greater scrutiny of legislation, providing more points of access openly and publicly to government, mobilising some expertise to scrutinise government activity, are all functions of the House of Lords. Merely to remove the House would be more likely to weaken than to strengthen Parliament as a whole. Furthermore, the difficulties inevitably involved in the process necessary to bring abolition about – at least if abolition were opposed by the Lords and by the opposition of the day – might weaken Parliament and the wider fabric of our constitutional arrangements even more seriously.

But the Lords as it stands, despite the gradual cumulative changes which have so altered its character and its place within the British constitution, remains a House composed in such a way as to invite ridicule. As much is widely recognised, and all major parties have formulated ideas for its reform. But so far no government has carried through fundamental reform. Such looked a real possibility in the late 1960s, but in the following decade the climate of opinion changed dramatically.

Proposals for Reform

The 1968–9 Attempted Reform

The most recent legislative attempt at comprehensive reform of the Lords was the Parliament (No. 2) Bill 1969, described in detail by Janet Morgan (1975). This bill was pre-eminently a rational attempt at evolutionary reform based upon the inter-party concord and reflected the mood of the 1960s when both major parties shared a predilection for institutional reform. In essence, the radical element in the legislative proposals was the ultimate complete exclusion of hereditary peers. The reformed House was to have a nucleus of about 230 full-voting regular members with an outer-circle of non-voting members who could attend and participate in the proceedings of the House. Thus reformed, with detailed proposals also made for bishops, and law lords, the House would retain the powers to delay bills (for six months) and to oblige the Commons to 'think again' (i.e. debate and vote again) on statutory instruments. If, on the Conservative side the abandonment of hereditary rights of membership was seen as the major concession, on the Labour side the retention of the House's power of delay was likewise a concession. And indeed it was on these grounds that back-benchers on both sides of the Commons objected to the bill, and eventually forced its abandonment.

Polarisation: Labour's decision to abolish the House

During the 1970s a polarisation of views about the House took place, a polarisation which made it hard to realise by the end of the decade that a mere ten years earlier there had been so significant an area of agreement, at least between the party leaders. Most notable was the Labour party conference vote in 1976 to abolish the House, the possible consequences of which were examined above. In order to set that vote in context, however, it is necessary to examine the way the House developed in the 1970s.

The experience of the Labour government in the period 1974–77 is of crucial importance to the understanding of the 1976 commitment to abolition. Unlike its predecessor of 1964, the Labour government's tenuous Commons majority after October 1974 did not prevent it from introducing controversial legislation. By the mid-1970s a government defeat in the Commons was no longer viewed as such a serious blow to government authority as in the 1960s, with the result that governments were prepared to take more risks in the lower House over legislation. As far as the Lords were concerned this meant more legislation came before it which had passed the Commons very narrowly – indeed in several crucial cases in 1975/76 by a single vote. The Upper House in exercising its right to amend legislation passed a great many amendments which the government resisted and sought to overturn in the Commons. In the 1974–77 sessions the proportion of Lords' amendments agreed by the Commons fell from its usual level – of over 95 per cent – to around 75 per cent. For many Labour MPs, with their wafer-thin Commons majority, securing the reversal of these amendments was a tiresome business which angered them.

In some cases this proved impossible; the abstention of small numbers of Labour MPs prevented the government securing the cancellation of Lords' amendments to the Dock Work Regulation Bill and the Housing Finance Bill in 1975. In these cases it was ultimately the failure of the government to secure a majority in the Commons which brought about the demise of its intentions. The government itself was somewhat confused over some provisions of the Trade Union and Labour Relations Amendment Bill also of 1975, particularly concerning the effect of a trade union closed shop in journalism; the Lords delayed this bill on the initiative of a prominent cross-bench peer, Lord Goodman. But the real wrath of Labour MPs was invoked by the Lords insistence on delaying the Aircraft and Shipbuilding Nationalisation Bill of 1976 until ship-repairing had been deleted.

The constitutional settlement pre-dating World War I, and the subsequent reduction in delaying power in 1949 had pre-supposed a House which *did* delay bills – not in any massive way, but simply by insisting on those amendments to which they attached particular importance. But over the years the reluctance of the House to use its suspensory veto – understandable enough in the light of its own unmodernised composition – resulted in a belief arising, at least within the Labour party, that a constitutional convention forbade the Lords from using its power, unless maybe in some last ditch defence of the constitution. One could argue that through failing to use its brief delaying power over so long a period, the House had really conspired in the creation of such a convention. On the other hand, the House had on past occasions shown itself ready to resist governments, and had certainly not itself articulated any such doctrine. Nevertheless, provoked by the delay inflicted on its major nationalisation measure by the Lords' action, Labour voted overwhelmingly at its party conference for the abolition of the Lords.

The irony was that from 1977 onwards the relationship between the Lords and the Commons was different again. Labour, by this time, lacked a Commons majority, so legislation only passed the Lower House if it had the support of some other party. The government made a pact with Liberal MPs which ensured its survival, but as a simple matter of Commons arithmetic it could no longer secure the passage of controversial and partisan legislation, as it had prior to 1976. When the Lords took a different view from the Commons, as it did for example on important questions arising during the passage of the devolution legislation, this was not simply a disagreement between a majority of peers and the governing party in the Commons, but between peers and a Commons majority made up from a variety of parties. Peers seemed more disposed to give way when opposed by a Commons majority made up from beyond the ranks of the Labour party, even if the issues were of a constitutional and machinery of government kind, rather than to do with, for example, industrial policy. But the damage had already been done, the Labour party conference was by 1977 committed to the reform of Parliament into an 'efficient *single chamber* legislating body'.

The Manifesto of the Labour party in 1979 did not reflect this commitment inasmuch as abolition of the Lords was not included. Instead there was a proposal for the removal of the remaining Lords' powers, while leaving the question of composition untouched. The 1983 manifesto included a commitment to abolish the House 'as quickly as possible' but as an interim measure to abolish its legislative powers forthwith. Terminating the power of the House is a simple, straightforward, easily understood proposal; as such it remains the most likely course of action a future Labour government would take. Because the great bulk of the Lords' work is now undertaken without any question of the use of its powers arising, it is arguable that little practical difference would be made to the working of the House; the House would still be able to ask the Commons to 'think again' about any item. But matters may not be so straightforward. A House without any formal power may be in greater danger than the Lords has been hitherto of not being taken seriously by the first chamber. This is not to defend a delaying power in the terms in which the Bryce Commission (Cmnd 9033 1917) did, charging the House with a responsibility to delay legislation which may be contrary to public opinion, but rather to argue that the capacity at least to threaten some delay may be a necessary pre-condition for an effective revising function. With its composition unchanged, the House would remain an easy target for criticism, even ridicule, and this would cast further doubt on its ability to ensure a fair hearing for itself, particularly in those hectic fraught days in which parliamentary sessions often terminate.

Other ideas have been expressed from within the Labour party. In particular a group of Labour peers in 1980 put forward a scheme for reform which involved the removal of any hereditary right to seats in the House, and the establishment of a Commons select committee to advise the Prime Minister about nominations for life peerage. Under this scheme not all peers would have voting rights, because at the start of a new Parliament each party group in the House would choose a body of voting peers proportionate to party balance in the Commons. Remaining peers could attend and take part in proceedings in the

House, but not vote. Such a House would have a six month power of delay. Voting peers would receive a salary. Underlying this proposal is the attempt to retain a House which might in the broadest sense be useful, but which because of its voting membership would be unlikely to find itself in conflict with the Commons. The House would in theory have the same functions as now. Legislation could be introduced and amended; the good and the great could continue to mingle with the politicians (semi-retired or otherwise) to debate issues of the day, sit on select committees and so on; the House would still be there as a pleasant place for MPs in need of a quieter life. But would peers who could not vote still bother to take part in the proceedings of the House? This problem is a recurring one for any scheme of reform which involves two-tier membership. It seems reasonable to suppose that peers would be likely to take part in proceedings, even when they could not vote, simply out of the desire to influence what goes on.

A much more fundamental objection to the plan put forward by the Labour peers concerns the way the voting House would be composed; the suggestion to make this proportional to the party balance in the Commons would aggravate the offence already felt by minor parties at their treatment under the existing electoral system. It also leaves unclear the position of cross-bench peers (one might unkindly suggest these should be proportionate to the non-voters in the election . . .!). A variation would be to compose the upper House according to the proportion of votes cast at the last election (rather than seats won). But this would be to emphasise the lack of proportionality in elections to the lower House, and might (at least in the eyes of some) embolden the upper House into making claims to be more representative of public opinion than the Commons. Such a scheme would result in the government almost invariably being in a minority in the upper House, while enjoying a majority in the lower, and it is doubtful whether this is a sensible basis upon which to carry through any reform. More fundamentally, any scheme which limits membership of the House entirely to those nominated by successive Prime Ministers implies a serious loss of independence for the House. Criticism was expressed of the 1968–9 proposals on these grounds, and such criticism probably would be sharper since Mr Wilson's resignation honours list was issued in 1976.

Within the Labour party, those who are not outright abolitionists are (on the whole) seeking a chamber which would be useful, even decorous, but incapable of being awkward. This objective, it can be argued, derives from a basic view about the purpose of Parliament as a whole. The question whether or not to have a second chamber, and if so what form this should take, returns us to the more fundamental question raised earlier in this chapter, namely, what is the proper role for Parliament? Is the chief purpose of Parliament to 'make a government' and once having fulfilled this electoral function, to strengthen the political arm of the executive? Within the Labour party – and beyond it – many would say 'Yes': paramount is the need for a strong executive, legitimised directly by an electoral mandate; checks and balances in reality already exist in profusion – within the civil service, local government, nationalised industries, and interest groups of all kinds. Parliament should not add to such checks; rather its purposes should be to strengthen the hands of ministers *vis-à-vis* other interests in the state. Select committees (if they have any role at all) are a 'forum for party political debate where outside opposition to the government's policies can be exposed as invalid' (never valid?); such committees are to 'strengthen the spine of weak cabinets' (Sedgemore 1980: 180). It is the wish to govern without parliamentary hindrance which determines the attitudes to parliamentary reforms (Lord Northfield 1978). A strong political executive is the dominant requirement and Parliament must be shaped to this end. 'It is not possible to continue if a Labour government has control over only half of Parliament' declared Mr Benn to the 1980 Party conference. Clearly, the implication is that ministers ought to control Parliament rather than the other way round. At what point does the concern for strong government become a denial of parliamentary government? This is a question which demands an answer in terms of Parliament as a whole, but the kind of answer given must have implications for any second chamber.

The Conservative Party

Labour's abolitionist stance provoked concern throughout the Conservative party, perhaps even alarm in places. Mrs Thatcher appointed a committee under Lord Home to advise on the future of the second chamber, and this reported in March 1978. Its two guiding principles seemed to be the need for continuity between a reformed House and the present House, together with the need to enhance considerably the legitimacy of the House. Eighteen months before the committee reported Lord Hailsham in his Dimbleby lecture had spoken of the need for constitutional reform to safeguard Britain from 'elective dictatorship'. The Home Committee (1978) spoke of 'mandated majority government' but meant the same thing. Many Conservatives were in this period acutely aware that the Labour government had, in October 1974, attained an overall Commons majority with the support of less than forty per cent of the voters (and less than thirty per cent of the electorate). The need for a more effective parliamentary check upon such a government was very much in mind. The Home Committee recommended that the upper House should include a substantial elected element – ultimately two-thirds of its membership. The electoral system used should be quite different from that for the Commons, with some form of proportional representation strongly preferred. Elected members would sit for lengthy terms, maybe nine years with one-third being re-elected every three years. The rest of the House would be life members nominated by the Prime Minister, who would be assisted by an initiatory and advisory committee of privy councillors. A reduced number of bishops and law lords would remain. Continuity with the present House would be emphasised by including all present life peers and fifty active hereditary peers. Other peers by succession might be chosen as prime ministerial nominees, but if carried through the proposals would have ended the right of hereditary peers to a seat in the House. Thus reformed the House would have its delaying power increased to two years and would possibly be given further powers (for example, to call a referendum) in the context of wider constitutional reform.

Between its two guiding principles – of enhanced legitimacy for the reformed House and continuity with the present House – the Home Committee probably attempted too extravagant a compromise. Under its proposals, for at least a decade, elected peers would be in a minority. More crucially, while it may seem logical to increase powers and at the same time reform composition, to attempt both would certainly provoke the jealousy of MPs, and it is most unlikely that such a reform would pass the Commons. Moreover, it is doubtful whether the powers of the House need to be increased. Certainly its existing power is sufficient to ensure that its revising function be taken seriously, and arguably sufficient to ensure that it can act as a constitutional watchdog.

The Home Committee (1978: paragraph 68) emphasised the need for reform: 'Maintenance of the status quo is not a prudent policy. Indeed we are doubtful whether it is a policy at all'. This drew attention to the urgency for reform felt by many in the party. It was not a feeling shared by Mrs Thatcher, who despite some concerted pressure brought to bear within the party after the 1979 election victory, declined to take up the subject. Mrs Thatcher's reluctance is in many ways understandable. Any scheme for fundamental reform acceptable to the Conservative party as a whole would be likely to meet with determined Labour opposition. During the passage of any reform through Parliament, the Labour party would almost certainly pledge itself to undo the reform, and very likely to abolish the House. When the subject was debated at the 1981 Conservative party conference, Baroness Young – then leader of the Lords – argued that all-party talks and agreement must precede any major reform and that such agreement would be unobtainable in the 1979 Parliament, which in any case had more pressing business more closely related to the country's problems.

An additional reason for Mrs Thatcher's misgivings about the subject probably lay in her known antipathy to electoral reform. Most recent suggestions for a reformed House which have come from within the Conservative party (e.g. Bow Group 1977; Society of Conservative Lawyers, 1978), have involved election, and invariably when this has been proposed some form of proportional representation has been advocated. If the House, or any of its members, were to be directly elected, a form of PR would undoubtedly be the right way to do this. But objecting to reform of the Lords in order to avoid raising the subject of electoral reform is short-sighted; it would be much wiser to recognise that different bodies with differing functions (second chambers, devolved assemblies, Euro-Parliament) may be best constituted through differing electoral systems. Failure to do this risks obscuring some valid cogent arguments which can be advanced for maintaining the present electoral system for the Commons.

Problems of Reform

The argument for an elected second chamber does need further clarification. Direct election is the method usually favoured by those whose chief concern is to strengthen the upper House. An obvious problem is that of potential rivalry between an elected upper House and the Commons. Sometimes it is implied that any House directly elected would inevitably engage in damaging conflict with the Commons, but such fears may have no more substantive ground than the dearth of thought hitherto given in Britain to methods of election. A House whose members were elected one-third or one-quarter at a time, for lengthy fixed periods of nine or even twelve years, could not claim the same popular legitimacy as the Commons. Nor would members of the upper House, if elected from large regional constituencies, trespass upon the constituency 'ombudsman' role which most MPs now seem to value so highly.

A system of election based on PR was advocated in a recent Fabian Tract (Bell 1981); the author of this proposal wished to see a House complementary to and not a rival of the Commons, and to this end suggested a House entirely composed of members elected from Euro-constituencies. The manner of election suggested (four members per constituency, two being elected every two years) would have severely limited proportionality, but such a House would have retained a six month delaying power.

It is when direct election is linked closely with increased power for the House that fears of damaging rivalry with the Commons become justified. The Conservative party conference in 1980 called for an upper House strengthened so as to act as a 'check upon arbitrary government'. There is a danger of blurring the constitutional principle that cabinet responsibility lies clearly to one chamber only; where a parliamentary system co-exists with bicameralism it is essential – or sooner or later inevitable – that this point be recognised (Wheare 1968: 135).

A phrase such as 'arbitrary government' could cover a multitude of things; that is part of the difficulty. In so far as 'arbitrary government' is to be checked then it is better to look to the Commons to do this. If the chief cause of concern is the fact that a government can come to office with an overall Commons majority based on the support of less than a third of the electorate, then the proper reform is one that involves the electoral system – a matter beyond the scope of this chapter, but one taken up elsewhere in this volume.

There remains, however, a sense in which the House of Commons *does* need a rival. Part of the purpose of Parliament is to hold government (and all its bits and pieces) properly and publicly accountable, and in this the lower House has done badly. While the main brunt of this task must rest with the House to which the government is directly responsible, a stronger second chamber could make a more effective contribution. What is required is that both Houses be stronger. Hence a possible pre-condition for the implementation of any proposals for a reformed upper House is a visibily stronger and more effective Commons, one likely to be less easily provoked into jealousy by the strengthening of a junior rival.

A number of suggestions for reform of the second chamber have been closely linked with wider constitutional reform, particularly that involving regional government. The minority report of the Royal Commission on the Constitution made by Lord Crowther-Hunt and Professor Peacock (1973) which recommended a regional structure of government for the United Kingdom suggested that reform of the House of Lords, though not essential to their proposals, was desirable. Under their scheme regional assemblies would have elected about 150 of their members to join existing peers in the upper House. This they argued would have a number of advantages, in particular it would enable regional governments to be better and more strongly represented at the national level. Such ideas have been discussed further in the context of devolution. Proposals for a second chamber, partly composed of members elected by regional assemblies have been put forward within the Social Democratic Party. Such suggestions have a clear rationale. But the real question in this context concerns provision for a regional tier of government; to discuss the whole subject from the point of view of second chamber reform is to make the tail wag the dog. Any reform of the second chamber which involved direct election from large regional constituencies (as mentioned earlier) would probably help generate and express regional feeling, and articulate regional interests at Westminster. Reform based on indirect election from regional assemblies would certainly do this.

Some proposals for reform appear to be based on the premise that the major task of the second chamber ought to be to mobilise consent for government policy. The chief obstacles governments face, so it is argued, are the power of major institutions in society, notably trades unions, professional associations, business groups and so on. Hence the second House should be reformed so as specifically to include representatives of such groups. This approach does attempt to build on an important aspect of Parliament's historical development, namely to include within it those who wield *de facto* power, the barons of the day (see Changing Gear 1981). Advocates of this view argue that it is desirable to 'bring into the open the concealed corporatism of so much of our political system' (Beloff, *Daily Telegraph*, 30 May 1980). There are obvious difficulties of detail involved in any such scheme: which groups would be represented, and in what proportions? How might these change in the future? If such a second chamber retained its existing formal power, or even had this increased, how would the choice of nominees not become a party political consideration? More fundamentally, would a House so composed adequately cohere? At present the House benefits from the presence of bishops and law lords – examples of professionals who owe their place in the House to their professional appointments. But a study of their contributions suggests a certain idiosyncracy. They are valuable as an element but a working House could not be entirely composed in this way. Even more fundamentally is it desirable to entrench within Parliament the *de facto* power such groups as the CBI, the TUC, and the professional bodies already possess? Is corporatism to be resisted, or is it to be recognised and formalised?

Conclusion

Drawing up a blueprint for a reformed House is not part of the purpose of this chapter. But nonetheless a number of points can be made by way of conclusion.

First, the upper House is very much the junior part of Parliament; government responsibility in a constitutional sense lies in the lower House, and it is the Commons which must carry the major weight of Parliament's total function. But within this structure it is reasonable to argue that the present House of Lords performs modest functions satisfactorily. It is valuable – given the state of the Commons – to have a revising chamber, and the House makes a good attempt at this task. It is desirable to have a second chamber which in a junior capacity complements the work of the first, in particular by tackling issues and dealing with problems which the first by-passes. Again the House has done this to a significant extent. When its work is examined alongside that of its senior partner – the Commons – the House of Lords need not feel embarrassed. A stronger Parliament requires both Houses to be strengthened. Developments in the Commons over the last decade have begun this process, and the Lords has in many ways been keeping in step as it has developed its own role (e.g. select committee work).

If this is to continue, and if damaging conflict is to be avoided, then the composition of the House needs to be tackled. The eccentric, even offensive, feature of the present House is the hereditary element. This should be removed; it was not part of the House when it first existed, and it is plainly anomalous today. That there are peers by succession whose work within the present House is valuable is not to be doubted; such could well find their way into a reformed House. Abolishing the hereditary right to a seat need not in other respects affect the peerage. Just as the Life Peerage Act was a simple measure introduced by the Conservatives, without opposition support but more in accordance with Labour than Conservative party values, so a Conservative government should now remove peers by succession from the Lords. To leave the House entirely nominated would be unwise. The only satisfactory alternative is some form of election. In the context of regional reform one could hope for a rational basis upon which to add an elected element to the House. Without such reform however it would still be right to elect members, and this should be done on a properly proportional system from regional sized constituencies. The nominated element would remain.

To abolish the House outright would be a difficult task to accomplish. The actual act of carrying abolition through would weaken Parliament probably even more than the loss of the present House. To abolish the House and replace it with an entirely new second chamber would be to violate the principle of continuity which has served the British constitution well, and any entirely new House would be vulnerable to further reform or abolition before its authority had been established.

There is a sense in which the Labour party has always been naturally an abolitionist party. The House of Lords has been inextricably bound up with hereditary rights, an honours system and privilege and reforming the House in such a way as entirely to eradicate these elements has seemed a remote possibility; hence better its abolition, which at least would have some symbolic significance. If abolition takes place it is likely to be for this sort of reason, and because of the symbolic value of such an action. The failure of Labour governments to achieve their broader objective – more equality in particular – may paradoxically increase the attractiveness of doing away with the Lords. In the same way the Conservative party in its heart would probably prefer to leave the House alone. It has symbolic value here too (reminding the nation of its history) and also perhaps some practical value from time to time. In any case, reform is never – to the Conservative – to be undertaken eagerly, but only reluctantly.

In the modern period no government has yet felt that the difficulties inevitable in replacing or abolishing the House would be outweighed by the advantages gained, nor has there existed between the major parties a sufficient degree of agreement to permit an agreed major reform to take place. Furthermore, almost any reform would be likely, at least in the short run, to enhance the House in some way, and to distract attention from the Commons, which has understandably been reluctant to allow this. While the House of Lords itself has been at times eager for reform, its behaviour has on the whole failed to give governments an adequate incentive to grasp the nettle of reform. Instead it has adapted to a very subordinate role in the parliamentary system and in practice has been more convenient than inconvenient to both major parties. If governments have a natural disposition not to strengthen Parliament, then they have been well advised to leave the House of Lords alone.

6 Devolution and the Parliamentary State
Michael Keating

Introduction

The United Kingdom has always found it extremely difficult to come to terms with the politics of territory. There are many reasons for this. The UK was constructed gradually over a long period by the absorption of peripheral territories under a variety of regimes pragmatically designed to suit the individual circumstances of each. There was never a UK 'national revolution' to establish a 'UK nationality' on the basis of popular sovereignty. Instead, the peripheral territories were absorbed within the *English* parliamentary regime, a process made possible by the weakness of their own political systems; and represented perfectly by Westminster's habit of dating its origins, for the purposes of celebrations and memorials, from 1254 rather than the strictly correct 1707. In the case of Wales, absorption took place before state formation and parliamentary development was possible. In Scotland, statehood and the political system were surrendered in exchange for commercial advantages and the preservation of valued features of civil society. Only in Ireland was assimilation to English political norms impossible so that political absorption would have been possible only by a transformation of the latter to accommodate the new element. Although this brought the UK to the brink of civil war in the early part of this century, the problem was, in the event, dealt with by granting independence to the larger part of Ireland and isolating the politics of the smaller part from metropolitan politics by devolution and parliamentary under-representation.

The development of the party system alongside the extension of the franchise and the rise of parliamentary government served further to obscure the politics of territory. It was by no means inevitable that – again with the exception of Ireland – party politics in the peripheral nations should develop along the same lines as those of England (Keating and Bleiman 1979; Morgan 1981); and the development owed as much to the ability of UK parties, especially those of the left, to incorporate the essence of many territorial demands into their politics (Jones and Keating 1979).

So the UK was able to develop pragmatically without clear principles to govern the nature of the state, held together by the symbol of the Crown and values and practices of a unitary and sovereign Parliament. This has made it possible for some English observers to deny that there is such an entity as the UK state; or to assume that underlying a unitary Parliament and (always with the exception of Ireland!) party system, there must be a homogeneous political culture (Finer 1970).

To the observer standing at the periphery, however, a different perspective unfolds. Westminster's unitary facade gives way to a complex pattern in which territorial, class and party politics intermingle and in which attitudes to the institutions of the state vary from outright rejection of its legitimacy (amongst many Irish Catholics and some Scots and Welsh) through conditional support in exchange for specific concessions (amongst Ulster Unionists and many Scots) to unconditional acceptance (among British nationalists in Scotland and Wales). The issues of territorial politics are many and we can do no more than cite a few examples: minority languages; rural depopulation and land reform; industrial decline and North Sea oil; education and religion; and, of course, territorial autonomy and the extent to which it can be traded off for material concessions wrung from Westminster (Keating and Bleiman 1979). For the UK political elites, however, this has not called into question the myth of the sovereign and unitary Parliament except when the regime itself (in 1912–14) or the party system which underlies it (in 1976–79) have been threatened. The ingenious experiments have been devised to accommodate territorial politics but without calling into question the essence of the system. It is the argument of this chapter that such attempts at squaring the circle are bound to fail and that providing for the politics of territory requires a transformation in the parliamentary regime.

States founded on the principle of popular sovereignty, whether unitary or federal, usually have clear principles laying down the relationship of the citizen to the state and the connections between territory and power, whether at the state or sub-state level. In post revolutionary France, popular sovereignty has been the basis of state sovereignty, of national identity, equality of citizenship and rights and of national unity. Territorial politics, while an important feature of the political process takes place within the framework of the unitary state. In the United States, popular sovereignty is the basis for the constitution and the legitimacy of both federal and state levels of government. The rules of territorial politics and the rights of the citizen are laid down and understood or, at least, are ascertainable. In the UK, I will argue, the principle of parliamentary sovereignty serves only to obscure these issues; and the myth of the unitary Parliament serves to distort territorial politics.

In the absence of any clear conception of the UK state, Parliament has had to undertake a variety of roles. It serves not only as an institution within the state but also as a stand-in for the state itself. There are many facets of this but as the focus of this chapter is on territorial politics, we will note merely that it is the institution of Parliament which defines the limits of the territorial state and that it is within Parliament that the territorial politics of the state must be played out. My argument is that it is ill-equipped to fulfil these roles and that radical change is called for.

Parliamentary Sovereignty

In theory, the sovereignty and supremacy of the UK Parliament has traditionally been regarded as absolute. In practice, it has been infringed, not only by the difficulties of exercising it effectively but also by the concession of authority to international and supra-national agencies, notably the European Communities. Yet, in spite of its erosion in practice, the principle continues to be defended vigorously in political debate, especially by the Conservative and Labour parties. It is defended on two types of ground – instrumental and absolutist.

Instrumentally, the supremacy of Parliament has been defended by Conservatives because of their concern with the internal and external security of the state and the maintenance of the established order. It has always been important for them to ensure that no powers which could potentially threaten this should be allowed to escape permanently beyond the control of the central authorities. Seen thus instrumentally, the principle is not an absolute one. There have been Conservatives, from the 1912–14 Irish Home Rule crisis to the more recent Rhodesian rebellion, who have been prepared to defy parliamentary authority where it conflicts with other beliefs or interests.

On the Labour side, instrumental support for parliamentary supremacy has come from the statism inherent in its policies. While radicals might in many circumstances be inclined to overthrow or drastically reform established institutions, Labour has traditionally preferred to keep the existing state intact in order to use it for its own purposes. As Nairn (1982) puts it, 'it was only rarely that the political leaders of "British Socialism" perceived a new state and constitution as the precondition of achieving class demands'. Instead, the centralised and seemingly authoritative UK state has been seen as a suitable vehicle for state socialism since the demise of syndicalist and guild socialist visions earlier this century. The state is defended from attacks from above as well as below. Many of the Labour left see the European Communities' bias towards free-market policies and free trade as incompatible with socialist measures in the United Kingdom. At a still higher level, many of them would like to see the UK state freed from dependence on international trade and capital to build socialism behind protective walls.

A widespread instrumental defence of parliamentary supremacy has been that it provides a guarantee of civil rights, of equal rights and of equity in the provision of state services. We examine the question of distributional territorial equity below. As far as civil rights are concerned, parliamentary supremacy has, in practice, failed to provide guarantees against the abuse of executive power. Indeed, by consolidating executive power with parliamentary authority it has served to reduce the status of the citizen *vis-à-vis* the state. Nor has it ensured equality of civil rights in all parts of the state. Both before and since the abolition of the Stormont Parliament, rights in Northern Ireland have differed from those in other parts of the UK. Even as between England and Scotland there have in the past been radically differing rights in matters like divorce or homosexual relations and in the last Parliament considerable differences in police powers were introduced in legislation.

Absolutist versions of parliamentary sovereignty are also evident on both sides of the political divide. For Conservatives, parliamentary sovereignty is associated with traditional authority and the inherited state form. In some conservative ideology, it is its antiquity and continuity rather than its elective character which give Parliament its legitimacy. Philosophers from Burke to Oakeshott have sought to justify traditional authority as superior to anything which could be derived from abstract principles; parliamentary supremacy as an element of traditional authority is not a rigid and unchanging mechanism but an entity whose essence remains even while its form is modified.

Stripped of its mysticism, this implies support for traditional elites. This being so, Labour's absolutist support for the doctrine of parliamentary supremacy is the more puzzling. Yet it is clear that many of its leading figures do subscribe to such an unqualified doctrine. As Michael Foot explained when defending the Labour government's devolution bill for Scotland, 'The fundamental explanation for the way we have devised the bill is that we want to ensure that this House retains its supremacy . . . We sustain the proposition that the House of Commons . . . and the decisions of Parliament must be respected' (Nairn 1982: 64).

Indeed, since the conversion of the Conservatives to support for the European Communities, it is on the Labour side that some of the most ardent expressions of support for parliamentary sovereignty have come. This, as we have seen, is partly an instrumental matter; but not entirely. Labour's vigorous contention that UK oil and fish stocks were a *national* resource to be used for the benefit of *UK* residents, contrasted with its equally vigorous denial of the validity of the same argument when put, *mutatis mutandis*, by the Scottish Nationalists, implies something wider than parochialism but less than internationalism. It implies a form of British (or perhaps UK) nationalism. As expressed in rhetoric from Gaitskell's 'thousand years of history' speech in 1962 down to Peter Shore's contributions to the 1975 referendum debate and beyond, this tends to equate the defence of parliamentary democracy, of parliamentary sovereignty and of national independence as an essential part of the British tradition. Similarly, for Conservatives, defence of national independence and defence of parliamentary sovereignty have often been equated. This is not surprising. Parliament is the only constitutional entity common to all parts of the UK and, unlike the Crown, confined to the UK. In a state lacking even a coherent law on nationality and citizenship, let alone a doctrine of national sovereignty resting on popular will, it is a vital basis of nationality. Yet, it is a curious one for radicals to adopt as their own; and, as we shall see, one ill-adopted to the reality of territorial politics.

Westminster and Territorial Politics
A unitary parliament in a unitary state might be taken to imply a territorially uniform system of government, with all parts of the state having the same relationship to the centre. Yet, in the United Kingdom, this is by no means the case. It is certainly possible to discern a 'Whitehall model' of government in which functional departments are responsible to ministers, themselves responsible to Parliament for policy and administration throughout the Kingdom. On closer examination, however, the exceptions loom larger than the rule.

Territorial differentiation in UK government goes back a long way. Neither Scotland nor Ireland has ever been administered in precisely the same way as England; since 1964, there has been a Welsh Office. In recent years, powers have been passed upwards to international and supra-national bodies, notably the European Communities. On another dimension, powers have shifted out of the hands of ministerial departments to a variety of *ad hoc* agencies and 'quangos' many of which have a territorial remit, bringing them within the scope of our examination.

The Scottish Office was established in 1885 for the twin motives of allowing Whitehall to govern effectively in the distinctive political environment of Scotland and of defusing Scottish agitation for more autonomy without questioning the basis of the parliamentary state. Since then, it has grown to take over responsibility for a large part of central administration in Scotland and to act as a lobby for Scottish interests within the governmental system. Both this lobbying role and the Office's ability to conduct a distinctive policy for Scotland raise serious questions about the role and purpose of the 'unitary' Parliament.

In a unitary state making no constitutional provision for territorial differentiation, resources should be allocated according to uniform criteria of need. Yet it has been firmly established that, in practice, territorial bargaining occurs within government as a result of which the Scottish Office has been able to obtain a larger share of resources than could result from any uniform set of criteria (Treasury 1980; Short 1981). On the other hand, our constitutional arrangements make no provision for this and lay down no rules as to how it should be conducted. Parliament was traditionally invited to endorse only the functional distribution of government expenditure, Scottish Office expenditure being expressed as a series of sub-headings of the functional categories. Until the devolution debates of the 1970s, Scotland's relative advantage thus escaped the attention of English parliamentarians. It was only the need for a mechanism to set the block allocation to be given to the Scottish Assembly which started a search for some *principles* for territorial distribution. Following the failure to implement the Scotland Act, the new Conservative government was left with a Treasury study (Treasury 1980) purporting to show that Scotland was over-privileged in terms of public expenditure and an 'English backlash' against this. The government was determined to bury the constitutional question. So it made permanent the technique of determining Scottish Office expenditure introduced towards the end of the Labour government, under which it is expressed as a single block which is increased or decreased by the same percentage as the corresponding 'functional' blocks of English expenditure (Heald 1980). This completely arbitrary means of establishing the Scottish total (which the Secretary of State *then* distributes functionally within the Scottish Office) has, not surprisingly, never been debated in Parliament; and both government and Parliament seem further away than ever from establishing *principles* of territorial distribution in the unitary state.

Policy differentiation in Scotland depends on the Scottish Office's ability to convince other departments that their own interests are not affected and, of course, is constrained by overall government policy. Within these limits, however, it can have considerable latitude, particularly where Scottish administrative practice is already distinct and there are few UK-wide considerations present (Keating and Midwinter 1981). Even where policy is uniform for the UK or for Britain, it may be the subject of Scottish legislation. There has, therefore, developed a whole area of Scottish political, administrative and legislative activity. To cope with this, Parliament has developed a series of special committees. The Grand Committee takes the second reading debates on most Scottish bills. The two Standing Committees take the committee stages. A Select Committee on Scottish Affairs scrutinises the work of the Scottish Office. Most Scottish MPs have become absorbed in this Scottish political arena, to the detriment of their participation in wider UK affairs except in a lobbying role (Keating 1975; 1978). Those who have 'escaped' into the UK political world are conscious of the hard choice they have made and usually refrain from participation in Scottish Affairs (Keating 1975).

This Scottish political arena is not – to revise my earlier view (Keating 1975) – a political system as it lacks the essential element of authority. All authority is retained by Parliament as a body, on Scottish as on other matters. Given the division of work within the House of Commons, this has given rise to a great deal of confusion.

To the extent that the Secretary of State is free to make his own decisions in response to distinctively Scottish demands, his responsibility to Parliament as a whole is weakened. Those wishing to achieve constitutional reform, whilst preserving the essentials of the Westminster model, have not always been aware of this. The Scottish Council of the Labour Party, in its anti-devolution days, recommended that 'the Secretary of State should be more answerable to responsible Scottish elected members through improved parliamentary Committee structures' (Labour Party 1973). Earlier, in 1948, the then Secretary of State, Arthur Woodburn, had recommended to Parliament a series of reforms which would 'give Scotland . . . more control over its own affairs' (HC Debates 1948, vol. 450). The Conservatives, too, have fallen into this trap. While their 1970 report on Scotland's government (Scottish Constitutional Committee 1970) was careful to say that a separately elected assembly could make the administration (i.e. the Scottish Office) 'more responsive', by 1977 Francis Pym was talking of a *separate assembly* to 'call to account' (*The Times*, 5 October 1977) the Scottish Office whose constitutional accountability to Westminster would, it appears, also remain. In fact, while the Scottish Office continues to be responsible to Westminster, inserting other types of accountability can only serve to confuse matters. Yet the problem remains; if all the Scottish Committees were abolished then government would experience tremendous difficulties in managing Scottish politics and government.

Within the limits of the sovereignty doctrine and the myth of the unitary Parliament, British parties have been able to accept a tremendous variety in the *procedures* for governing. The Conservatives were for some years able to support the Douglas-Home proposals for a Scottish Assembly, which, though separately elected, would be part of Parliament, taking some stages of bills whose remaining stages, including the vital second and third reading votes, would be taken at

Westminster (Scottish Constitutional Committee 1970). The obvious anomalies of such a scheme and the built-in potential for conflict were seen as less important than the tying of the Assembly to Westminster to ensure that no questions could be raised about parliamentary supremacy.

Labour's devolution plans of the 1970s can also be seen as a way of altering the procedures of governing while leaving the essence of the system intact. The Scotland Act purported simultaneously to transfer power and retain Westminster's supremacy. There was even a declaratory clause stipulating that nothing in it would affect the sovereignty of Parliament or the unity of the United Kingdom. It was defeated by an alliance of Conservatives who considered such a stipulation right but untrue and nationalists, who considered it wrong but true (Keating and Lindley 1981). The government appear to have been persuaded that, in the end, it did not matter anyway. In one, purely formal, sense this is true. There is no way in which Parliament can constitutionally restrict its own sovereignty or that of future Parliaments – this is implied by the doctrine of parliamentary sovereignty itself. On the other hand, the government showed a marked lack of willingness to spell out what parliamentary sovereignty and the unity of the United Kingdom meant in practical terms. The nearest government spokesmen came to this were references to Stormont and the fact that the retention of parliamentary sovereignty had permitted its suspension and abolition. No account was taken of the fact that parliamentary supremacy had failed to guarantee civil rights under Stormont or that its abolition had been made possible only by the political circumstances. With the exception of a few supporters of UDI, the dominant Unionists had nowhere else to go and so felt obliged to acquiesce in Westminster's demands. The lessons of that experience for Scotland were, to say the least, ambiguous.

If official reasoning has had difficulty accommodating Scotland – and, to a lesser extent, Wales – within the doctrine of the unitary and sovereign Parliament, in the case of Northern Ireland it has hardly tried to do so. Northern Ireland – and Ireland as a whole before it – has long been treated as an exception. Early supporters of the 'homogeneity thesis' of British politics dismissed the Northern Ireland case as an argument against them on the grounds that it was small, sparsely populated and remote. Certainly, one can accept with Blondel (1975) that the predominance of England and, within it, of London, has profoundly affected the conduct of politics. It means that Westminster politics can – at least some of the time – be carried out without reference to the peculiarities of the periphery. Yet this itself is evidence of Westminster's inability to handle the territorial dimension of politics or to come to terms with the heterogeneity of the United Kingdom.

Northern Ireland can, in fact, be seen not as a minor exception to the norms of the UK state but as a test of the state itself. It raises in acute form the question of whether the UK is a nation state. If it is, it is one with an extremely arbitrary border running through another nation and incorporating a non-allegiant minority. If it is not, then the defence of parliamentary sovereignty as an expression of the will of 'the nation' falls. Assuming that Parliament's legitimacy does not rest on individual consent by each citizen, it thus presumably rests upon the consent of the constituent 'nations' or parts. This, of course, has been conceded in the case of Northern Ireland but the implications of this have, as we have seen in our discussion of the Scotland Act, been rejected for the UK as a whole.

If the UK were really a unitary state, then the problems of Ireland would be an integral part of political life in the sovereign Parliament. In fact, Westminster politicians have been unable or unwilling to face up to this and have usually tried to hive off Irish questions in order to preserve its own unitary myth. In the process, many of the rules which are brought to bear to sustain this myth on the mainland have been broken. A measure of quasi-federalism in the shape of the Stormont Parliament was sustained for fifty years. Proportional representation has been introduced though at Westminister it is regarded as a threat to the adversarial politics on which the system thrives, and which allows the linking of executive and legislature. A constitutional convention has been assembled to consider the governmental arrangements for the province, an idea treated with derision in the Scottish context. In 1979, the Conservative government and Parliament repealed the Scotland Act on the grounds that, despite its majority endorsement in the refer-endum, it allegedly did not command widespread support and posed a threat to the unity of the UK; since then the same government has sought to re-establish devolved government in Northern Ireland where, without a referendum or any attempt at sounding out opinion, the people are alleged to favour it.

If the unitary Parliament can preside over this sort of inconsistency, one is led to demand what the essence of its 'unity' is. It appears either as a fig leaf for those unable to admit that the Westminster emperor has no clothes; or, more seriously, a device to preserve the dominant metropolitan political culture from the consequences of the fact that the UK is indeed a heterogeneous polity.

UK entry into the European Communities raises more problems about the traditional parliamentary doctrine and practice. Much has been written on whether Parliament has surrendered its sovereignty, or part of it, to the institutions of the EC, as implied by the Treaty of Rome; or whether it has not done so because by definition Parliament cannot alienate its own sovereignty. If the latter then, once again, the doctrine has been saved only at the cost of emptying it of all practical content. For it is clear that EC membership raises serious questions about some fundamental features of parliamentary practice. The doctrine of ministerial responsibility holds that ministers are collectively and individually accountable to Parliament for their actions and those of their departments. Yet the EC Council, consisting of government ministers and with considerable legislative powers, is not accountable to Parliament. UK ministers attending the Council may continue to be answerable to Parliament but it is impossible for them to accept responsibility for the actions of a body whose members are severally responsible to nine other legislatures. So there is both confusion of executive and legislative roles and confusion of accountability. When we add the Commission, with its initiating and executive roles beyond the control of national parliaments, we can see that the Westminster model totally fails to meet the circumstances. No number of investigative committees can obscure this basic finding.

Of course there is the directly-elected European Parliament, but its establishment and constitution have served to obscure rather than clarify the situation. It does have the powers, inherited from the old indirectly-elected body, to dismiss the whole Commission and reject the budget. It does not have legislative powers, nor are the Council or the Commission accountable to it.

To re-establish coherence in this field requires either a move back from European integration, the re-assertion of parliamentary supremacy and the voluntary negotiation by responsible governments of any international agreements; or a move towards a European federalism. In the latter case, there would have to be a European executive responsible to a European Parliament co-existing with the UK government and Parliament. This, however, raises the federal principle which Westminster parties have always refused to admit. So, as in territorial relations within the UK, we are left with an untidy compromise. Unity and sovereignty are vigorously asserted yet in practice they are continually denied.

Finally, as a threat to traditional parliamentary doctrines, there is the growth of regional administration and 'technocracy'. Since the Second World War, regional bodies, including regional offices of ministerial departments, regional water authorities, Regional Economic Planning Boards and, until 1979, Councils and sundry *ad hoc* agencies have grown up, especially in England, serving a variety of purposes (Hogwood and Keating 1982). Regional offices of ministerial departments are extensions of Whitehall into the regions and so accountable to Parliament. Water and health authorities raise more difficult problems. They have been described (Keating and Rhodes 1981) as 'technocratic' devices to subordinate political choices to technical criteria, the judges of which are the technical experts. Of course, 'technocracy' occurs at all levels of government. What is significant about the English regions, however, is that there is no corresponding *political* authority, so allowing political judgement to be subordinated almost entirely to professional judgement. The ambiguity of the role of the local authority member on health and water boards illustrates this well (Elcock 1978).

The existence of regional administration has consequences for territorial distribution as well as for political choices. Despite being called a *National* Health Service, the NHS has preserved a very inequitable territorial distribution of resources and its structure has proved unamenable to efforts to redistribute (Haywood and Elcock 1982). Parliament, removed from control on two dimensions – as health authorities are devolved both functionally and territorially – has been unable to come to grips with this issue.

The traditional unwillingness of governments to face up to the territorial dimension in politics and administration is well illustrated by the history of the Regional Economic Planning Councils and Boards. These were set up in the 1960s to provide the regional element in the National Plan. The Councils consisted of representatives of local government, industry and unions, together with 'independent' members. The Boards comprised civil servants from regional offices of government departments. From the start, there was an ambiguity about the political relationships involved. Were the Councils there to carry out the policy of central government? If so, why were locally-elected members included? Or were they there to *modify* the centre's policies? This is something that central government was unlikely to permit as it involved precisely that intrusion of territorial politics into the centre that Whitehall and Westminster have traditionally sought to prevent. In the event, it is not surprising that the Councils failed to establish the political weight necessary to exercise any influence and gradually declined until their abolition, with scarcely a murmur of protest, in 1979. The exception was in Scotland where the Council, having a politically significant interlocutor at the same territorial level – the Secretary of State – had managed to establish some influence.

Establishing political control over regional administration entails setting up elected regional assemblies. Elsewhere (Keating and Rhodes 1979) I have argued against Crowther-Hunt and Peacock's (1973) suggestion that there is a regional level of government which could be placed under regional assemblies; rather, there is a complex regional *network*, reaching up to the centre and down to the localities. Crowther-Hunt and Peacock, like Mackintosh (1968b) however, were right to stress the weakness of the political input at the regional level. Regional assemblies, precisely because they would not take over a ready-made, functionally distinct level, however, present a grave threat to the Whitehall/Westminster traditions of government. Elected regional governments would affect not only administration in the regions themselves but also the conduct of national government. They would thus reduce the isolation which permits the centre to ignore the territorial dimension of politics.

Towards a New Territorial Politics

There is a long tradition in UK politics and government of denial of the territorial dimension in the interests of preserving the myth of the unitary state and the parliamentary regime. The result is the incoherence and muddle noted above. How, then, can parliamentary reform help to improve matters?

Territorial politics is most explicitly recognised in federal systems where there is an explicit division of responsibilities, the federal level looking after 'national affairs'. Sovereignty is divided according to the spheres of responsibility, with each level supreme over its own range of affairs. Common or overlapping problems must be settled judicially or by negotiation. Usually, the inter-dependence of levels is recognised by the representation of the lower level in the second chamber of the federal legislature.

The problem with federalism, however, is that, designed for a liberal age of limited government, it is difficult to adapt to the needs of the modern state. Governments' responsibilities for economic management have led them directly, or through attempts to control expenditure, into all areas of policy; and the welfare state demands equal provision of services irrespective of location. So the distinction between national and sub-national affairs has broken down (Keating 1982a). Areas of 'single jurisdiction independence' have shrunk (Wright 1978) and the area of negotiated policy has grown.

Interdependence of levels of government is an inevitable feature of modern political systems. The centralisation which often accompanies it, however, is not. Policy making may demand coherence and co-ordination but this can be negotiated as well as imposed. This is where the federal principle is still useful.

The principle of parliamentary unity and supremacy precludes bargaining and negotiating and the possibility that Parliament may, at the end of the day, be unable to get all its own way. Yet in practice UK governments have frequently conceded these very principles. Policy must be negotiated in the European Communities – though the gaucherie of British negotiating methods often astounds our European partners. Even the Conservative government, which officially favours continued membership is unable to bring itself to play the subtle negotiating games which this requires to replace authoritative *fiat*. It is widely accepted now that public policy measures are effectively negotiated with domestic interest groups. Territorial politics is played out within central government. In Northern Ireland, there has even been negotiation and bargaining over the constitution itself. So to introduce the federal principle would not be to force an alien element of territorial politics into a homogeneous UK. Rather it would be to make explicit and subject to democratic sanction what is at present suppressed or denied.

I do not intend to present here a blueprint for constitutional reform though I have elsewhere (Keating 1982b) examined alternatives. What the argument does clearly point to, however, are elected assemblies for the nations and regions of the UK, and for the European communities if we should decide to remain a member. This would have to be accompanied by entrenched powers of some sort or else the assemblies would be no more than existing local government – free to agree but not to disagree with the centre. Such entrenched provisions could also include stronger safeguards for individual and collective civil rights than are available in the parliamentary system. Provision could be made for a second chamber ensuring the representation of the nations and regions at the centre and the protection of their constitutional position.

Whether such a system would be *called* federalism is not important. I have already suggested that much of the emphasis would be on negotiation and bargaining rather than on purely autonomous action at each level. Entrenched powers would serve not just to safeguard the latter sphere but to provide bargaining levers for each level, making cooperation necessary and removing the temptation for central government to attempt to regulate everything from the centre. Such a development would clearly involve a radical change in the parliamentary regime. The doctrines of parliamentary sovereignty and unity would need to be replaced by those of popular sovereignty and free association. Democratisation of the whole system of government and transformation of a range of other constitutional principles would be needed to prevent the system degenerating into one of purely *inter-organisational* bargaining by unaccountable and ill-understood units.

Finally, such radical changes are unlikely to come about consensually, through the efforts of detached reformers. Constitutional change is about the redistribution of political opportunities and these have substantive effects in terms of policy and party advantage. Territorial politics itself is intimately mingled with class and party politics, making it extremely difficult to consider one in isolation from the other. Up to now, the major British parties have placed all their investment in Westminster politics. Only when threatened from the periphery have they responded, hesitantly and clumsily, to the need for change. The SDP/Liberal Alliance has talked about the need for constitutional change but the SDP, at least, remains locked into the Westminster model. The impetus for change can come only from the periphery whether from a revived nationalist party or from a Labour party driven from the prospect of Westminster power and forced back on its peripheral strongholds, obliged to think again about its strategy for power.

The result of the 1983 General Election raises the possibility of such a development. The collapse of Labour's vote in the south of England and its continuing strength in Scotland have already led to speculation about the party adopting a strategy going beyond mere 'devolution' which, as we have seen, was really a means of preserving the essence of the parliamentary regime. Certainly, there are tactical advantages for Labour in pushing for a federal system; but it will still require an ideological revolution to tear it away from its attachment to the unitary Parliament.

PART TWO
Comparative Perspectives on Reform

One of the traditional failings of British reformist tracts is that they are normally monofocal, focused exclusively on Westminster, or at best are bifocal in their squints across the Atlantic to the US Congress. Other legislatures might as well not exist for most British academics and parliamentarians. Yet as S.C. Patterson (1973: 378) has convincingly argued 'students of the British House of Commons could learn a great deal more about that institution by conducting comparative studies . . .' A sentiment which fits well with the affirmation of the value of comparative study made in the Introduction of this book. But which legislatures warrant analysis? Obviously, the US Congress has been a persistent reference point for many reformers – but often for the wrong reasons. Thus rather than searching for congressional procedural transplants British reformers would be better advised, according to Malcolm Shaw in chapter 7, to discover the dynamic of reform in the negative sense that 'by identifying what Parliament **is not** one may obtain insights into what Parliament **is**'. The Canadian Parliament has been chosen to illuminate the process of reform in a Westminster derivative parliamentary model. In this manner the practical operation of canvassed reforms for the British legislature can be studied in a similar parliamentary setting. Yet the real value of Anglo-Canadian cross-national study is the recognition of the impact that different political and social contexts have upon these parliamentary systems. As Michael Rush points out in chapter 8: 'mechanistically there is no great difficulty in transferring institutional arrangements from one political system to another, but the **appropriateness of** and the **reasons for** such a transfer need to be the subject of close scrutiny'. Finally, the West German Parliament provides valuable insights into the operation of a parliamentary system distinctly different from that of Britain. The West German model has many elements, in its committee system, its electoral arrangements and the public financing of parties, desired by British parliamentary reformers. But the true lesson of comparison with Germany is the acknowledgement of the differing party, executive-legislative, and centre-periphery relationships which account for these structural differences. Most importantly, once again, Tony Burkett identifies the major lesson of comparative study to be the location of the movement for parliamentary reform within the political, economic and social networks within which legislatures operate.

7 Reform of the American Congress
Malcolm Shaw

The American Congress is in many ways the quintessential legislature. As the grand inquest of the nation it functions on a grand scale. From the points of view of expertise, political clout, facilities, interest articulation and constituency service, it is in a class by itself. In view of this, it is particularly instructive to examine Congress from the broad perspective of reform. In this chapter I shall examine, therefore, the context within which reform of the American Congress occurs, some reforms which have been effected in the recent past and the relationship which the process of congressional reform bears to the reform of the British Parliament.

Comparisons

Comparisons between British and American political institutions and processes are commonplace. They are found in the literature of Western political science more frequently than comparisons involving any other pair of countries. They are often thrown in without any explanation as to why they might be apt, as if this is self-evident. Moreover, the tendency is equally strong on both sides of the Atlantic and has survived the demise of the parliamentary-presidential dichotomy as a principal reference point in cross-national analysis.

What are Anglo-American comparisons thought to be so appropriate? There are a number of relatively obvious explanations: Britain and the United States are unusual in their importance on the world scene. They are two of the six countries which can be characterised as major industrial democracies (the others being France, West Germany, Italy and Japan). Moreover, unlike three of the others, their governing arrangements have been emulated throughout the world. Therefore, these arrangements are unusually influential and are thus important to understand both in their indigenous settings and in conjunction.

What is particularly intriguing and enlightening about comparing the British and American political systems concerns the factor of systemic distance. Conceptually and behaviourally, the two systems are so near and yet so far. Looking first at similarities, they both incorporate entrenched liberal democratic values, governing arrangements which make these values operational, a common historical and ethnic inheritance and a constant interactive relationship. Looking at differences, on the other hand, the systems are influenced by social circumstances and cultural norms which have become markedly differentiated as 170 years of a colonial relationship has given way to 200 years of national divergence. Accordingly, these divergences in the British and American social environments have resulted in variations in their respective governing arrangements, making the two systems markedly different despite the aforementioned elements of similarity. As far as the legislature is concerned, it follows that the differing contexts have made Parliament and Congress dissimilar in important ways.

Discussions of the working of the British Parliament often include references to the American Congress. Such references are sometimes coupled with an acknowledgement that the American context is not only dissimilar from the British context but also too dissimilar to make it relevant to what happens at Westminster. Crick (1968: 251), for example, maintains that, '. . . it is misleading (and usually deliberately so) to suggest that greater use of committees of advice, scrutiny and investigation [in the House of Commons] would lead to their controlling the policy of the Executive, as happens in the United States.' Similarly, when discussing the reform of Parliament, Punnett (1980: 259) asserts: 'Certainly, to draw parallels with the United States Congress can be misleading, as Parliament's role in the system of government is very different from that of Congress'.

Such observations are not usually amplified. It is the purpose of this chapter to provide amplification by suggesting what the main factors are that make attempts to change Congress a different exercise from attempts to change Parliament. In doing so, it is hoped that some illumination of the reform process in Parliament (and in Congress) may occur. By identifying what Parliament is *not*, one may obtain insights into what Parliament *is*.

At the same time, I am not looking at the British Parliament from the perspective of the Malagasy Assembly. I do not wish to suggest that the reform of Congress, on the one hand, and Parliament, on the other, bears no relationship whatever to one another. The members of Congress and Parliament are territorially-elected representatives of mass electorates who discuss policy questions and legitimise the outputs of government in an effort to achieve the kinds of accommodations that become necessary in industrial democracies. People engaged, mutually if separately, in such endeavours must have common points of reference which override even such disparities as the quantitative gulf that separates Congressmen and their British counterparts in the provision and utilisation of research, constituency and secretarial staff. Similarly, in a study of committee systems in the national legislatures of eight democracies it is suggested that overlaying the distinctiveness of committee arrangements in different legislatures there are broad tendencies that may be identified generally with the working of committees in certain kinds of legislatures. For example, in all eight legislatures it was found that members were assigned to committees in proportion to party strengths in the plenary chamber (Lees and Shaw 1979: 364, 392).

Before turning to specific contextual constraints in Congress, it should be mentioned that the concept of 'reform' will be broadly construed. Reform will be taken to refer not only to changes in standing orders and other formal rules of procedure but also to changes in practices, such as the use of staff, which arise alongside the formal rules and, like them, have an important bearing on the working of Congress.

The Historical and Social Context

When the American colonies broke with Britain in 1776, they rejected more than their political connections. It was already evident – as would also prove to be the case in Canada, Australia and New Zealand – that a new and different society was in the making. While there were loyalists in America at the time of independence, as there are Anglophiles today, a non-European, if not anti-European, society was emerging. It would require governing arrangements different from those of the mother country.

Authoritarian rule has prevailed during most of England's history, together with, at various time, feudalism, extreme social stratification, severely constricted occupational and educational mobility, deferentiality and limited space. None of these conditions has been conspicuous during America's historical development. American society, in contrast with Britain's, has evolved in a less self-consciously stratified way. It has also been more ethnically diverse and more individualistic and participatory in its culture. The latter tendencies are reflected in the family and in education, as well as in political life. The ambitious use of the referendum in the United States and the infrequent use of it in Britain is illustrative in relation to several of the aforementioned themes.

As far as the two economies are concerned, there are differences which contribute toward making the agenda of politics dissimilar in important ways in the two countries. While both countries are highly industrialised, the United States in this century has been less collectivist, has had a weaker trade union movement, has had a larger agricultural sector and is potentially more self-sufficient. Moreover, the development of heavy industry in the United States came after workers were enfranchised, not before as in Britain.

These relatively disparate settings have produced distinctive constitutional and procedural ground rules for the conduct of politics and government. At the same time, historical events peculiar to one or the other country have resulted in different political agendas, although at times, as with monetarism and supply-side economics, the politics of one "kissin' cousin" seems to resemble that of the other rather closely.

For present purposes history rather than procedure is being examined, and in that connection it is clear that specific political events that provide the substance of deliberation and action in the legislature constitute a variable of great importance. As Davidson, Kovenock and O'Leary (1966: 34) have suggested, 'The rules of the political game, as defined by the structure of institutions, cannot be divorced from the stakes for which the game is played'.

Thus the curbing of the powers of the Speaker of the House of Representatives in 1911 arose in relation to Speaker Cannon's identification with the obstruction of progressive legislation, just as the curbing of the powers of the House of Lords in the same year arose in relation to the Lords' obstruction of Liberal tax policy. Likewise, a change in the composition of the House Rules Committee occurred in 1961 after the Committee had blocked a series of social welfare and other bills. Similarly, the identification of filibustering in the Senate with the obstruction of civil rights legislation by southern senators resulted in 1959 in a change in the rule relating to unlimited debate. One might also mention the tendency for Congress to be assertive immediately after it has been liberated from the domination of a strong President. Thus Andrew Johnson had unprecedented difficulties with the Congress that he inherited from Lincoln, and Truman likewise had a rough ride immediately following Franklin Roosevelt's lengthy reign and 631 vetoes.

It is instructive to consider the relationship between reform and policy during the postwar years. It is generally agreed that the passage of the Legislative Reorganisation Act of 1946, which re-organised the committee system, was followed by twenty years of relative inaction on the congressional reform front. Then, in the late 1960s, an era of major procedural change in Congress began. Two issues had a great deal to do with this development: Vietnam and Watergate:

> Actions by Lyndon Johnson in relation to Vietnam and by Richard Nixon in relation to Watergate produced a strong reaction in Congress. Specifically, the exercise of the war powers by Johnson and the extraordinary use of various 'powers' of the presidency by Nixon precipitated an effort within Congress to redress the balance between the legislature and the executive.

The impoundment of funds by Nixon and his interpretation of the doctrine of executive privilege were particularly important in provoking this reaction, with pressure for change being most pronounced in 1974–75 in the wake of Nixon's resignation.

(Shaw 1981: 272–3)

Because Vietnam and Watergate did not happen in Britain the attendant pressures for parliamentary reforms did not happen either. More accurately, such reforms as were effected in Parliament in the late 1960s resulted from entirely different circumstances and took different forms.

It can be argued, then, that an important reason why the context for parliamentary reform differs as between Britain and the United States is that the social order, historical development and policy agenda are different for the two countries. There is, of course, a sense in which the broad sweep of Anglo-American political evolution bears some resemblances. Both Parliament and Congress were stronger relative to the executive in the 19th century than in the 20th century. Moreover, nations which experience the social and economic consequences of industrialisation and fight on the same side in war touch some of the same bases. But in general the dissimilarities are far more significant.

Entrenched Procedures

Any attempt to understand the reform process in Congress must take into account the entrenched nature of its procedural norms. Some rules date from the 18th century. When an institution has been doing things in the same way for a long time, it does not lightly alter its ways. If procedural changes can be got through at all in Congress, they tend, with some exceptions, to be at the margins.

An example of an entrenched procedure is the right of unlimited debate in the Senate. Although this right was sometimes abused, it was not until 1917 that the Senate adopted its first cloture rule. Subsequently, abuses continued in the form of filibusters, and efforts were made from time to time, successfully in 1959, to make it easier to obtain cloture. By the 1970s filibustering was being resorted to by opponents of the Vietnam war, military spending, legislation relating to busing, the extension of the draft and various other matters. Cloture was often moved and often failed to carry. In 1975, when there were twenty-three cloture votes and only eleven of them passed, a successful effort was made to change the existing rule. The new rule provided that cloture could be invoked by a vote of three-fifths of the *full* membership. This compares with the previous requirement of two-thirds of those present and voting. The point is that the new rule was not much more liberal than the one it replaced. It was a case of chipping away at the margins. By 1979, however, the Senate was forced to act to close the post-cloture loophole left by the 1975 rule. Some senators, thwarted by cloture, engaged in post-cloture filibusters. This loophole was closed when the Senate ruled, in 1979, that time spent on procedural manoeuvres would count towards the 100-hour limit which applies to post-cloture debate.

A reluctance to alter procedures was encountered when members of the House of Representatives were interviewed in 1963–64 (Davidson *et al.* 1966: 94). Thirty-two proposals for reform were put to a sample of members, and few of the proposals received the support of a majority of the respondents. Only five of the proposed reforms were given at least an even chance of adoption by the House during the next decade. The authors of the survey concluded that 'reformism does not seem to be the dominant mood of the House', and they speculated on why representatives should consider procedural reform 'a hazardous and unproductive commitment'.

About the time of this survey Cater (1965: 171) observed that one reason for the 'substantial resistance' to reform in Congress was that past reforms had had unanticipated side effects. Cater suggested that the overthrow of Speaker Cannon had freed the Rules Committee to develop in a troublesome direction, liberated as it was from the Speaker's control. It is significant that a decade after Cater wrote the Speaker regained some of his influence in the Rules Committee. In 1974 he was authorised by the Democratic caucus to nominate the Democratic members of the Committee, subject to ratification by the caucus. Cater cites the Legislative Reorganisation Act of 1946 as another instance of reform producing side effects. He says the Act 'helped consolidate the dominion of the standing committee chairmen'. One might also mention the proliferation of subcommittees as a side effect of the 1946 Act.

Procedure in Parliament is similarly entrenched. In fact few parliaments in the world can match Parliament and Congress in the matter of procedural continuity as well as continuity as legislatures. In this connection it is interesting to return to the matter of committees. As far as Congress is concerned, a commitment to devolve substantial authority to committees is very long-standing. Eight of the existing committees in the House of Representatives were created before 1820, with two of them (Ways and Means and Interstate and Foreign Commerce) dating from 1795. Clearly the idea of working through committees is very entrenched on Capitol Hill. As far as the House of Commons is concerned, the opposite tradition is equally entrenched. The floor of the House has traditionally been the focus of activity in the Commons.

Thus the idea of working through committees, congressional style, is as alien to Westminster as keeping the important things on the floor, Westminster style, is alien to Congress. Moreover, these contrasting predispositions are much more than casual preferences. Therefore anyone who proposes transferring congressional-type committees to Westminster is going against the grain in a fundamental way. Accordingly, the departmental committees created by the House of Commons in 1979 bear only a limited similarity to their counterparts in the House and Senate in Washington. In 1979, for the first time in the 700-year history of Parliament, the Commons acquired committees designed to oversee the activities of government departments in a comprehensive way, whereas Congress began doing this virtually from its inception. Indeed, the different patterns of committee development are a manifestation of fundamental differences between the two legislatures. Congress has developed an extensive system of committees, through a formal division of labour, in order to facilitate decision-making in the absence of consistent leadership from the executive or the party leadership in Congress.

The Great Divide
After nearly 200 years the separation of powers remains a powerful doctrine in American government. Despite inroads by strong presidents and by all presidents since the New Deal, Congress still considers itself to be an equal partner in relation to the executive. In a century of worldwide legislative decline Congress has not escaped its measure of lost influence. But it has been determined to maintain its discretionary and co-ordinate role in the face of burgeoning agendas, increased statutory complexity and enlarged executive establishments. The Supreme Court as well as Congress takes the doctrine of the separation of powers seriously. This was made clear when the Court declared the National Industrial Recovery Act unconstitutional in 1935 on the ground that authority of an essentially legislative nature had been delegated to the President.

Whereas the House of Commons has accepted its subordination to the part of it that forms the government, in the United States the leaders of the executive are, physically and attitudinally, outside Congress and therefore in a fundamentally different relationship to the legislature than the executive is in Britain. In any consideration of parliamentary reform which examines it from the perspectives of Britain and the United States the existence of the separation of powers in the latter and its absence in relation to legislative-executive relations in the former must never be forgotten.

Numerous consequences derive from the great divide that separates executive and legislature in Washington. One of the consequences relates to career expectations. While MPs at Westminster are reluctant to press for reforms which could get in the way of their elevation to ministerial office or their exercise of power once they get there, such considerations are not normally relevant to the congressional context. Congress itself provides the posts to which senators and representatives aspire in the form of committee and subcommittee chairmanships and party posts. The latter include the office of Speaker, whose occupant is sometimes characterised as the second most powerful politician in Washington. The fact that Congress itself provides the arena for promotion – except for a handful of presidential hopefuls – produces attitudes towards reform quite different from those of a backbench MP with an eye on Whitehall.

Another consequence of the separation of powers relates to the procedural development of Congress. Separation from the executive means, among other things, that Congress can develop internally much as it pleases. Specifically, it may develop free from control by the executive branch. The position is formalised by the stipulation in the Constitution that 'Each House may determine the rules of its proceedings'. This entitlement is elaborated in the Legislative Reorganisation Acts of 1946 and 1970, which include provisions recognising the right of the Senate and House to make changes in their rules on their own authority.

It is significant that such autonomy is not normally exercised in parliamentary democracies in which ministers are members of the legislature and thus in a position directly to influence its procedural development. At Westminster the government must give its blessing to important procedural developments, and since governments do not wish to make life more difficult for themselves than is necessary, their controlling influence tends to be more than nominal. This has been the case at various times in the matter of the development of a system of specialist committees in the House of Commons. In Washington, by contrast, the executive must normally acquiesce in however many subcommittees, office buildings, swimming pools and other extravagances Congress may deem to be politically acceptable.

It is true that some of the more important changes within Congress require the enactment of statutes, which in turn require the President's signature. But Presidents tend to have enough difficulties with Congress in relation to public policy without being heavy-handed about 'housekeeping' matters. There are occasions, however, when a President may feel compelled to intervene, as Kennedy did over the move to enlarge the House Rules Committee in 1961 (MacNeil 1963: 410–88).

In general, 'American legislatures have tended to become autonomous organizations, existing without domination by other agencies such as party organizations or political executives' (Jewell and Patterson 1977: 30). By contrast, Walkland (1979b: 244) notes in relation to the House of Commons:

. . . the organization and procedures of the House of Commons have been structured into the activities of the executive to an extent that has produced a strong organic relationship between them. There has developed a close – almost a symbiotic – connection between parliamentary procedure and administrative practice that has largely determined the main characteristics of the modern British Parliament. The House of Commons has retained areas of independent criticism in relation to government, but largely within a basic procedural system that has been evolved to support and facilitate government administration and control.

Congress has taken elaborate steps, including the creation of a counter-bureaucracy, to ensure against a 'symbiotic' relationship with the executive. Some modest steps along this path have also been taken in the House of Commons, to be sure. MPs are better paid, better accommodated and better serviced than used to be the case. Nevertheless, the arrangements are very modest compared with those in Congress. To understand the congressional context for reform, one must appreciate that a sizeable congressional bureaucracy exists and that this makes Congress fundamentally different from any other legislature.

The total staff of Congress is now more than 23,500. This counter-bureaucracy on Capitol Hill incorporates the following components: central administrative institutions; a staff in Washington for each senator and representative; field offices in members' constituencies; and a staff for each committee. The central institutions include the Congressional Budget Office, the Office of Technology Assessment, the General Accounting Office, the Congressional Research Service, and the House Information System, and employ some 2,790 persons working directly for Congress.

Staff personnel for senators, representatives and committees has increased eight-fold since World War II. The overall total at present is about 16,000. There are 4,200 staff aides working for senators; 8,700 for representatives; and 3,000 for committees. Anyone who deals with Congress is aware of the powerful role that this bureaucracy plays in congressional life and policy-making. As concern is sometimes expressed that senior civil servants usurp the powers of heads of executive departments, so one might express concern about the influence of senior congressional aides. Yet, notwithstanding the buoyant position in which members of Congress find themselves relative to members of other legislatures, one must not lose one's perspective: '. . . legislative staff aides [in Washington] are by no means a match for the enormous pool of experts upon whom an executive officer can call for intelligence and information. The personnel of executive agencies not only are more numerous but also have a greater opportunity to specialize; they . . . have a tremendous advantage over the congressional committee staff' (Jewell and Patterson 1977: 453). If this is the situation in Washington, one can imagine how much more one-sided the corresponding relationship is in other national legislatures.

The Party Factor

The relationship of legislators to their political parties is a factor of great importance for present purposes. In this, one finds another vital disparity between the Westminster and congressional situations. Just as the presence of ministerial responsibility and the absence of the separation of powers at Westminster contrasts with the absence of ministerial responsibility and the presence of the separation of powers in Washington, so, too, the position in relation to party is markedly differentiated. In a range of situations the party factor conditions the behavior of MPs, on the one hand, and senators and representatives, on the other, in different ways. First, for example, Britain normally has party government while the United States normally does not. The party which wins a majority of seats in the Commons governs Britain, with the cabinet and its parliamentary majority working together. In America this kind of collaboration is not usual. Second, debate tends to be two-sided in the Commons whereas it tends to be every-man-for-himself in Congress. There is an official opposition in the Commons but nothing corresponding to this in Congress. These contrasts arise from a situation, on the one hand, where 'party is indeed king' to a situation, on the other hand, where party allegiance, while significant, is often muted. Third, the two-sided, adversarial style of deliberation extends to committee work in the Commons, inhibiting committee integration and the emergence of a committee point of view. With looser party allegiance in Congress, committees are freer to develop a life of their own and exert strong influence (Fenno 1966; Fenno 1973).

It follows from the loose nature of party affiliation in Congress that congressional autonomy has not been unduly compromised by party cohesion, particularly since about 1890. From time to time forceful presidents or exceptional circumstances or both have united executive and legislature through the leadership of a party majority from the White House. But the stronger tradition of an independent legislature has made such arrangements difficult to sustain for long.

Party relationships within the Senate and House are significant as well as party relationships between Congress and the President. Within the chambers control by party leaders has been difficult to sustain in the face of the strong constituency and committee orientations of members and other decentralising tendencies. Moreover, such congressional party organisation as exists operates independently of extra-congressional party bodies. Majority and minority leaders must not become too deferential to the White House if they are to maintain their influence on Capitol Hill.

The general picture that emerges is one of an atomised Senate and House. Although party identity is important, members are sufficiently on their own to function as independent operators, to form factional alliances and to pursue their special interests. In this free-wheeling situation spokesmen for organised interests find Congress a useful venue. While it is sometimes suggested that one reason for the decline of Parliament is the tendency for such spokesmen to devote their attention to their opposite numbers in Whitehall rather than to MPs, it can be said, conversely, that a reason for the continued influence of Congress is that Washington lobbyists seek out their opposite numbers on the congressional committees (as well as in the executive depart-ments). It follows that the style of interest articulation is related to legislative influence within government.

The congressional parties took the initiative in bringing about one of the more important procedural changes in the 1970s. This was a modification of the seniority principle. Prior to 1970 the convention was that seniority determined who would be the chairman and the ranking minority member of Senate and House committees. In both parties in both houses the changes were instituted during caucus meetings. In 1971 and 1973 the House Democratic caucus voted to permit the nomination of candidates for committee chairman during caucus meetings. The procedure was elaborated in 1975 when the Democratic caucus decided to conduct these elections by secret ballot and to extend the procedure to nominations of chairmen of the powerful subcommittees of the Appropriations Committee. The 1975 caucus then proceeded to depose three incumbent committee chair-men. In 1977 another chairman was deposed. Modifications of the seniority principle were also agreed by Senate Democrats and by Republicans in both houses.

The retreat from strict seniority was one manifestation of a general attitude in Congress favouring a deconcentration of power. In various ways traditional norms of deference were giving way to arrangements whereby junior members could exert more influence. How can this change be accounted for? First, there had been campaigns outside Congress in favour of increased political participation and devolution, and these pressures were reflected in Congress. Second, the number of subcommittees in Congress had been increasing. By 1977 there were 304 chairmanships of committees and subcommittees to be allocated to 535 senators and representatives, or at least one for every two members. As subcommittees increasingly became discrete policy-making units this meant a retreat from the traditional exercise of autocratic power by the chairmen of full committees. Third, Lyndon Johnson had instituted a scheme whereby junior senators could obtain desirable committee assignments, and this whetted the appetites of junior members. Fourth, there was more turnover than usual of members in both houses in the 1970s, and the newcomers tended to be dissatisfied with the status quo.

Oversight

It is generally acknowledged that the amount of oversight of the executive by Congress increased markedly during the 1970s. The stress on oversight is an indication of Congress' determination to maintain its authority in the face of administrative complexity. Oversight was effected in a number of new ways. For example, the Legislative Reorganisation Act of 1970 directed committees in both houses to submit biennial reports on their oversight activities. The Act also strengthened the Congressional Research Service and the General Accounting Office in an effort to enhance the investigative capability of Congress. In 1974 the Budget and Impoundment Control Act gave new authority to congressional committees to evaluate executive programmes.

A method of effective oversight which has seen increasing use in recent years is the incorporation in legislation of provisions for a 'legislative veto' or a 'committee veto'. Statutes incorporating such provisions extend new authority to the executive while providing for Congress' right to approve or disapprove the exercise of it. In the case of a 'legislative veto', approval must be obtained from one or both houses. In the case of a 'committee veto', executive decisions must be reviewed by a particular congressional committee prior to execution.

Congress has also been less deferential than previously in the field of foreign affairs. The Executive Agreements Act of 1972 requires the President to inform Congress about any executive agreements with foreign governments he enters into, while the War Powers Act of 1973, which was enacted over Nixon's veto, entitles Congress to review any commitment of armed forces abroad by the President.

One of the most significant procedural developments in Congress in recent years is the development of a new method for dealing with the President's budget. The Budget and Impoundment Control Act sought to give Congress more influence over the raising and spending of money. Previously, taxation policy had been determined with little reference to spending policy, and spending policy had been determined on a compartmentalised basis with little effort to consider federal spending as a whole.

The 1974 Act created three new congressional structures: the House Budget Committee, the Senate Budget Committee and the Congressional Budget Office. The new committees, aided by the Budget Office, are intended to guide the budget process in a rational direction, with expenditure related to income. Specifically, the Budget committees are authorised to adopt concurrent budget resolutions in April and September, setting targets for spending, tax receipts and the size of the public debt. The April targets can be adjusted in the September resolution. Throughout the session the Budget committees monitor the relevant recommendations coming from the authorising, appropriations and tax committees to ensure that they conform to the guidelines. The idea is to fix overall goals early in the session, to be followed by binding figures, confirming or revising the initial targets, shortly before the fiscal year begins in October.

What does this budgeting procedure illustrate? First, it makes clear Congress' determination to play a more assertive role in central government after the traumas of the Johnson and Nixon administrations. Second, it is significant that the new arrangements did not replace existing arrangements but, rather, were grafted onto them. The Appropriations, Ways and Means and Finance committees remained intact. Thirdly, Congress was reacting to a specific executive abuse – the impoundment of appropriated funds by Nixon. Fourthly, the arrangement builds on previous efforts to cope comprehensively with the national budget, beginning with the Budget and Accounting Act of 1921.

But these budgetary reforms, which were designed to redress the balance in congressional relations with the executive branch, have recently been subjected to criticism. In 1981 Congress failed to meet its own deadline for the passage of a final budget resolution and appropriation bills providing money to run federal agencies in the new financial year. Alan Grant (1982: 63) ascribes these delays to 'the split in party control of the two houses, the independence of members and the proliferation of sub-committees'. Indeed, an increase in the number of committees and subcommittees, both in the budgetary and wider decision-making processes, has had the negative pay-off of making coherent and cohesive policy-making in Congress difficult.

Nonetheless, the predisposition in Congress towards engaging in rigorous oversight is a consequence of the long-standing suspicion in the United States of the exercise of executive power and the equally long-standing stress on the legislature as a maker of substantive policy. When the nation's worst suspicions are realised, as during the Watergate crisis, Congress renews its determination to keep the executive on an even shorter leash in future. As far as the predisposition towards legislative policy-making is concerned, the following observations are pertinent:

> The large part played by colonial legislatures in the . . . 1760s and 1770s made them far more potent policy-making institutions than the British House of

Commons on which they had been modeled. On American soil the representative assembly . . . became a more powerful institution of government than it had been in Europe, a 'legislature' in the true sense of a body making the laws, rather than a parliament, a place first and foremost *parler*, to talk.

(Loewenberg and Patterson 1979: 14)

In the matter of the role of the legislature things have not changed all that much as between Britain and the United States since the 18th century.

Dealing with People

To understand Congress and the possibilities of reform, one must keep in mind that American constituents are unusually, perhaps uniquely, demanding. They frequently expect their senators and representatives to intervene in government on their behalf, and these demands have been increasing. A study of mail coming into the House of Representatives showed that it increased three-fold between 1971 and 1977. Outgoing mail, not surprisingly, has also been increasing. About 40 million pieces of franked mail were sent out by senators and representatives in 1954. By 1970 the volume had increased to 200 million.

In the earlier discussion of the congressional counter-bureaucracy mention was made of members' field offices. It is significant that the use of such offices to deal with casework has been increasing. Senators and representatives have been hiving off staff personnel to offices in their states and districts. As constituents have generated more work, members have ensured that staff personnel are conveniently located to deal with it. In 1960 the proportion of representatives' staffs assigned to their district offices was 14 per cent. By 1977 the proportion had risen to 36 per cent. Senators have established more than 300 state offices, and most representatives have more than one office in their districts.

It is clear that the boundaries between the legislative system and the executive system differ as between the United States and other democracies such as Britain. American citizens go to senators' and representatives' staff aides with problems that would go to civil servants elsewhere. As I have written, 'In the largest states there are formidable numbers of congressional 'field offices' dealing with administrative problems which are the concern of ministerial field offices in other countries. Senators from New York and California . . . deal with 30,000 to 50,000 items of casework a year' (Shaw 1981: 281).

Related to the foregoing is the fact that congressional facilities at both the constituency and national levels are extravagant by the standards of the British Parliament and other legislatures: 'The fact is that facilities available to American senators and representatives are so much more elaborate than those available to lawmakers anywhere else that the

American case must be regarded as deviant and not a 'norm' against which British practice should be measured' (Rush and Shaw 1974: 252–3). For the 1980 session the appropriation for the operation of Congress was in excess of $1,150 million. For the 1980/1 session the appropriation for the operation of the House of Commons was £12.6 million. These figures speak for themselves.

A further aspect of congressional relations with the people concerns what might be called open government. Various steps have been taken since 1970 to make Congress more open to the public and the press. This retreat from secrecy took four forms.

First, the proceedings of committees were made fully open rather than, as previously, open only for certain aspects of their work. Decisions in 1973 in the House and 1975 in the Senate required that all meetings of committees and subcommittees devoted to bill-drafting, which were previously closed, should in future be open unless a committee majority, voting in public, decided to close them. Whereas committee hearings had long been held in public, the bill-drafting (i.e markup) meetings were also now to be conducted in public.

Second, the proceedings of conference committees were made open where previously they had been closed. These important committees, which reconcile bills passed in different forms by the two chambers, deal with about 10 per cent of bills passed by both Houses, including most major legislation. In 1975 the House and Senate adopted rules requiring that conference meetings be open unless a majority of the conferees from either chamber voted in public for closed sessions. In 1977 the House ruled that any move to hold closed conference meetings would require the approval of the full House.

Third, voting procedures on the floor of the House were changed so as to ensure that there would be a public record of members' votes. Previously, much of the voting in the House was recorded in aggregate total but not in relation to individual members. With the change to individually recorded votes, practice in the House was reconciled with that in the Senate where the recording of individual votes had long been commonplace.

Fourth, electronic voting was introduced in the House in 1973. This means that a member inserts a card into one of some forty voting stations and presses a button marked 'Yea', 'Nay' or 'Present'. As voting progresses, the votes are displayed on the walls of the House. The electronic system is also employed to record quorums. This development, which speeded up the voting process, has resulted in a dramatic increase in the number of recorded votes.

As with the retreat from seniority, the retreat from closed procedures reflected a tendency found elsewhere in American political and social life. The intention was, as with the Freedom of Information Act, to admit 'sunshine' into public proceedings and to make public servants more accountable to the public. Such accountability was felt to be desirable when memories of the Watergate cover-up and aspects of the conduct of the Vietnam war were fresh. Secrecy associated with these events were precipitating factors in relation to moves towards open government.

Structure and Reform
There are a number of aspects of the way in which the American political system is structured which have not yet been mentioned but which are relevant to the reform process. For example, unlike the position in most legislatures where one of the chambers is dominant, Congress has what might be called equal bicameralism. In view of this, reform of the Senate and House of Representatives are equally important. In Parliament, on the other hand, reform of the Commons became more important than reform of the Lords after 1911 when the Lords' legislative veto was changed to a delaying power. About the time that the Lords was becoming less important within Parliament, the Senate was becoming more important within Congress. In 1913 the Senate's prestige was enhanced as a result of one of the most important reforms affecting Congress in this century. The instrument of this change was a constitutional amendment which made the Senate a directly elected chamber, thus enhancing its standing much as the office of President of the Fifth French Republic was enhanced when it was made directly elective.

The federal arrangement in the United States provides another significant variable. While changes in the working of Parliament may be instituted in the knowledge that the potential exists to deal with public matters at all territorial levels, this is not the case as far as Congress is concerned. The American constitution reserves certain matters for the states. It is true that various ways have been found to circumvent the formal requirements of a federal system, but nevertheless the federal spirit remains as an important conditioning factor in American governance.

Electoral arrangements are relevant to the politics of reform. The fact that representatives must stand for election every second year makes them potentially vulnerable and may predispose them for or against particular reforms. The possibility of being deposed in a primary election is a further hazard. In practice incumbent representatives are rather difficult to unseat, but their position nevertheless differs markedly from that of senators whose terms – six years – are lengthy by international standards.

Finally, there is the matter of reforms of elements of the political system other than the national legislature. Such ancillary reforms can have an important spin-off effect on the working of the legislature, and various reforms of this type have been introduced in the United States during this century. Examples are the introduction of primary elections; the creation of the Executive Office of the President; the increased use of the referendum and initiative; and innovative financial arrangements involving the national government, on the one hand, and state and local governments, on the other.

There is an interconnectedness between the various elements of a nation's political system which makes it inadvisable to consider reform from the perspective of the legislature alone. Therefore the afore-mentioned characteristics of American governing arrangements – old and new – are conditioning elements distinctive to the congressional situation.

Toward the American Model

An unconscious theme of much of the reformist writing on the British Parliament is the desire for changes which in many respects echo the ways in which certain things are done in the United States. It is an unconscious theme because British advocates of reform usually focus only upon their own parliament and political system. When their attention is directed towards the United States, it is often no more than a sideways glance at a specific feature of Congress rather than a protracted gaze at the panorama of the congressional system. One consequence is that British reformers tend to admire the congressional foliage without analysing the political soil in which it is rooted.

It is instructive to work through current proposals for parliamentary reform in Britain and to check their intentions against American practice. Hence, those advocates of electoral reform who seek flexibility and self-renewal in the British party system can, and do, look to the United States for their example. Similarly, evidence in support of the hoped for effects of more 'independent' voting in the Commons can be found in Congress. In particular, some of Philip Norton's prescriptions have a familiar ring when considered alongside congressional behaviour. It would be accurate to say that an American administration tends to be responsive to anticipated congressional reactions. It would be valid to say that there is a more balanced relationship between the executive and Congress than between the executive and the Commons as a result of independent postures struck on Capitol Hill. Moreover, to ask whether senators and representatives feel free to exercise their right to defeat the administration would have to produce an affirmative reply. Overall, therefore, increasing doubts of legislators on both sides of the Atlantic about executive claims to 'know best' may be moving the Commons and Congress closer together in the 1980s.

When attention is turned to the advocacy of a comprehensive system of departmental select committees, again an apparent desire to see the Commons follow congressional practice is manifest on the part of many British reformers. Experience in the Commons since 1979 reflects, albeit hesitantly, moves towards this practice. It is reflected in increased numbers of members taking part in committee work, in the number of committee meetings and committee reports, in the use of specialist advisers, in the taking of evidence in public, and in the questioning of ministers and civil servants. In addition calls on the part of 'internal' reformers for the Commons to control its own pace of reform independent of executive control likewise reveals a wish 'to do it the congressional way'. Finally, advocacy of elected assemblies for the regions and nations of the UK with entrenched powers of some kind clearly can draw upon the American experience of federalism.

So where does this checklist leave us? My chapter began with assurances that the congressional context is sufficiently alien to the Westminster context to make prescriptions based on American experience suspect. I went on to detail the factors which produce these dissimilarities. It became clear that Congress is not like Parliament and that therefore the American experience is not an apt one for parliamentary reformers in Britain unless the entire congressional *system* is considered. Yet reformers in Britain keep coming up with proposals which bear strong resemblances to trans-Atlantic practices. Where this leaves us, it seems to me, is with different reformers describing different parts of an elephant. When you put these parts together you do not produce an elephant. It follows that the value of comparative analysis lies in the opportunity it affords to consider reform from the perspective of the complex contextual settings of different legislatures.

8 Parliamentary Reform: The Canadian Experience
Michael Rush

Whereas the Provinces of Canada, Nova Scotia and New Brunswick have expressed their Desire to be federally united into One Dominion under the Crown of Great Britain and Ireland, with a Constitution similar in Principle to that of the United Kingdom.

(Preamble to the British North America Act, 1867)

The British North America Act planted in Canada a living tree capable of growth and expansion within its natural limits. The object of the act was to grant a constitution to Canada.

(Lord Sankey 1930)

It would indeed be surprising if the Canadian political system did not resemble to a considerable extent its British counterpart. Not only was this the intention of the British North America Act, 1867, as the preamble to that act makes clear, but, to pursue Lord Sankey's metaphor a little further, its roots extend and the seed was planted many years prior to 1867. It is not, however, the purpose of this chapter to trace the detailed history of the Canadian political system or the Canadian Parliament, but to examine in its widest sense parliamentary reform in Canada, to relate it to its historical and political context and to consider the relevance of Canadian experience to the United Kingdom Parliament.

Nowhere is the resemblance between the two political systems more apparent than in their respective Parliaments. A visitor to the Parliament Building in Ottawa is swiftly made aware of the British connection. The layout of the two chambers of the Canadian Parliament mirrors Westminster, with government and opposition facing each other in traditional adversary fashion. Like its British counterpart, the Canadian House of Commons is fairly sombre in its decor, with seats upholstered in green leather, whilst, like the House of Lords, the Canadian Senate is more sumptuously decorated, with red-upholstered seats and, of course, a royal throne. Already, however, one difference has emerged: the Canadian upper house has a different name – not a difference of great significance, although an indication of the Canadian attitude towards honours. More immediately striking is the fact that Canadian MPs and Senators have individual desks and seats in their respective chambers, whereas British MPs must crowd themselves onto benches which do not provide sufficient room for the full complement of members. Perhaps most striking of all would be the frequent use of French as a language of debate and record, with those members who are bilingual often using English and French within the compass of a single speech. More detailed investigation would reveal that Canadian legislators are better paid and have more extensive services and facilities than their counterparts at Westminster. In broad terms the two Parliaments are procedurally similar and many Canadian standing orders and practices would be familiar to British practitioners and observers, but closer scrutiny would once more reveal significant differences in procedure. Again, it is not the purpose of this chapter to detail these differences – they can be found elsewhere (Dawson 1962; Stewart 1977), but to pursue those which are relevant to the specific question of parliamentary reform.

Just as it would be surprising if the Canadian Parliament did not resemble Westminster, so it would be surprising if it did not differ significantly from the latter, for Lord Sankey's 'living tree' was planted in a different soil, a different historical and political context and from the very outset differences were apparent. This is partly because the Dominion of Canada was a union of already-existing political entities – Upper (Ontario) and Lower (Quebec) Canada (themselves separate Crown colonies before 1840), New Brunswick and Nova Scotia, each of which had had varying degrees of self-government prior to 1867 and going back into the latter part of the eighteenth century. These provinces of the newly-formed Dominion had not only enjoyed a separate political existence, but were and remained physically separated by vast tracts of land, reinforced in the case of Quebec by ethnic, linguistic and religious separateness. It was these differences that were largely responsible for the most important constitutional difference between Britain and Canada – the fact that Canada had adopted *federalism*.

Federalism and Parliamentary Reform

Federalism inevitably looms large in Canadian politics. The original four provinces have expanded to ten and the limited powers the Fathers of Confederation originally intended for the provinces have been vastly expanded, largely through a combination of the growth of governmental intervention and the process of judicial review, with the result that the provinces have become powerful, though not equal partners in the Canadian political system.

The impact of the federal system on parliamentary reform has been limited yet profound. In direct terms its main impact has been to delay pressure for reform, since federalism, by definition, divides the responsibilities of government between regional and national levels. The exact nature of that division varies, of course, but such a division inevitably limits the responsibilities of national government, thus reducing the workload of the national legislature. Moreover, in Canada's case the development of 'welfare state' policies came later than in Britain and significant areas of such policies became matters of provincial rather than federal responsibility. Changes in parliamentary procedure produced by a growing legislative workload therefore came a good deal later in Canada than Britain.

The principal result of this lower workload was that, whilst the adversary system of government versus opposition is the major operational feature of the Canadian Parliament in general and the House of Commons in particular, the procedural means enabling the government to secure the passage of its legislative programme are less developed in Ottawa. The closure was not introduced until 1913, more than thirty years after its introduction at Westminster. Furthermore, it has never been regularly used or threatened and remains 'a dirty word', a weapon of the very last resort. In addition, less use has been made of committees to spread the legislative workload and, until fairly recently, considerably more business was taken on the floor of the House compared with Westminster. There can be little doubt that the legislative workload was a major factor in postponing the need felt by the *government* for procedural change. It was also an important factor in limiting the development of the 'usual channels' as the principal means of securing procedural co-operation between the government and the opposition, although here, as will be related in due course, the party system was of crucial importance.

This rather negative impact of federalism is seen again in the role of the Canadian Senate, which, apart from its decor, shares a rather more important characteristic with the House of Lords in that it has remained unreformed, largely because, like the Lords, there is no agreement on how it should be reformed. In both cases, of course, there are those who advocate the abolition of the second chamber (on the Senate see Campbell 1978), but reformers are divided between those who wish to modify significantly the existing second chamber and those who wish to replace it with a totally new model. However, the vested interests of those with the political power to effect change and the fear of a more powerful second chamber are major stumbling blocks in the way of reform. There are other similarities: both the Senate and the House of Lords have non-elective memberships, both perform some useful services and both have problems of equitable party representation, but these similarities can be pressed too far, for there is little doubt that it is only a limited exaggeration to describe the Canadian Parliament as a bicameral body operating as though it were a unicameral one – a description which could not reasonably be applied to the British Parliament.

The Canadian Senate has 104 members, but unlike its American counterpart, representation is not divided equally amongst the basic units of the federal system, the provinces. Instead, Ontario and Quebec, which are much the largest provinces in terms of population, with over 60 per cent of the population between them, have equal representation with the four Maritime provinces on the one hand and the four Western provinces on the other. Although these groupings are of considerable political importance, they have no *institutional* significance beyond formal representation in the Senate. In fact, the Senate is dominated by party rather than regional or provincial considerations, so that neither individual senators nor the Senate as a whole are generally regarded as representing provincial interests in the context of the federal system.

However, the Senate is not an entirely moribund institution and performs a number of useful services. Its committees have conducted useful investigations, rather in the style of royal commissions, into a number of matters, such as the mass media, drugs and, in conjunction with the House of Commons, constitutional reform. It has a useful role in dealing with private legislation, mostly relating to the incorporation of companies and, more controversially, acts as a channel for business interests (Campbell 1978). The Senate's role as a revising chamber for legislation passed by the House of Commons is, however, more limited than that of the House of Lords. Moreover, since almost all government legislation in Canada is introduced first in the Commons, its use as a forum for non-controversial legislation is also limited. In short, whereas the creation of a unicameral Parliament in Britain would significantly increase the workload of the Commons, its impact in Canada would be much more limited.

Unlike the Senate, the Canadian House of Commons broadly reflects the provincial distribution of the country's population, although there has always been a provision for minimum representation, which in practice applies only to the smallest province, Prince Edward Island, with 1.4 per cent of MPs and only 0.5 per cent of the Canadian population. Because the House of Commons is broadly representative of the provincial distribution of population, the eastern half of Canada (i.e. all provinces from Ontario eastwards) is numerically in a position to dominate the Canadian federal system. Indeed, the two provinces of Ontario and Quebec control no less than 62.4 per cent of the seats in the

House of Commons and the electoral control of these two provinces is a crucial factor in all federal general elections. In practice, of course, much depends on the nature of the federal party system, which is in turn significantly affected by the way in which the federal system institutionalises regional differences in Canada. Whilst this is largely the case in physical and economic terms, it is significantly the case in terms of the ethnic origins of the population. Each province, and in some cases a group of provinces, such as the Maritimes or the Prairies, is a distinctive socio-economic and political entity which is reinforced rather than fragmented by the federal system. Historically, demographically and ethnically Canada can be described as a 'vertical mosaic' (Porter 1965). Whilst the French-Canadian dimension is the most well-known feature of this mosaic and has, of course, a significance far greater than any other, it is by no means unique. Indeed, it is a part of that mosaic precisely because nearly three-quarters of the French-Canadian population are found in Quebec and each province has its own distinctive ethnic pattern or mix, whether it be the predominantly British stock in Newfoundland, the Scots in Nova Scotia, the significant French minority in New Brunswick, the almost American style 'melting pot' in Ontario, the continental Europeans of the Prairie provinces, or back to British stock in British Columbia. These differences in ethnic origin are reinforced by the physical and economic differences, all of which combine to give each province its own distinctive political flavour, reflected most markedly in the provincial and federal party system.

Political Parties and Parliamentary Reform

It is a commonplace in textbooks on Canadian politics to say that Canada has not one party system, but eleven in that not only do the party systems of the ten provinces differ one from another, but each is different from the federal party system. Cynics have been known to suggest that Canadian voters must be schizophrenic on the grounds that they will vote for one party at national level and for a different party at provincial level, often within a remarkably short period of time. The true explanation is almost certainly less psychological and more complex than this cynical view suggests. One explanation offered is that Canadian voters, or sufficient of them at least, believe that the real opposition to the federal government in Ottawa comes not from the official opposition, but from the provincial governments, who are therefore best formed by parties other than that in power federally. One writer has noted an apparent cyclical process at work by which whichever party may be in power in Ottawa gradually loses control of those provinces it also governs until it is itself replaced in Ottawa, following which the process begins all over again (Muller 1968), but this seems to attribute to the voters a greater degree of calculated behaviour than reality will sustain. Nonetheless, there seems little doubt that a significant proportion of Canadian voters see federal and provincial elections as distinct decisions involving different choices. In any case, it is an assumption that parties of the same name at federal and provincial level are for all intents and purposes the same party. Quite apart from the fact that such parties are organisationally separate, they do not necessarily pursue similar policies.

This divorce of the federal and provincial party systems would be of less significance were it not for the most important feature of the Canadian party system. Like Britain, Canada has a two-party system, but it is a two-party system with an important difference: since 1921 the Liberal Party has, more often that not, been the party of government and the Conservatives have been the party of opposition – in short, at national level Canada has a system of 'ins and outs' not found in modern Britain. In Britain for most of the period since 1868, not only has the government been formed by one of the two major parties – by the Conservatives or Liberals, or later by the Conservatives or Labour parties, but for most of the time *both* parties in the two-party system have had a reasonable expectation of achieving office at the next election, whatever the eventual outcome may have been. This has not been the experience of the Conservative Party in Canada since 1921. Ironically, it was the Conservatives under John Diefenbaker who, in 1958, achieved the largest federal parliamentary majority in Canadian history, but it proved to be an aberration rather than a fundamental shift in the party system. It is also true that since the loss of the massive Conservative majority in 1962 Canada has experienced several periods of minority government, but these have been predominantly Liberal rather than Conservative periods of government.

The contrast between the period 1867–1917, when Canada had a two-party system similar to that in Britain, and the period since 1921 is clearly shown in Table 8.1, whether measured in terms of share of the vote, elections won or years in office. Moreover, the Liberal domination extends to the Senate, since nomination to the upper house is effectively in the hands of the government and, given that senators hold office until retirement at 75 and that Liberal governments have shown only a limited inclination to appoint non-Liberals, it is hardly surprising that two-thirds of senators are Liberals and only just over a quarter Conservatives.

The *prime facie* cause of the distinction between the Conservative and Liberal parties since 1921 is the growth of support for a variety of third parties who made greater inroads into Conservative than into Liberal support. These include the United Farmers of Alberta, the progressives (remnants of whom eventually joined the Conservatives to form the present Progressive Conservative Party), the federally-defunct Social Credit, the Co-operative Commonwealth Federation (CCF) and its successor, the New Democratic Party (NDP). The Canadian House of Commons elected in 1980 consisted of 147 Liberals, 103 Progressive Conservatives and 32 NDP MPs (there have been some

Table 8.1 Selected electoral statistics relating to the Conservative and Liberal parties in Canadian federal general elections, 1867–1980

		Cons.		Party	Lib.	Difference (Lib.–Cons.)
A.	Highest & lowest percentage votes, 1867–1911*	%	Year	%	Year	%
	Highest vote	52.5	1878	53.8	1874	+ 1.3
	Lowest vote	45.4	1874	45.1	1896	− 0.3
	Mean	48.90		48.93		− 0.03
	Range	7.1		8.7		+ 1.6
B.	Highest & lowest percentage votes, 1921*–80	%	Year	%	Year	%
	Highest vote	53.6	1958	51.5	1940	− 2.1
	Lowest vote	27.4	1945	33.6	1958	+ 6.2
	Mean	36.0		42.7		+ 6.7
	Range	26.2		17.9		− 8.3
C.	No. of elections won	n		n		n
	1867–1911	7		5		− 2
	1921*–80	6		13		+ 7
D.	Years in office	%	n	%	n	%
	1867–1917	62.0	31	38.0	19	−24.0 (−12)
	1921*–80	22.0	13	78.0	46	+56.0 (33)

Note:* The general election of 1917 was fought between a coalition government headed by the Conservative leader, Sir Robert Borden, consisting of Conservative and English-speaking Liberals who supported the introduction of conscription, and mainly French-speaking Liberals who opposed conscription. The coalition broke up after the First World War, with many coalition Liberals reverting to their former party. The 1917 election has therefore been excluded from the analysis shown in the table.

changes in by-elections since the general election). Although there is no significant difference in the number of parties represented in the House of Commons compared with Britain, not only are the 'usual channels' less developed in Ottawa as a result of the lower workload, but their development has been profoundly affected by the experience and attitudes of the two major parties.

The Liberal party is not only more often than not the governing party, but it tends to regard itself as the party of government. Conversely, the Progressive Conservative Party, more often in opposition than government, tends to regard itself as the party of opposition. The expectation of the governing party in Britain that sooner or later it is likely to find itself in opposition and of the opposition party that it is likely to find itself in power, encourages inter-party co-operation through the 'usual channels'. Any such incentive in Canada is severely curtailed by the attitudes of the two parties: neither has much experience or expectation of fulfilling the other's role, with the result that the Liberals are essentially government-minded and the Conservatives opposition-minded. Consequently, as a growing legislative workload increased the pressure for procedural change, there was little that Liberal governments could offer that was attractive to Conservative oppositions and little that the Conservatives were willing to concede that the Liberals wanted. In spite of a continuing growth in the legislative burden during and after the Second World War, the party system effectively stood in the way of parliamentary reform.

Of course, the same could also be said of the Conservative and Labour parties in the British Parliament: neither had much incentive to concede the demands of parliamentary reformers for more effective means of scrutinising the executive; any such concessions, however limited, seemed positively masochistic. This is partly true in Canada in that the concession of an effective committee system was likely to make the government's life more difficult, but in the Canadian case there was another dimension, for successive Liberal governments in the 1960s sought procedural changes which would bring about the more effective dispatch of business, changes which would strengthen rather than weaken the position of the executive. The Conservatives, however, opposed a strengthened committee system, since they regarded committees as aiding the government rather than the opposition. The Conservatives wished to retain as much business on the floor of the House as possible, for it was there that they could more effectively harry, obstruct and oppose the government and with far greater publicity than normally accompanied any committee proceedings. Procedurally there was little or no advantage to the government in making much use of committees, especially for dealing with legislation, since the then standing orders stipulated that, even when a bill had been referred for its committee stage to a standing committee, it still had to have a further committee stage on the floor of the House, in a committee of the whole. Similarly, whether or not they had been examined by a committee, the estimates also had to be dealt with on the floor of the House. There was thus no advantage to the government and no desire on the part of the Conservative opposition to see a greater use of committees, except in *addition to* the powers of scrutiny they already enjoyed on the floor of the House.

Ironically, however, it was a Conservative government which first experimented with a revitalised committee system between 1958 and 1962. The first Conservative government since the defeat of R.F. Bennett in 1935 was formed by John Diefenbaker in 1957. Initially it was a minority government, but the following year Diefenbaker's Conservatives won an unprecedented 208 seats in a further general election. One of the factors which had contributed to that success was the contempt with which the previous Liberal government and its predecessors had tended to treat Parliament. This had been shown particularly vividly in what became known as the Pipeline Debate in 1956, in which the Liberals had sought to secure the passage of a bill to authorise the establishment of the Northern Ontario Pipeline Company to construct a natural gas pipeline. Apart from accusations that the government had vested interests in seeing the bill passed, there was bitter criticism of the government's attempts to force the bill through the Commons with minimal discussion, especially after the government had similarly forced another bill through the previous session. This and a general dissatisfaction with the extent to which the government's actions and policies were subject to parliamentary scrutiny prompted the Conservatives to pledge themselves to strengthening the role of Parliament, notably through the greater use of committees. Once in power the Conservative government strengthened the Estimates Committee, which had existed only since 1955, and made greater use of the existing system of standing committees by referring the committee stage of more bills and more subjects for investigation to them. It was said, both at the time and later, that the principal motive in the revived use of committees was a desire on the part of the government to keep its vast number of largely unoccupied backbenchers busy. Whilst there may have been some truth in this suggetion, there seems little doubt that the government genuinely felt that parliamentary scrutiny needed strengthening.

However, it would be a mistake to make too much of this revitalisation of the committee system, since it involved the *greater use*, not the *reform of* the committee system. The powers of committees were not increased, nor were their resources, but most importantly of all, they remained at the periphery of the legislative arena and in no sense did committees become an integral part of the operation of the Canadian House of Commons. In the event, after two parliamentary sessions of widespread use, there was a limited and then a sharper decline in committee activity in the two succeeding sessions. In part this was due to the increasing difficulties and criticism that the Conservative government faced, but of greater significance was the realisation that the greater use of committees was of little advantage to the government, since, far from expediting parliamentary business, the committees tended to prolong its passage. Quite apart from this the committees were large and unwieldy bodies, ill-suited and ill-equipped to perform the task of parliamentary scrutiny. Revitalisation had failed; what was now required was reform (Rush 1974a).

During the Diefenbaker administration the Liberals, in opposition for the first time since 1935, had been distinctly lukewarm about parliamentary reform in general and committee reform in particular. With only forty-nine MPs in a total House of 265, committees were seen as a considerable drain on resources and of limited utility, but some Liberal backbenchers saw parliamentary reform, including a reformed committee system, as not only desirable but necessary. Nor did their views change as the prospect of a return to power seemed likely, with the eradication of the massive Conservative majority in the election of 1962 and a reversion to Conservative minority government. The following year that prospect became a reality in the form of a minority Liberal government, but the very fact that it was a minority government made the need for reform all the more pressing. As a minority government the Liberals were reasonably secure, since they could normally rely on sufficient third party votes to sustain them in office, but the procedural limitations on the government's control over parliamentary business were more severe for a minority as opposed to a majority government. The Liberal government therefore set up the first of what became a series of procedure committees. These committees produced a series of reports which formed the basis of extensive procedural changes between 1965 and 1968.

On the one hand, these changes markedly strengthened the government's ability to secure the passage of its programme and, on the other, a reformed committee system laid the foundation for improved and more extensive parliamentary scrutiny. The Canadian Parliament, which had hitherto operated *ad hoc* parliamentary sessions, now adopted the British practice of regular sessions beginning and ending in October or November. This necessitated the development of more effective 'usual channels' and the revision of the closure rule. Indeed, the new closure rule partly formalised the 'usual channels' by allowing for closure to be introduced through standing orders by all-party agreement, two-party agreement or, ultimately, on the governing party's initiative alone. The committee system was a crucial part of the strengthening of the government's control over parliamentary business, since all estimates and, unless the House ordered otherwise, which it does not normally do, the committee stage of all public bills was now to be referred to committees. The second committee stage on the floor of the House was abolished. In return twenty-five supply days were allocated to the opposition, to be used to debate such matters as the opposition wished, thus basically following the long-standing British practice. Estimates had to be reported back to the House by a date set in standing orders otherwise the committee would be deemed to have reported and, should it be necessary, the House could require a committee to report on a bill by a set date or a bill could be recalled from committee. Moreover, committees lacked direct means of initiating investigations, so that each inquiry required a specific motion of the House. At the same time the assistance given to committees was increased and committees were now an integral rather than a peripheral part of the legislature. There can be no doubt that apart from improving the government's ability to secure the passage of its programme, there was also the firm intention that by involving committees automatically in the consideration of estimates and legislation, parliamentary scrutiny would become more systematic and effective (Rush 1974b).

The Liberals, as the governing party, found much in the changes to commend them, but the Conservatives were divided. Their ability as an opposition to frustrate the government was significantly reduced, although some Conservatives saw the committees in particular as a means of subjecting governmental policy to closer and therefore more effective scrutiny. Most Conservatives, however, saw the changes as a means of frustrating the opposition and did not see them as an advantage to a future *Conservative* government, all the more so now that the Liberals were back in power with a majority, following the election of 1968. The Conservative attitude towards committees in particular was well-illustrated on the return to minority government in 1972. Although still in opposition, the Conservatives failed, except in one or two cases of isolated initiative, to capture any committee chairmanships or vice-chairmanships, which in a minority government situation would have strengthened their position in opposition. The fact that the Conservatives were within a single seat of parity with the Liberals and felt that power was within their grasp, blinded them to the opportunity that the committee system offered (Rush 1979).

Parliamentary Reform and Institutional Change – the Canadian Experience
In spite of the limited ideological gap which divides the Liberals and

Conservatives in Canada (Christian and Campbell 1974), the adversary system of government versus opposition is deeply entrenched in the Canadian Parliament. If anything, the prevailing system of 'ins and outs' serves only to reinforce it. In such circumstances the ground for more extensive or fundamental parliamentary reform is not particularly fertile. Of course, much hinges on what is meant by terms like 'parliamentary control', so often the reformers' catchphrase. Leaving aside constitutional niceties concerning the definition of parliament, it is usually taken to mean legislative control over the executive, but this leaves open the nature and, more particularly, the extent of that control. It is, of course, fully accepted that in a parliamentary system the government can remain in office only so long as it retains the support of a majority of the members of the legislature, but it is what happens whilst it exercises power by virtue of retaining that support which is ultimately at issue. No one suggests that the life of the government should depend on the outcome of every vote, the fate of every policy or proposal, but this leaves much to be decided. In short, constitutional doctrine asserts that the executive is responsible to the legislature, but it leaves open the question of the extent to which the executive should be responsive to the views of the legislature.

Parliamentary reality is, of course, dominated by parties and in the normal everyday sense of 'control' it is not Parliament which usually controls the government, but the government which controls Parliament. That control is all the greater where the government is formed by a single party which has an absolute majority in the legislature. On the other hand, it is quite possible to conceive a situation in which the government is willing to allow Parliament a significant degree of influence. Indeed, the experience of both the British and the Canadian Parliaments is that it is misleading to draw too stark a picture of the relationship between the government and Parliament, in that it is a relationship which is complex rather than simple, and one in which it is notoriously difficult to trace paths of influence. Nonetheless, parliamentary reform in Canada has reached a stage not unlike that in Britain, in that the prospect of further significant change brings increasingly into view the relationship between the executive and the legislature and the attitudes of ministers and MPs (Rush 1982).

The stark picture of the government always prevailing, aptly summarised in the aphorism 'the opposition has its say, but the government gets its way', is an oversimplification. Parliament is more than an opposition forum; it is the arena in which the government is expected to justify and defend its policies and actions and, although the government's success in this task is ultimately judged in the polling booths, the immediate test is not the reaction of the opposition but the government's ability to carry its own supporters with it. In a survey of

Canadian MPs, conducted in 1970, nearly half of all backbench MPs and nearly two-thirds of government MPs thought that committees had an influence on government policy. Majorities of government MPs, ranging from 85 per cent to 58 per cent, regarded committees as being effective in examining legislation, investigating policy, examining the estimates and providing information, and nearly half in scrutinising the activities of the civil service. Even substantial majorities of opposition Conservatives regarded committees as effective in examining legislation and providing information (Rush 1979). Nonetheless, few observers would argue that the standing committees of the Canadian House of Commons are particularly powerful or influential and, as in the British case, reformers continue to seek greater powers and influence for committees. What Canadian experience does demonstrate, however, is that committees can greatly improve the *degree* of public scrutiny to which government policies and actions are subjected and to that extent, at very least, enhance the effectiveness of that scrutiny. In addition, both generally and in the examination of legislation in particular the standing committees provide a valuable forum for outside interests to present their views and to be questioned about them in public. There is also no doubt that the systematic and integrated use of committees in the Canadian House has greatly increased the involvement of MPs in the work of Parliament. Finally, and in spite of only a limited coverage in the media, the committees have substantially increased the amount of information made available to MPs, to interested organisations outside Parliament and to the public at large.

Of course, it could be argued that committees in the British House do much the same and there is a good deal of truth in this, but the Canadian House has a longer experience of a more or less full range of departmentally-oriented committees and in this sense has a greater experience of a committee *system*, whereas Westminster was still using a range of committees which in no sense could be described as part of a coherent *committee system*. Moreover, whilst the use of the same committees to deal with legislation, the estimates and policy investigations may have much to commend it, Canadian experience is more important in demonstrating the viability and value of hearing witnesses at the committee stage of bills, a practice only rarely used at Westminster.

In January 1983 the Canadian House of Commons sought to strengthen its committee system by allowing committees to choose their own subjects for investigation, thus bringing them into line with Westminster practice, and, more importantly, stipulating that the government would in future have to respond to committee recommendations within 120 days. Proposals to enforce a maximum period for a government response have been made, though not adopted, at

Westminster and it will be interesting to see what impact its introduction has in the Canadian House.

There are other procedural areas in which much could be learned from Canadian experience, such as that of oral parliamentary questions, which, in the Canadian House, are usually without notice, in contrast to the practice at Westminster. This gives Canadian question time a spontaneity which supplementary questions do not necessarily provide at Westminster, but of greater importance is that many Canadian MPs see this as a more effective means of keeping the government and individual ministers on their toes. Both arrangements have their advantages and disadvantages and it is not so much a question of arguing that the British House should adopt this Canadian procedure or that, so much as arguing that Westminster should be prepared to look at what is happening in Ottawa (and for that matter elsewhere), a point which will be taken up again at the end of this chapter. There are other examples which could be cited, but it would be more useful at this point to turn from internal parliamentary reform to consideration of the wider reform of the parliamentary system.

In this context Canada can offer a variety of experience, of which the most important are those of minority government, federalism and a written constitution. For three short periods, 1957–58, 1972–74 and, more recently, from July 1979 to February 1980, and for a longer period, 1962–68, Canada experienced minority government. Indeed, the longer period led some writers to suggest that minority government had become the norm for Canadian politics. In the longer term that may well prove to be the case, especially as the Liberal Party has steadily lost support in Western Canada since 1972, which means that much will depend on the nature of the party system which produces minority governments. Thus far Canada's experience of minority government has been one of stability rather than instability and of continuing Liberal rather than Conservative rule. The three Conservative minority governments of 1957–58, 1962 and 1979–80 have all been short-lived, the first because the government quickly took advantage of growing electoral support to win a majority, but the other two collapsed because of the failure to secure sufficient third party support in the House of Commons. Conversely, the Liberal minority governments of 1963–68 and 1972–74 did not find it difficult to reach an accommodation with the NDP and Social Credit. There was, of course, a degree of uncertainty in the absence of a formal coalition or legislative pact, but in terms of the survival of the government, stability was maintained. There is no doubt that the third parties found it much easier to co-operate with the Liberals rather than the Conservatives. Indeed, the operation of minority government undoubtedly rests heavily on the nature of the party system, which might itself be significantly affected by a prolonged period of minority government, leading, possibly, to a formal coalition between two or more of the parties. However, the main lesson of Canada's experience of minority government is that it should not automatically be equated with instability, either in terms of frequent changes of government or in terms of constant uncertainty as to the government's survival. It is likely to produce somewhat more frequent elections, if only because the governing party may seek an early opportunity to win an overall majority.

Much has been written about Canadian federalism, not only because of the French-Canadian presence and the continuing threat of separatism in Quebec, but because historically it has moved a long way from the more centralised union envisaged by most of the Fathers of Confederation. In addition Canadian federalism provides many contrasts with its American neighbour, especially in the number of units that make up the federal system and in the extent to which the federal system institutionalises the regions. It is worth pointing out that the original American union had, with its thirteen states, more units than modern Canada has, with its ten provinces. The number of units in a federal system almost certainly affects relations between those units and the federal government. On the one hand, a large number of units may find it difficult to co-operate sufficiently to defend their interests against the federal government, but, on the other, the federal government may find it difficult to secure the co-operation of a large number of units. Of greater importance, however, is the extent to which those units reflect wider divisions in the country as a whole. It would, of course, be foolish to suggest that regionalism has been or is of no importance in American politics, as the Civil War and assertions of Eastern domination, to cite but two examples, demonstrate, but in general the state boundaries in the United States do not, as such, institutionalise regional divisions, whereas provincial boundaries in Canada most certainly do. In short, Canada offers extremely useful experience on the advantages and disadvantages of institutionalising regions; whether through a federal system, as in Canada's case, or through some form of devolution. Thus Canada's experience of regionalism is particularly pertinent to the question of what special institutional arrangements should be made for Scotland, Wales and Northern Ireland on the one hand, and England on the other, for those who favour a federal United Kingdom or one in which there is a significant degree of devolution. The problems faced by a national government formed by one party, faced with regional governments formed by other parties, for instance, are very familiar to Canadian politicians. The development of formal and informal mechanisms for co-operation between the two levels of government is another area in which Canada has much experience.

In a more formal sense Canada, like other federal systems, also has considerable experience of the problem of dividing powers and responsibilities between the two levels of government. This is important in at least four senses: first, in formulating an initial division of powers and responsibilities; second, in devising a means of re-allocating such powers and responsibilities as conditions and circumstances change; third, in allocating new powers and responsibilities which were not originally anticipated or the necessity for which has since developed; and fourth, in devising a means of settling disputes between regional and national authorities over the right to exercise particular powers and responsibilities. Canada's experience in these areas has been mixed. The original division of powers and responsibilities in the British North America Act, 1867, proved to be somewhat ambiguous and, understandably, did not anticipate various matters for which modern governments more or less automatically assume responsibility. To add to these difficulties the procedure for amending the British North America Act was unsatisfactory and, subject to some changes in 1949, remained formally in the hands of the United Kingdom Parliament until the federal government and most of the provinces were able to agree on an amending procedure in 1982. Finally, the settling of disputes also remained in the hands of a primarily non-Canadian body, the Judicial Committee of the Privy Council, until 1949, when the Supreme Court of Canada became responsible for judicial review. Nonetheless, constitutional amendment and judicial review have played an extremely important part in Canada's political, economic and social development and both provide valuable positive and negative experience of the problems of federalism and, by implication, devolution.

Given its federal arrangements Canada has, of course, a written constitution or, to be more accurate, a partly written constitution, for most of the institutional arrangements relating to *parliamentary government*, as distinct from federalism, are the product of constitutional conventions rather than specific provisions of the British North America Act 1867, and subsequent amending acts. In the circumstances it is hardly surprising that, whilst many of the conventions of parliamentary government found in Britain are also found in Canada at both federal and provincial levels, conventions peculiar to Canada have also developed. The most important example of such a convention is that which requires each province to be represented in the federal Cabinet. Indeed, the convention goes further and stipulates that a balance should be achieved between the representatives of Ontario and Quebec, between French and English-speaking ministers and to a lesser extent between Catholics and Protestants. From time to time this convention has not been fully observed, usually when the governing party has no MPs from a particular province, but it usually prevails, offering yet further thought for those favouring greater regional representation in Britain.

In spite of emulating Britain in relying heavily on constitutional conventions, Canada has also demonstrated, if only in theory, that there is no reason why many of the constitutional arrangements that fall within the purview of conventions should not be incorporated in a written constitution. As part of its long campaign to effect various changes in the Canadian constitution, including the introduction of a wholly Canadian-controlled amending procedure, the government of Pierre Trudeau introduced a Constitutional Amendment Bill in 1978 as a basis for discussion. Had it, or a similar bill, been passed by the Canadian Parliament and had the United Kingdom Parliament made the necessary changes in the British North America Acts, it would have given Canada a written constitution which would have included various provisions previously the subject of constitutional conventions, such as the formal existence of the Cabinet, the responsibility of the Cabinet to the House of Commons and certain aspects of the power of dissolution. In addition, the bill contained a Charter of Rights, which, together with a number of other provisions, was entrenched in the constitution by being subject to a special amending procedure.

The 1978 bill was merely an important step in the discussions eventually leading to constitutional change, but many of its provisions found their way into the Constitution Act, 1982, which was the culmination of Trudeau's long-held wish to patriate the Canadian constitution. As is happens, the Constitution Act does not incorporate various constitutional conventions to the extent that the 1978 bill proposed, but it does include a Charter of Rights and Freedoms, which, by being part of the Constitution Act is entrenched under a new amending procedure involving the consent of Parliament and seven of the provincial legislatures representing at least 50 per cent of the population of all the provinces. Ironically, Canada has had a Bill of Rights on the statute book since 1960, but it suffered from not being entrenched and, more particularly, from applying only to matters that came under federal jurisdiction.

There can be no doubt that the major steps that Canada has now taken along the road to a written constitution and her experience of a Bill of Rights provide further lessons for those who would follow a similar route in Britain. The feasibility of a written constitution and the entrenchment of rights is clearly demonstrated by Canadian experience, though their efficacy has yet to be tested.

The question that is all too seldom asked about change and reform is, why? Why change? Why reform? To what purpose? To this end comparative examples offer both a comfort and a warning. To those who advocate or oppose particular reforms, whether it be the greater use of parliamentary committees, electoral reform, the adoption of a written constitution, fixed term election, or the passing of a Bill of Rights, the apparent success or failure of such reforms in other political systems provide invaluable ammunition, but all too often successes or failures are chosen with judicious selectivity. For many Liberal MPs in Canada the reformed committee system was a welcome widening of the opportunities for participation in the decision-making process; for many Conservatives it was a means of strengthening the government's control over the House of Commons and therefore over its financial and legislative programme. Similarly, it was only by making considerable concessions that Trudeau was able to secure sufficient provincial agreement to secure the passage of the Constitution Act, 1982. Reform is not divorced from politics, it is at the very heart of it and what one man argues is a matter of the highest principle, another denounces as seeking personal or partisan gain. Viewed dispassionately comparative examples can provide invaluable insights into the problems of reform, but they need to be viewed within the context of the political system and society in which they operate. Mechanistically there is no great difficulty in transferring institutional arrangements from one political system to another, but the *appropriateness of* and the *reasons for* such a transfer need to be the subject of close scrutiny.

It is one of the failings of many British politicians that they are markedly reluctant to look abroad: 'abroad', apart from holidays, is foreign policy and what happens in other countries' political systems is all too often overshadowed by an assumption that, except where judicious selectivity creeps in or where it affects foreign policy, there is nothing to be learned. To argue that politicians, whatever their views on reform, should look beyond their national boundaries is not to advocate the slavish adoption or adaptation of other countries' political practices – indeed, such an examination can lead to a well-argued rejection – but to plead for a willingness to consider their practices with an open mind and to learn from them.

9 Reform and the West German Bundestag
Tony Burkett

The reformist movement in Britain has drawn some inspiration from the West German model and certain features like the electoral system and the public financing of political parties have clearly influenced some proposals. The specialised committee system adopted by Westminster since 1979 is a limited version of the system used in the Bundestag. This latter case aside, the influence exerted by the Bundestag and the West German political system as a whole has been to evoke envy for its style, one of avowed anti-adversarialism, rather than for its mechanics.

It is not difficult to see why West Germany's political style should be so widely admired. The broad consensus between the parties, over-whelmingly endorsed by an affluent electorate, and the effectiveness of the political system to process demands made upon it have given the Bundesrepublik over thirty years of stability which few other EEC states have enjoyed. Yet it remains an open question whether this co-operative style of politics and the benefits it has accrued for its electorate is a result of the effectiveness of the political system laid down in 1949 or of the changes in public attitudes within German society that have evolved in the post-war years (Rausch 1980: 39–43).

Perhaps the most marked cultural change has been the demise of ideology which has occurred since 1949. In contrast to the situation in the period 1919–33, the social bases of West German politics no longer reveal deep divisions of class, religion and regionalism which evinced themselves in the multi-party system of Weimar and which were the root cause of its parliamentary strife and unstable executives. Certain institutional reforms introduced by the Basic Law of 1949 or under its influence – the strengthening of the political executive, the enhanced status and constitutional position of the parties, to name but two – have clearly assisted the stabilising process. Nevertheless, the most crucial changes have been attitudinal ones, by political elites and by the electorate, fostered by the Economic Miracle but also by the international context. West Germany's vulnerability in the period of the Cold War, the existence of a rival, 'mirror image' Germany led eventually – through membership of NATO, the pivotal roles in the founding of the EEC and the detente movement – to the Bundes- republik's emergence as a major actor upon the international political stage. It is these influences that have fostered the German political miracle, and attitudinal changes rather than the institutional reforms of 1949 that have welded a hitherto fragmented society together. It is the adhesive of the economic upsurge that has fused almost universal support for the political system. In this sense the limited reforms made to the parliamentary and party systems in 1949 were but a part of the wider changes, largely those in public attitudes to politics, that are the basis of the present and stable political system of the Bundesrepublik. Within that movement public admiration for the political system has generally lagged behind the high ratings accorded to the economic system (Huebner, Oberreuter, Rausch 1969). The Bundestag itself had to wait a long time to achieve public recognition of its impressive legislative record and it is clear that its pivotal role in the political system has not always been appreciated or indeed understood. However unpopular Westminster and its inhabitants may be in Britain its centrality if not its reputation is better recognised by the British than is Bonn by the West Germans.

There are solid and substantial barriers against the Bundestag in focusing public attention on its work and in winning public esteem. It is not seen to occupy the dominant position in the political system enjoyed by Westminster because it does not occupy one (Thaysen 1972: 353–7). The West German Parliament like its predecessors has never possessed that constitutional supremacy generally referred to in the British context as parliamentary sovereignty: it was never accorded it, German political theory never recognised it, nor indeed does it aspire to it. Within the Republic's political system the role played by the Bundestag is subject to constitutional and legal constraints which not only confine its ostensibly strong powers over legislation and its ability to check the executive but which also formalise and thus control its procedures and practices. The constitutional role accorded to the Bundestag is a limited one, like that of Congress, but those limitations, perhaps with the unconscious acquiescence of generations of parliamentarians, reduce the educative and informative role of the legislature. No German Parliament has ever achieved the high standing as a national forum of debate that Westminster has enjoyed in its heydays.

Constitutional and Legal Constraints

In that it uses a parliamentary model within a federal system West Germany has affinities with federations of the British Commonwealth like Canada and Australia. The federal system shares features in common with that of the USA, those of parameters, a prescriptive and regulatory constitution, a system of judicial reform carried out by a body of senior jurists sitting in the Federal Constitutional Court. German federalism and the American version spring from the same philosophical prescription, the limitation of the powers of central government and the constitutional devolution of power to states or provinces. Thereafter, however, German federalism goes its own way. Powers are divided horizontally not vertically as in the USA. The Federation has legislative and administrative powers over such matters as defence, foreign affairs, citizenship, the issue of currency and postal and telecommunications. In respect of all other matters its powers are limited to legislative competence. It is the governments of the *Laender*, the constituent provinces, which administer these federal laws passed by the Bundestag, the federal Parliament, but which are executed by their own administrative machines (Merkl 1959).

It is this unique form of federalism that limits the role of the Bundestag to a largely legislative one and this has further implications for its deputies and their constituents. The latter do not look to Bonn for redress of grievance against the actions of administrators and bureaucrats but to their own local, provincial diets, the *Landtage*; or even more likely to the profusion of administrative courts that exist in the *Laender*. The powers of the Bundestag to exercise control over the federal government and its ministries is clearly limited by the narrow range of administrative responsibilities which that government exercises (Johnson 1973: 7–16). The nature of the German federal system therefore limits the Bundestag to a primarily legislative role. It is this primacy which has given the House its procedural shape and style.

Yet the Bundestag does not enjoy a legislative monopoly. In all save those matters for which the Federation has exclusive and total powers as mentioned above, it shares the legislative function with the Federal Council, the *Bundesrat*. In a German context this second chamber is not an upper house, not a facsimile of the US Senate. It is an indirectly-elected body made up of 41 members, all of them ministers of the *Laender* governments who exercise the powers given to the Bundesrat by the Basic Law as the body through which the *Laender* participate in federal legislation. As such it shares with the Bundestag the right to scrutinise all bills which the provinces will administer, often exercising close scrutiny over them and having a veto over most of them, as well as the federal budget. A complex system of mediation is used where the two houses cannot agree on the final form of bills. Where agreement is not reached bills often fail. Where the Bundesrat exercises its veto it can be overruled by a vote of the Bundestag. When the Bundesrat's veto is by a two-thirds majority, however, the Bundestag can only overrule that veto by a similar two-thirds majority of the whole house. In a case of 'opposing majorities' controlling the two chambers the SPD/FDP coalition has often had some problems with the passage of bills through the CDU controlled Bundesrat. If the CDU had been able to achieve a two-thirds majority of votes in the Federal Council it could, in theory, have blocked the passage of all the coalition's legislation. This 'politicisation' of the Bundesrat has been seen by some authorities as a regrettable introduction of party politics into a body intended to protect and nurture the rights of the provinces not as an arena for a replay of a game lost in the Bundestag. The Basic Law does not foresee such a development although its framers scarcely foresaw it. In any case it appears to be part of the centripetal forces that have manifested themselves within the federal system.

If the Bundestag shares the legislative function with the Bundesrat that role is exercised within other parameters beside those imposed by the federal system laid down in the Basic Law. That document's specific constitutional limitations upon the legislature also restrain, in form and scope, both what the Bundestag does and how it does it. Just as the house does not exercise total and final powers over bills but must accommodate them through negotiation with the amendments made by *Laenders'* representatives in the Bundestag, so too it must frame law that is acceptable to the constitutional precepts established by the Basic Law and enforced by the system of judicial review exercised by the Federal Constitutional Court. Each act of the federal Parliament must conform to those precepts both in form and in procedure (Schaefer 1975: 127). The established procedures of Parliament must be used during the passage of a bill or the Federal President cannot sign it. If he does the court may declare that law invalid. Thus the Bundestag is constitutionally constrained in what it does, its procedures must conform to legal precepts or norms specifically prescribed or inferred by the Basic Law and interpreted by a judicial body. Moreover, the tradition of the *Rechtsstaat*, older and more deeply entrenched than those of the republican, parliamentary or even democratic values within the Basic Law, exercises legal constraints over both function and structure of the Bundestag (Smith 1979: 187–9).

With its constitutional and political role limited both by the federal model and by the legal positivist traditions of the *Rechtsstaat* the Bundestag is neither sovereign nor supreme. What softens its focus as a forum for public debate and has hidden its productive legislative records, however, has been the style of the House, its mode of operation, not least of all the dominance of its committee system. If adversarial politics have not manifested themselves so sharply in the Bundestag as in the Commons, this is not solely a reflection of the broad consensus on policy goals between the parties, nor of a commitment to 'co-operative politics' *per se*. Rather it is because the resolution of conflict is seen to be a legal prerogative in the last resort and that the qualitative value of law is the primary one (Edinger 1975). The final effect is to transform the legislative role into a managerial or technical one. Just as West German parties compete for votes in terms of expertise – especially in economic affairs – so within the Bundestag the parties compete to bring that expertise to bear upon the final form of laws. This predilection, the procedures of the House and even to some degree the recruitment of its members have contrived to minimise the pivotal position played by the Bundestag within its political system.

Recruitment and the Electoral System

If parliamentary reform is not a hotly debated issue amongst the public in Western Germany, it is not of major concern to the parliamentarians nor the parties. A lack of interest or understanding of the Bundestag by the electorate as a whole may be reinforced by an innate conservatism or a wish to leave well alone. In any case the reforms to the system introduced in the Basic Law or under its influence in the formative years of the Republic have worked well and needed little supplementation.

The legacy of the Parliamentary Council of 1948 which framed the Basic Law was essentially a reformist one. Its work can be seen largely as a re-working of the Weimar Constitution of 1919; as an attempt to correct or avoid the deadly errors of the first German model of parliamentary democracy. Basically those errors were a combination of constitutional cautiousness and executive instability. The first rested in the reserve power of the President to appoint chancellors above the heads of the warring fractions in Parliament and eventually to rule by decree. The second lay in the multi-party system produced by a truly 'pure' proportional voting system. A third perhaps lay outside anyone's control, the deep ideological differences that had long divided German political parties, some of whom – the Nationalists until 1925, the Nazis always – were opposed to the democratic and parliamentary forms of the state.

There was little done by the Parliamentary Council that was intended to reduce the number of parties. Indeed in many respects the Basic Law seems to make the assumption that a multi-party system would emerge and it set about to mitigate its excesses by strengthening the political executive in the form of the Chancellor against both the Head of State and a fractious parliament (Golay 1965).

What the Basic Law did was to place the parties within the framework of law, imposing the legal positivist traditions of the *Rechtsstaat* upon the parties, using that tradition to give sanction to political activity through the form of constitutional specifics but also by the regulation of organisational and political practices. Article 21 sanctions the establishment of political parties requiring that their organisation and conduct shall be subject to specific federal laws which were subsequently framed not only to regulate that conduct but also to lay upon the parties certain specific obligations and duties for the maintenance and advancement of democratic values (Smith 1979: 65–72). Thus the Basic Law laid the foundations upon which political parties have been raised to the status of constitutional pillars of the state whose popular legitimacy, based on electoral strength, is founded upon legally defined activities and forms. For at the same time as sanctioning what later became a three-party monopoly, the Basic Law also lays down what does not constitute a political party – any group whose constitution or aims are at variance with the democratic basis of the state. Article 21, paragraph C gives the Federal Constitutional Court the duty to outlaw any such group, even on the basis of their supporters' behaviour alone. In tit-for-tat judgements of 1953 and 1956, one right wing party and the old communist party (KDP) were both outlawed. Other parties of various sizes and importance have been crushed by the nutcracker of the party monopoly exercised by the three large parties. This constitutionally sanctioned legitimacy accorded to 'democratic' parties is further underpinned by the law governing party finance. West German parties receive generous subvention at federal, provincial and local levels based on the number of votes they receive (3.50 DM at federal level). By these standards the proposals made by the Blake committee in Britain look very small beer indeed but the impecunity of British parties is the least striking of the comparisons to be made. British and German parties occupy the same pivotal position in interest representation and articulation as well as in providing the personnel from which political executives are recruited and elected. The latter however operate within a context of closely-defined constitutional precepts, whereas the former's position and activity rests largely upon popular legitimacy and constitutional convention. And this is equally as true within the parliamentary context as it is outside.

It is against this context of constitutional recognition and the structure of the federal system that West German parties seek to organise, recruit and mobilise their support. The electoral system, which has had some influence upon the reformers' lobby in Britain, is not laid down in the Basic Law although there is the presumption therein that it too must conform to the democratic precepts of the state. The system that has evolved since the first Bundestag elections can be seen as a retreat from the overscrupulously proportional system used in Weimar which manifested itself in a profusion of splinter parties. Adaptations since 1949 assisted the demise of minor parties and the growth of the present three-party monopoly. The system has been fully-exploited by those three since. It is fair to say too that when it suited them the two major parties, the CDU and SPD, have raised the prospect of further adaptation usually to produce the British system. Such a step would be likely to lead to the demise of the FDP at federal level and has thus been used, particularly in the 1960s, as a threat to goad or intimidate the Liberals during coalition negotiations.

The electoral system used in West Germany at federal level can be described as a mixed system. It is intended to produce parliamentary parties in the same proportion as the votes that have been cast. Yet within those proportions the system allows for half the deputies to be elected by a simple majority in single-member constituencies as in Britain. Each voter therefore has two votes. The first he casts for a named party candidate, the second for a party (the voter is permitted to cross vote if he wishes). It is the second vote it receives that decides the proportion of total seats allocated to each party. If a party qualifies for 250 seats and has won 150 constituencies its remaining seats are chosen by taking one hundred names from the party's ten *Land*-lists of candidates. In fact, once a party's total of seats has been determined by the size of its national vote that figure is split into the ten constituent totals received in the *Laender*. The size of the party's vote in each of the *Laender* determines how many seats the *Land* party has in the overall number won nationally by the party (Burkett 1975: 131–5).

Parties must win at least five per cent of the vote nationally or three constituencies to gain representation. The Liberals have not won a constituency since 1961 (unlike their British sister party) and they have only once attained above twelve per cent of the national vote. What they have won more often than not is the balance of power and with it representation in more governments than either the CDU or SPD.

It is clear why this electoral system has attracted the attention of British reformers, although none has gone so far as to advocate its total adoption. The ability to top-up from a party list enables a party to ensure that its leaders, if they fail to win a constituency, can still gain a seat in the Bundestag nevertheless. It also allows for experts, who lack charisma or who eschew the rough and tumble of the hustings, to find their way into Parliament. Perhaps because it does not offer party supporters alternatives between candidates of their party by allowing them to choose a 'moderate' over a 'radical' if both are on the list, the full adoption of the German system has been modified into the 'additional member' system advocated in Britain by the Social Democrats. However, if German parliamentarians have a reputation for moderation and have rejected adversary politics it is because of the nature of the party system, the narrow range of policy options between the parties, the electorate's elemental conservatism that precludes radical change, especially any that might threaten the economic plenitudes of the

Miracle; these and the control exercised by the party elites at all levels.

It needs to be stressed that it is post-war cultural attitudes more than the mechanics of the electoral machine that have produced the three party, stable and effective party system that is so widely admired. The Nazi experience, the confinements of the Cold War, the threat of a rival, repressive and communist East Germany and the accelerated and burgeoning expectations rewarded by the economic system produced the *Volkspartei* concept, Adenauer's catch-all, anti-ideological formula that drew the German parties onto the same margin of political competition based on claims of managerial expertise and the maintenance of law and order, security and rising living standards. If the mechanics of the electoral system, like the five per cent hurdle, played any part in reducing the number of parties it cannot necessarily permanently maintain the party monopoly that has existed since the mid- to late-fifties. The rise of the Green parties, the combination of radicals, ecologist and anti-nuclear groups has begun to challenge the comfortable, conformist and complacent elites of the party monopoly.

Ironically enough the challenge of the Green parties underlines what the framers of the Basic Law feared, lessons drawn from the Weimar experience. Though they did not specify the mechanics of the voting system, believing at that time and with some justice that a multi-party system was almost inevitable they tried to mitigate the effects of such a system by strengthening the political executive in relation to both the Head of State and the Parliament itself. What, looking back from 1949 to Weimar, had to be avoided was the frequency with which parliamentary coalitions had broken up. In the Weimar Parliament, the *Reichstag*, there had been a profusion of parties, many of whom were warring camps reflecting deep cultural divisions in German society which a 'pure' proportional voting system faithfully reflected. These antagonisms so affected the Parliament that eventually the power to appoint Chancellors passed from the *Reichstag* and into the hands of the President of the Republic who in the person of von Hindenburg showed a preference for men who often enjoyed little parliamentary support. The Reichstag lost the power to appoint and then the power to control. Government in the latter days of Weimar was government by presidential decree.

The lesson was not lost. Since they could not guarantee that another multi-party system would be re-established the framers of the Basic Law chose to protect and strengthen the political executive through safeguarding its head, the Federal Chancellor (Golay 1965: 146–8).

The Elective Function

The major and correct assumption made in 1949 was that federal governments would be based on coalitions of parliamentary parties.

Although events and the changing attitudes of the electorate were to produce a much reduced number of parties there were clear attempts to strengthen the hand of the Chancellor once installed against sudden withdrawal of support by a coalition partner, a situation common in the French Fourth Republic, post-war Italy as well as pre-war Germany.

Provisions of the Basic Law (Article 63) invest the elective function upon the Bundestag alone. The President's power is only to nominate, and the convention is now firmly established that he puts forward the name of the candidate acceptable to that combination of parties which has during the election campaign, or after, announced the intention of forming a government based on a majority in the house. The mechanics of coalition-building were largely established by Adenauer; the major change being that since 1969 the SPD and FDP, bowing to the pressure of public opinion, have announced their coalition intention before, rather than after, the elections. Once elected by secret ballot the Chancellor is invested with the reins of government. He alone lays down the guidelines of policy, nominates all ministers for presidential appointment and allocates portfolios according to agreements reached with his coalition partners. The stability of those coalitions have ensured that most Chancellors, once elected, are unlikely to have their four-year stint in office cut short. Three have resigned from office however before their terms had been completed.

What guarantees a Chancellor's tenure from the threat of dismissal is the constitutional device called 'The Constructive Vote of No-Confidence'. This apparently contradictory phrase is a device contained in Article 69 of the Basic Law and intended to protect Chancellors from the vagaries of unstable coalitions. Basically it lays down that a Chancellor cannot be dismissed unless at the same time his opponents can agree upon a successor and establish another coalition with a majority in the House. The device has only been resorted to twice. On the first occasion, in 1972, Brandt, whose thin majority had been eroded by defections, survived such a vote in a dead-heat ballot. Article 69, intended to safeguard the Chancellor, had produced a deadlock since the SPD/FDP no longer commanded a sure majority. Indeed, the government had already lost a Budget vote. Clearly this impasse could only be resolved by a dissolution and a new election. But on this point the Basic Law is vague and the pressures against dissolution on the President's initiative are great. The impasse was solved when Brandt tabled a vote of confidence in his government on which his Cabinet abstained. Defeated technically, he then requested the President to dissolve the Bundestag and went on to an electoral triumph.

The second occasion was in 1982 and followed the break-up of the Social-Liberal coalition. Here the vote succeeded in removing the incumbent Chancellor (Schmidt) and replacing him with the CDU's leader, Kohl, with whom the Free Democrats had subsequently made a coalition agreement. But Kohl then found himself in the same position as Brandt had been. He sought to dissolve the House for fresh elections in order to win a clear mandate from the electorate. Like Brandt he had to engineer his own defeat in order to get a dissolution for new elections in March 1983.

Thus the parliaments of 1969–72 and 1980–83 are the two which have not run their full course although in both cases some constitutional juggling was necessary to overcome the deadlock which the Constructive Vote of No-Confidence has twice produced. What, one wonders, might have been the result in March 1979 had the British Parliament had recourse to such a device as the Constructive Vote of No-Confidence? (Birke 1981).

The Opposition

Eager as it was to reduce presidential power, to strengthen the position of the Chancellor and protect the office from fractious or petulant coalition partners, there is one element of parliamentary democracy (strongly entrenched in the practices of Westminster) upon which the Basic Law is silent. There is no mention of the role of opposition nor any specific guarantees for the rights of the minority parties in the federal parliament. Alone amongst the constitution of the *Laender* the city state of Hamburg mentions such matters and therein somewhat piously. This is not to say that there is not a general acceptance of a role to be played by an alternative party of government but rather that it is new and the focus is far less sharp than it is in Britain.

The inability to establish a clearly-defined role of leader of the opposition is a reflection of Germany's past when, more often than not, opposition was forced or chose to be opposition of principle to the form of the state. The early years of the Bundesrepublik saw the SPD vainly trying to establish the concept of a loyal opposition but when it embraced Adenauer's *Volkspartei* concept as well as most of his pragmatism, it never succeeded in finding a leader to match Adenauer's charisma. In any case, the development of parliamentary procedures and not least the 'co-operative' style of the Bundestag do little to encourage the development of the role of a loyal opposition. Very often too the parties have chosen to divide leadership functions into three:– party chairman, parliamentary leader and Chancellor candidate. The latter on occasions has not even been a member of the Bundestag when selected by his party to lead its election campaign (Kirchheimer 1968).

What softens the focus on the role of opposition is not the federal form of the state as in the USA but rather the function assigned to the Bundestag within the German political system. Furthermore, the formalism of German parliamentary practice conforms to closely defined procedures and practices which are themselves a reflection of the legal positivist norms of the society in which the Bundestag operates. Though superficially performing the same functions within their respective political systems, the *Bundeshaus* and the Palace of Westminster, because of their national, political traditions, their contrasting cultural contexts and the differences in the frameworks in which they operate are as diverse as the nations they represent.

The House and its Work: Legislating

If there is a central weakness in the Bundestag it is its failure to establish itself as a forum for national debate. In this respect the size and shape of the chamber and the fact that its members are addressed as if they were a public meeting by ministers and colleagues from a podium have combined to elevate oratory above debate. Aside from lowering by four inches the rostrum where ministers sit flanking the President of the House there have been no physical alterations to the chamber. Indeed, until 1949 the chamber was the assembly hall of a ladies' college. Plans are well-advanced for a new parliamentary building elsewhere in Bonn.

If the House is not noted for producing great debating occasions, and it is not, then it is not a matter of great concern to all parliamentarians or observers. One noted academic classifies the Bundestag as 'a working parliament' and Westminster as 'a talking parliament' without pejorative intent (Steffani 1973: 81–3). The Bundestag's major role is the processing of legislation and its function of checking the federal executive is more effectively pursued elsewhere than on the floor of the House.

Perhaps the most striking feature of the Bundestag's proceedings is the relative lack of formal control exercised by the government over them. The long-established Council of Elders (which also acts as a committee on procedure and privileges), together with the President of the Bundestag control the parliamentary timetable and programme. They react to the government's wishes rather than merely acceding to them. Although the Basic Law imposes little procedural or institutional arrangements upon the House's work, they are expected to conform to constitutional precepts. Some, like the election of the President (Speaker), are governed by convention – it is filled by a nominee from the largest caucus; others like the filling of committee places are decided by proportional voting by the members. Standing Orders, the subject of frequent amendment since 1949 are the strict and legal guidelines within which the House operates and covers even the establishment of parliamentary caucuses (the *Fraktionen*) whose own rules must also conform to constitutional precepts. Following from this the formalism of rules and procedures demands that the processing of bills must be conducted scrupulously within the House's coded practices: the requirement to ensure that a bill has been properly processed is a duty placed upon the Federal President before he signs it.

Needless to say, the power of the House over its work and timetable is not as total as it appears to be. By virtue of its parliamentary majority the government can use its influence to get priorities for some of its bills. Party cohesion is strong in the Bundestag. The power of the *Fraktion* over individual members remains significant even though the prospects of eventual office are smaller than in Britain because of the fewer number of portfolios available. Indeed, though the Basic Law specifically guarantees the independence of deputies the opportunities afforded private members to table bills or even major questions or initiate debates are more limited than in Westminster. Such rights are exercised only through the *Fraktion* and with the support of its leaders. The opportunities for the individual to make his name as a parliamentarian are limited and lie elsewhere rather than on the floor of the House; within the *Fraktion* itself or more especially within the closed confines of the parliamentary committees.

The specialised committee system is the strength of the Bundestag and the major cause for the weakness of the plenary session as an effective check on government. It is within the committees that bills receive close, detailed and expert scrutiny, where ministers are questioned and officials and departments rigorously examined. Here, too, the concept of 'co-operative' parliamentarism has developed to smother the definitive lines between government and opposition. Party lines become blurred by the technicality of the material scrutinised. Here the role played by the minority's experts can be, and often is, the major influence in amendment and adaptation of government bills. Coming between the first and second readings the committee stage of a bill is the most crucial for its survival through the legislative process. Since the rules of the House allow the parliamentary caucuses, though not individual members, to propose bills and even though most are government bills (which have the highest survival rate) there is a potential overload to the legislative function. Indeed it has become the practice on some issues for the opposition *Fraktion* to table detailed alternatives to government bills and seek to insert their proposals during the committee stage of the process (Schaefer 1975).

The Basic Law requires the Bundestag to establish certain committees like those on Foreign Affairs, Defence and Petitions to the House. In practice, however, it may set up as many as it wishes. The number has varied since 1949 between forty and seventeen; there are twenty at present and chairmanships are shared between the three *Fraktionen*.

Despite a proposal by the FDP in 1969 that the committees be open to the public, they continue to meet behind closed doors. The principal argument against this proposal is still as strong now, namely that it would increase party conflict if the sessions were open to the public. What it would also endanger is the cherised system of 'co-governing' that allows the opposition to participate in the detailed framing of legislation. Partisanship over bills is so reduced within a closed system that ninety per cent of all bills are approved unanimously at the end of the committee stage. Moreover, the co-operation between government, its majority and the opposition within the committees ensures a high degree of continuity when governments change. Certainly it removes what is often regarded as the central evil of adversary politics, the tendency of governments to undo the work of their predecessors. These benefits of 'co-governing' are not inconsiderable but they tend to encourage the opposition to act not so much as an alternative government but as if it were in some respects part of the government already (Thaysen 1976: 44–5).

Nor are these waters always placid. It is not unknown for the opposition or part of it when, having failed to defeat government proposals in both Houses, to pursue the bill by referring it to the final arena of conflict, the Federal Constitutional Court. And if the Court is not resorted to as a block on government legislation the opposition of late has used its majority in the Bundesrat to amend both the form and spirit of bills already passed by the Bundestag. The process of conciliation, involving the Joint Mediation Committee, can indeed be tortuous; a fact which in the view of some authorities serves further to prevent the public's understanding of parliamentary procedures and the mysteries of the checks and balances built into the federal system. In any case, the technical nature of much legislation – legal, administrative or economic – does not lend itself easily to simple exposition. It is fair to say that the confusing complexities of its procedures, their secretiveness and the esoteric nature of its material are seen by some parliamentarians to be the root cause of public apathy towards its work.

Control of the Executive
Conscious efforts to improve the working conditions of members and provide facilities to enhance parliamentary performance were made between 1961–65, during the Presidency of Eugen Gerstenmaier. Efforts to engage public interest by the introduction of television in the Bundestag have been as unsuccessful as the radio broadcasting of Westminster debates. Though it pays its members more handsomely and gives them excellent facilities for their work there is still a lingering admiration for Westminster amongst many German parliamentarians especially in respect of its ability to focus public attention on the errors and deficiencies of government.

Control of government by the system of judicial review of legislation as well as of the administrative powers of ministers by lower courts is seen as separate rather than supplementary to that exercised by the Bundestag. The public accountability of ministers for their actions can be ensured by the device of summoning ministers to attend the House but is one that is rarely used (only twenty-seven times since 1949). The use of the interpellation requires a written reply to questions by the government which is then debated. Resorts to this device have fallen sharply (save in the 1980 pre-election period) because, like the summoning of ministers, it has been superseded by the opportunities for more vigorous questioning allowed in the closed committee session.

The use of questions both written and oral has enjoyed some success amongst deputies, because, unlike the two former devices, they can be employed by the individual without backing from the *Fraktion*. The introduction in 1965 of the *Aktuelle Stunde* – debates on acute problems – was an attempt to meet criticisms that the House's debates were boring. It has enjoyed some success when its issues have had an immediacy that has attracted good speakers. And these successes have led to demands that it be extended. Again however it is a device that can only be employed by a *Fraktion* or a combination of members and not the individual deputy.

In 1975 a law was passed to strengthen the Petitions Committee giving it extensive powers to investigate grievances raised by citizens. The result of this reform was to swamp the Committee which in the legislative period 1976 to 1980 received 49,000 petitions.

There is no parliamentary commissioner in the Bundesrepublik although there is a defence ombudsman based on the Swedish model which was established in 1956. Proposals have been made for a civil commissioner but they have not been implemented (Bundestag 1976: 175).

Budgetary control has grown weaker in the past decade. Since the Bundesrat has a veto over the federal budget and that chamber is controlled by the CDU, the tendency has grown for budget proposals to be leaked publicly, to be challenged by the opposition publicly and debated in television studios whilst horse-trading continues between the parties outside the parliamentary framework. Both houses are then presented with the compromise which by that time is no longer negotiable and therefore not subject to parliamentary amendment. A further reduction of parliamentary control over the federal executive has been a result of EEC membership and which, incidentally, affected some powers of the *Laender*. The need to respond immediately in the horse-trading that occurs in Brussels at all levels has tended to reduce any control by the House over the federal government's negotiations with its eight partners and this control is in any case *post facto* and therefore ineffective (Schuettemeyer 1978). In this respect however, the Bundestag's sister parliaments in the Community have also been adversely affected and it is part of a general and universal trend of the weakening of parliamentary control of government in Europe.

Since 1949 there have been no major reforms to either parliamentary practice or the constitutional framework laid down in the Basic Law. The decision to arm the Republic and enter NATO resulted in some evaluation of the Basic Law in 1956 to enable the federal government to assume powers in respect of defence. The reforms proposed by the Troeger Commission to regulate financial arrangements between the federation and the provinces promulgated in 1969 were important technically but scarcely altered the balance between the two spheres of government. Proposals to give the Federal President powers to issue decrees in a state of emergency, introduced in 1968, were in a watered-down form and have not as yet been exercised.

What proposals have been made beyond these have scarcely been far-ranging. Reforms made to parliamentary procedure in 1969 have proved to be nugatory and their effectiveness debatable (Rausch 1981). They dealt with five main factors: (i) reform of procedures for plenary debates; (ii) redrafting to increase the opposition's rights to raise certain issues; (iii) improvement of working conditions and especially information and research services made available to members by the *Wissenschaftliche Dienst* (Research Office) of the House; (iv) the proposal by the FDP to open up committee sessions (and not implemented); (v) increasing the rights of the minority *Fraktion* to propose bills and establish inquiries (a demand made by a quarter of the deputies will establish an inquiry).

These proposals were followed in 1980 by some revisions to standing orders intended to guarantee the rights of government and the majority to enact legislation and of the minority to perform its function as an opposition (Bundestag 1976: 183). There were over sixty amendments designed to strengthen debating procedures, committee rights and lengthen question time.

Proposals made by a Committee of Inquiry on Constitutional Reform in 1973 were scarcely fundamental. In relation to the Bundestag they sought to increase the powers of investigation of the House and strengthen its powers of control. The Commission was concerned to increase popular participation in the political processes and to relieve the House of the burden of detail which conceals its real and vital function from the electorate (Rausch 1981). Some of these proposals were influential in the 1980 reform of standing orders.

In general, therefore, neither the political system as a whole nor the Bundestag in particular are seen as in need of major reform. Perhaps the most pressing problem, and it is not a specifically German one, is the encroachment of federal power and influence in spheres traditionally accorded to the *Laender's* authority. This process has been accelerated by the growing interaction of party politics in the two spheres of government, the infiltration of the federal parties into the arena of provincial politics and which evinces itself in the increasing partisanship within the Bundesrat.

Conclusion

For the reformist lobby in Britain the Federal Republic can offer lessons or give examples but they are inspirational rather than exact. The voting system and state aid to parties have already attracted and influenced some British reformers. But the devolutionists who often see German federalism as a system of administrative devolution alone – which it is not – have scarcely dared to suggest the adoption of this totally German form of federalism which would require a constitutional earthquake for its implementation in Britain.

Proposals for a Bill of Rights similar to the preamble of the Basic Law might indeed codify the citizen's rights to protect him against government. But they would certainly accelerate and enlarge the role of courts and judges in the arena of conflict which is one of the distinctive features of German government.

In curbing the powers of the 'elective dictatorship' the German parliamentary system seems to have little to offer. The Bundestag's control of government is in some senses weaker than that of Westminster and it shows no signs of being able to reverse this trend.

Above all else, however, the German experience shows that institutional reform has been a secondary influence in the development of a stable, legitimate and effective system of government. What has made West Germany the model of both political and economic success have been fundamental and relatively swift changes in political attitudes by elites and their electorate. It took a dictatorship and the rupture of war to break the old divisions that wracked and destroyed the first German parliamentary democracy. The new Republic has been established on a new society that has not been inhibited or restricted by the failures of the past.

The true lesson to be drawn from the experience of the Federal Republic is that institutional reform of itself is at most an ally but more often a by-product of reformed habits and attitudes. There are social and economic roots to Britain's industrial and political decline which parliamentary and constitutional reform alone cannot eradicate.

PART THREE   Conclusion

10   Considerations on Reform
David Judge

Inertia has been the defining structural characteristic of 20th century British parliamentary democracy. Judgements on decline and predictions of collapse have been aired and rapidly evaporated; schemes for reform have risen and quickly submerged, but throughout, Parliament has demonstrated its institutional indifference to such concern. It would be facile to believe that this book will break this indifference. Yet the explanations of parliamentary inertia and its consequences contained within the preceding chapters should at least have convinced the reader that such inaction is hardly to be lauded. If anything binds the contributors of this work together it is their acceptance of the need for parliamentary revitalisation and re-activation. The problem is how? There are, as Part One reveals, as many answers as authors.

Groundrules
This concluding chapter therefore seeks to assess the various schemes outlined in the first part of the book. To this end each contributor has been asked to examine the political premises of contending proposals and to comment critically upon the other chapters. In this sense what follows is the product of collective effort. However, the editor has had the responsibility of selecting, structuring and reporting these criticisms. So that some statement of the editorial groundrules adopted is appropriate here. First, where opinions represent a general view, even though the specific idea might derive from a direct quotation of a single author, then contributors' names are not mentioned in the text. Second, direct quotations are only cited where the comments are particularly forceful or sufficiently idiosyncratic to warrant identification. In this manner repetition of ideas and the 'personalisation' of the clashes of opinions are avoided. Overall, however, a fair degree of consensus emerges in this chapter – the contributors can all recognise the deficiencies of the various analyses (other than their own!). Indeed, a

curious form of academic immobilism emerges wherein the weight of opinion is always stacked against any specific proposal. This immobilism in itself may help to explain the institutional inertia of Parliament!

Lest, in the general flow of criticism that follows, the individual force of each chapter in Part One appears to be dissipated, the internal strengths and logic of each reformist scheme should be acknowledged at the outset. Criticism of the respective arguments is not intended therefore to be merely negative. Its positive purpose is to prompt the advocates of reform to re-assess and re-analyse their own simple panaceas; the cold splash of criticism is intended to taughten their analytical muscles. Indeed, if in the questioning of simple reformist faiths this chapter develops an awareness of the complexity of parliamentary reform then some benefit will have accrued. Parliamentary reform is not a simple matter; and acknowledgement of this fact alone would constitute an advance in the reformist debate in Britain.

A further point to be borne in mind when reading the following pages is the experience of other legislatures in effecting therapeutic change. The lesson to be derived from Part Two of this book is clear and simple: legislatures have to be considered within their wider political, economic and social contexts. To paraphrase the words of Tony Burkett, the true lesson to be drawn from comparative experience is that institutional reform of itself is at most an ally but more often a by-product of social, economic and political change.

Party Realignment and Electoral Reform

Stuart Walkland's discursive chapter stimulates a lively response from the other contributors. His broadside against the internal procedural reforms of the 1960s, and especially against specialised committees, is countered in George and Evans' argument that the incrementalist approach of the 1960s, whilst producing only minor gains at the time, was of crucial importance in establishing precedents for the select committee system of the late 1970s and 1980s. Not surprisingly, they also object to Walkland's blanket dismissal of the new committees' achievements. Indeed, they strongly recommend that he considers the Liaison Committee's view that committee endeavour since 1979 has 'considerably extended the range of the House's activity, strengthened its position relative to that of the Government, and deepened the quality of debates' (HC 92 1982: 8). But these are minor details in comparison to the protracted criticism of the underpinning premises of Walkland's analysis. Three crucial and interrelated assumptions are queried; first the primacy of political action over the economy; second, the nature of the 'new liberal consensus' to be built around the SDP or other 'centre' parties; and, third, the likely parliamentary consequences of electoral reform.

Starting with the parliamentary effects of electoral reform, Walkland clearly envisages that the development of coalition politics will bring in its wake a transformation of executive-legislative relationships in Britain. This belief is clearly premised upon the development of coalition government in the first instance. The expectation is that the electorate would maintain similar voting patterns under proportional representation as under the first-past-the-post system. But it is equally conceivable that the very introduction of PR itself would have an effect upon voting behaviour; for as Geoffrey Alderman (1978: 39) notes: 'Many calculations about what might have been under PR . . . are made on the assumption that people would have cast their votes exactly as they did under the plurality system. This is a most unlikely hypothesis'.

Even if coalition government did result, the exact degree to which the ties of party loyalty would be loosened in the Commons is open to dispute. Walkland obviously believes that there would be a significant slackening of these ties, with a subsequent reassertion of backbench independence and the reincarnation of the House as a corporate check upon the government. Yet, as David Judge (1981a: 189) has argued elsewhere, it is equally conceivable that a change to a multi-party Parliament might not alter the present position in which policy is the result of intra-party, rather than intra-House, compromises. Under the conditions of coalition government the bargaining process may well remain confined to Members of the governing coalition – to the exclusion of Members in the opposition parties. This would particularly be the case if intra-party cohesion was maintained within the respective governing parties and if, generally, loyalty to the coalition itself was invoked. Indeed, as long as the convention of collective ministerial responsibility persists, with governments prepared to make every major division in the House a vote of confidence, then rigid voting patterns conceivably would continue to differentiate government supporters (whether single-party or coalition) from their opponents in the opposition parties. Moreover, as Hugh Berrington (1975: 279) has pointed out, the introduction of PR might actually serve to increase discipline at Westminster 'by enabling moderate MPs to defy their local parties, and to express their loyalty to the parliamentary leadership in the division lobbies'. In which case the parliamentary hopes of electoral reformers would remain unfulfilled.

Indeed, the very unpredictability of the results of electoral reform concerns Philip Norton:

> From my perspective, I reject Walkland's approach because it lacks substantiation. It would constitute not only a leap in the dark, but a dangerous leap in the dark. It could – I am not saying it would (no-one knows, which is precisely my point) – lead to weak coalition government. It could produce coalition government, a coalition provided by post-election

bargaining to which other parties – let alone electors – were not privy. It could actually produce strong coalition government of the type favoured by Walkland, a strong coalition in office continually, leaving one large party permanently excluded from government. In all such situations, consent for the political system could be undermined either among a significant fraction of the population or more widely.

This latter point also worries Michael Keating who fears that if all but centrist forces are to be excluded from effective power in government then the prospects of extra-parliamentary opposition would be increased significantly.

If the anticipated changes in executive-legislative relationships and in the development of popular consent are less certain than Stuart Walkland maintains, several contributors also find his claims on behalf of SDP/'centrist' government unconvincing. Keating in fact identifies 'the central weakness of the SDP case as being the basic fallacy of Walkland's whole argument'. Still others note that his claim, that successful economic management has been frustrated in the frequent policy reversals wrought by the present party system, wantonly ignores, or cavalierly dismisses, recent research. Richard Rose (1980: 106–40), for example, has analysed, if not to the satisfaction of Walkland, the most important economic variables including minimum lending rates, PSBR, public expenditure, output, take-home pay, distribution of incomes and wealth, and unemployment and found that the basic trends in all of these are secular and resistant to party influence. Moreover, Andrew Gamble (1982: 20–1), one of Walkland's collaborators on an SSRC funded project on adversary politics, has already stated a 'few tentative conclusions' of his own. These are that: 'there is only limited evidence that there have been significant discontinuities in economic policy-making caused by the adversary positions adopted by the parties'; 'the idea of an invariant cycle of policy-making is also not at all convincing'; and 'the major failures of British post-war economic policy are found in areas which have not been issues between the parties'. Only in the areas of incomes policy and the reform of industrial relations does the adversary politics thesis appear to come into its own. Walkland's concentration upon the need to relate trade unions more to 'public purposes' and his hope that PR will provide a 'new and permanent political context to which powerful economic interests, especially the unions, would need to adjust' is perhaps tacit recognition of these findings.

Walkland also prompts further comments in his portrayal of over-bearing trade union power over 'pliable Labour governments' and their capacity to disrupt the continuity of the development of a permanent incomes policy. First, for over two-thirds of the last twenty years an incomes policy in one form or another has been in operation under successive Labour and Conservative governments. Second, under the last Labour government, incomes policy was administered largely by the trade unions themselves. On this occasion the trade union leaderships acted as the 'pliable arms' of the Labour government rather than vice-versa as Walkland maintains. Moreover, David Judge expresses the opinion that Labour governments generally have been committed to prevailing economic orthodoxies and a definition of the 'national interest' couched in terms of a healthy capitalist economy. Hence, such governments have acted not as the parliamentary arm of the trade union movement but as a major institutional mechanism integrating and socialising the working class into, and controlling it on behalf of, the established capitalist order. In this manner the interests of trade unionists have been treated as sectional rather than class interests and subordinated to the 'national' interest by Labour governments. All of this reflects Leo Panitch's (1979: 59) contention that the Labour party actually *demobilises* 'the working class at critical junctures in its development . . . at those very moments when economic militancy threatens profitability'. Indeed, the very fact that all post-war Labour governments have experienced conflict with trade unions over wage restraint in the ebb years in office points to the instability of incomes policy – not because of the party or trade unionist leaderships' fundamental hostility to such policies, but because of increased shop-floor militancy in the face of real losses in wages offset only by other, marginal, social and economic gains. That so few other gains have been realised reflects accurately the wider economic environment which both engenders and ultimately overwhelms incomes policy. Britain's competitive weakness within the world capitalist order also needs to be examined in the discussion of incomes policies.

By this argument the failure of incomes policy in particular and economic planning in general cannot be laid simply at the door of the trade unions or of one, or both parties. The failure to establish lasting consensus on crucial areas of incomes and industrial policy is not *caused* by party antagonisms but is a reflection of deeper social and economic divisions. Indeed, the very reason why the two major parties in opposition have increasingly forsaken the centre ground of the mixed economy, indicative planning and incomes policy is because of their inability in office to arrest Britain's economic decline. Political failure in this instance in an epiphenomenon of economic failure. Economic failure which in turn manifests the 'politics of Catch 22' (Coates 1982: 54). The 'catch' is that in restructuring British capitalism to make it internationally more competitive, governments are led to threaten the work practices and jobs of trade unionists, and in so doing release tensions which 'make clear that the interests of industrial capital and labour which the politicians sought to harmonise were not so much

similar as incompatible' (Coates 1982: 54). In their attempt to break out
of this circle both major parties have sought alternative strategies. In
this sense it is they, as Michael Keating argues, 'who have broken the
mould which the SDP is trying to stick together'. Whether a future
SDP or Alliance government could secure the compliance and co-
operation of the major corporate groups in the face of such tension is, of
course, open to speculation. Stuart Walkland believes so, several of the
other contributors remain unconvinced.

The Norton View

The very title of Philip Norton's chapter raises enquiries from a couple
of authors as to whether the Norton nomenclature is appropriate given
that the phenomenon of cross-voting was an established feature of life
in the Commons before it was appropriated as his research specialism.
In defence of Norton the editor should explain that Dr Norton was
requested to provide a statement of 'his' view – though this does not
absolve him of his initial presumptiousness! Nevertheless, this charge
against him is of little significance to the main thrust of criticism against
the 'Norton view'.

From Stuart Walkland's perspective, to argue that parliamentary
parties, through the occasional dissent from their leadership on the part
of a few MPs, can enhance consent for the parliamentary system is the
'equivalent of applying a sticking plaster to a broken leg'. Even if
cross-voting has been increasing it does not modify what, in Walkland's
opinion, is a growing disparity of views between the parties to the point
where on all important matters they seem to have no point of contact.
Any temporary consensus brought about by cross-voting cannot fundamentally breakdown these rooted party antagonisms. The spectre
haunting Walkland, and upon which he finds Norton strangely silent,
is that if no new mediating forces emerge then increasing policy
discontinuity will simply accelerate the decline of Britain:

> Philip Norton has nothing to say on this basic concern – he seems happy to go
> on playing the old two-party game provided that the rules are modified from
> time to time by small groups of MPs. It is not enough. Moreover, such
> dissidence cannot be commanded – it is at the mercy of the vagaries of
> day-to-day politics, usually the politics of minor issues. Even less can it be
> institutionalised. Norton seems to believe that cross-voting can mediate
> between the concepts of consent and authority. It can, in a minor way. But
> the only strength of two-party politics as I see it is that it provides a
> disciplined basis for executive authority, in the short-term, anyway. Yet
> Norton seems to want to destroy this only virtue.

Walkland then proceeds to argue that for all the illusions that attach to
the two-party system it just has not been working of late. In particular
the party system in the 1980s has failed in the important function of

producing a believable opposition, 'an alternative for a hard-pressed electorate to turn to in times of stress and hardship'. The decline and disorder of the Labour party, Walkland maintains, has deprived the country of a feasible alternative government. The lack of strong opposition in turn has sustained and enhanced Mrs Thatcher's position and 'Dr. Norton please note' has cut the ground from under the feet of the Conservative government's most severe internal critics. Walkland concludes his attack by asking what has happened to the Norton thesis since 1979? To say that the government has been defeated once and modified measures under the threat of defeat on approximately ten occasions simply reinforces the point that backbenchers have been unable to redirect government policy in any systematic or continuous manner. Dissent in the 1979 Parliament has not led, therefore, to a reappraisal of the relationship between parties and leaders nor of that between the House and the government. At best dissent has been symbolic, at worst it has been squashed with ease. Walkland is thus left ill at ease with Norton's 'complacency' in drawing upon 'what is as the basis for what can be' in the parliamentary arena without addressing the wider determinants of 'what is' in the political and economic spheres.

Similarly, Michael Keating is troubled by Norton's conclusion that Parliament can change by MPs changing their attitudes. Whilst Norton recognises that 'Parliament and parliamentary reform cannot be seen in isolation from the wider political, economic and social changes which affect society' there is no theoretical linking mechanism in his analysis to connect parliamentary change to the wider economic and political conditions necessary for a stable polity. What concerns Keating, therefore, is that the modest contribution of attitudinal and behavioural change in the Commons is in danger of becoming largely irrelevant to the solution of the country's fundamental economic malaise.

Equally important for Keating, and other contributors, is Norton's 'simplistic dichotomy' of MPs and whips. A dichotomy moreover founded upon largely unexamined behavioural assumptions. To take but one example, there is an implicit assumption that constituency parties would be expected to take action against dissenting Members. But in the Labour party, at least, this expectation may well be reversed, for as Keating observes it is often constituency party pressure in the first place which leads Labour MPs to rebel to the left against centre/right leadership. If anything, this tendency is likely to be accentuated by mandatory re-selection and other moves to 'activist democracy' in the Labour party. In other words, rebellion is by no means due to an abstract desire for 'independence' on the part of backbenchers. Yet there is no consideration of the type of issues upon which MPs of either major party rebel, nor for that matter the ideological pedigree of dissenting Members. Precisely this criticism has been raised by David

Judge (1981a: 3) against Norton's claim, repeated on page 64, that 'the manner of the leadership of Edward Heath served to transform covert dissent into public dissent in the division of lobbies' between 1970–4. Clearly, Mr Heath's style of leadership was of importance, yet Norton's own evidence (1978a) allows for the conclusion that ideological divisions within the party, as manifested over the issues of Northern Ireland, Rhodesia, Europe, immigration and counter-inflation were as important, if not more so, than the frustrations felt on the backbenches with Mr Heath's style. Correspondingly, ideological tensions within the Labour party help to explain many of the 23 defeats attributed to Labour backbenchers' dissent against the 1974–79 Labour government. When the issue of devolution is excluded from consideration, then many of the remaining defeats inflicted upon that government reflect cross-voting by members of the Tribune Group on the left of the party. In particular, the Group consistently opposed those economic and defence policies which transgressed adopted conference policies. But in voting against the Labour government in this way it can hardly be maintained that the House as a corporate entity had a collective, and positive, view to counterpoise that of the government. On such occasions the 'No' lobbies included opposition Conservative MPs voting against the government from the right and Tribunite MPs voting against it from the left. The unifying factor was 'opposition'. Opposition moreover which was both negative and variegated in its intent. Control in these circumstances simply served to stop the government from acting. Norton's claim that these circumstances will enable future governments 'to indulge in forward planning on the assumption that it [will be] . . . more responsive to anticipated parliamentary reaction' has a hollow ring to it. The point is that backbench power in his schema is negative, so that the positive actions of governments may well be blocked by shifting, temporary and, hence, unpredictable coalitions of backbenchers.

One of the clearest, and most recent, examples of the negative face of dissension (and indeed of the Norton view itself) was the defeat of the Conservative government's immigration rules in December 1982. On this occasion 23 right-wing Conservative backbenchers voted against the government, with at least another 28 abstaining, in support of their belief that the draft rules constituted a relaxation of entry requirements and hence a betrayal of election promises on immigration. The Labour opposition on the other hand voted against the new rules for precisely the opposite reasons; namely, that they were substantially more oppressive than the ones they were intended to replace. However, when the Home Secretary re-introduced the rules in February 1983, with the minor concession that they would be subject to continuous re-examination, the number of Conservative rebels fell to five, with a further ten abstentions. Hence, the government successfully pressed its policy through the House in spite of the determined opposition of a significant section of its own backbenchers. One consistent rebel, Harvey Proctor, ruefully enquired: 'Why should some of my colleagues, who pledged themselves unto the stake in December for fear of losing an arm, fall over themselves in the rush in the Government lobbies . . . at the prospect of losing two?' His answer was short and should be heeded by Philip Norton: 'The modern techniques of the parliamentary thumb-screw are many and varied – a whisky here, a trip to the Far East there, the friendly chat, the unfriendly chat, appeals to party loyalty – these are the stock in trade of [ministers]' (*The Guardian*, 15th February 1983).

A further weakness of the 'Norton view' is the assumption that dissidence *in itself* generated 'a change of attitude on the part of Members as to what they could achieve in their relationship to government'. But this 'tends to neglect', as Michael Rush notes, 'changes in pay, services and facilities which have in all probability helped to foster greater independence on the part of MPs'. George and Evans also make the related point that the positive forces for attitudinal change, such as experience on select committees and exposure to the limited improvements in research facilities, have been of importance, alongside Norton's negative perspective, in persuading backbenchers of their own potential power.

Finally, there is a residual scepticism amongst some of the contributors as to the actual extent of attitudinal change within the House. Whereas Norton, and backbenchers such as Bruce George, believe that 'the old assumptions have been dispelled', the countervailing view is that 'old habits die hard'. Importantly, the norms of the House and the career aspirations of most backbenchers are still determined by, and focused upon, the executive itself (see Judge 1981a: 12–13). It still remains true that most ambitious backbenchers conceive of their career patterns in terms of securing tenure of government office. Repeatedly, MPs have pointed to the fact that 'at present the route that ambitious . . . Members have to take if they wish to increase their influence is through Government and ministerial office. That in itself can often lead to a blunting of [a backbencher's] questioning and examination of a Government's performance' (D. Stoddart, HC Debates 1979, vol. 962: 312). If attitudinal change is to be brought about in the House then one major obstacle, unconsidered by Norton, is 'that so many people in [the] House are either Ministers or would-be Ministers' (W. Benyon, HC Debates 1979, vol. 962: 148).

'Internal' Reform

Given the acknowledged empathy between the perspectives of Norton and George and Evans it is not suprising to find that they prompt common criticisms. The failure to develop a theoretical foundation, or to consider the necessary political preconditions for the fulfilment of the House's ascribed controlling and scrutinising roles, are evident weaknesses in both chapters 3 and 4. One contributor goes so far as to suggest that George and Evans, like so many other practitioners, are so engrossed in the practice of parliamentary politics that they do not take the time to contemplate exactly what it is that they are doing. The danger is that activity becomes a substitute for analysis. Yet this attack is a little unfair as George and Evans do recognise the need for attitudinal change and the importance of identifying the obstacles in the path of reform. Nevertheless, they do not specify or analyse the forces frustrating attitudinal change, neither do they examine the inter-connectedness of the impediments themselves.

In linking the prospects of further procedural reform with attitudinal change on the part of backbenchers, George and Evans encounter similar problems of analysis as does Norton. They overlook, for example, the point that the normative system of the House, as with any other dominant value system, reflects the predilections of the most powerful actors and so supports the existing distribution of power: in other words the norms, aspirations and practices of most backbenchers are defined by reference to the executive. David Marquand (1981: 125) recently asked the question: 'Why not ask all MPs . . . to testify on oath which they would prefer to be – parliamentary secretary at a ministry or the chairman of a select committee?' His own answer was that 'until backbench Members of Parliament would rather be a chairman of a select committee than part of the executive, then [internal] reforms . . . are not going to make such a real difference'. In this context, it is significant that the 1977/8 Procedure Committee sought to develop an alternative career structure within the House and to develop a normative backbench 'sub-culture' in opposition to the hegemony of the executive. One important recommendation made by the Committee therefore was that the chairmen of select committees should receive extra payment for their parliamentary duties in order to 'provide some element of a career opportunity in the House not wholly in the gift of party leaders' (HC 588 1978: lxxix). As important as this recom-mendation itself was the government's rejection of such a threat to its own hegemony.

Generally those recommendations of the Procedure Committee which challenged executive control in the House did not find reflection in the standing orders of the new departmental committees: the power to compel the attendance of ministers was denied, no time limit was specified for the submission of departmental observations, nor were eight days set aside for the discussion of committee reports. Yet it is important for the argument of 'internal' reformers not merely that they note that these recommendations were not enacted by the government but that they explain *why* they were not backed. One reason Michael Rush suggests is that it would be masochistic for governments to support such reforms. If it is part of the 'internal' reformers' case that backbench control improved in the 1979 Parliament nonetheless, then this is not necessarily an indication of backbenchers' power. Power entails the capacity to change the actions of others in intended ways that they would otherwise not have chosen; and, significantly, the government has successfully frustrated, thus far, those reforms in which it saw no advantage for itself. Thus to argue that there is now in existence a system of select committees as a result of backbench pressure is only partly accurate. That there is such a system may also have something to do with the fact that departmental committees could be rationalised as an invaluable *ministerial aid* in the monitoring of Whitehall departments. The ideological commitment of key cabinet ministers, including the Prime Minister, in 1979 to 'rolling back the state' through cuts in public expenditure, decreased numbers of civil servants and greater restraint upon bureaucratic discretion in policy formulation and implementation, arguably increased the receptivity of Norman St John-Stevas' cabinet colleagues to his proposals for the new committees. In this instance parliamentary reform may have been countenanced, initially, to the extent that it was *compatible* with executive objectives.

Another area which George and Evans skate around in their chapter is the ability of bipartisan committees to function within a partisan chamber. Several contributors indeed note that the discussion of the operation of the new committees is politically neutered. It is unclear whether George and Evans favour bipartisan proceedings in these committees or partisanship whereby committee investigations are used to 'open up' the assumptions and criteria employed in departmental policy-making and then these findings are used for party purposes. Either way party relationships cannot be ignored by internal reformers. If the new committees are seen as essentially bipartisan bodies then their basic conceptual weakness has already been identified by Stuart Walkland (see page 45). In a House seldom so polarised the departmental committees have encountered difficulties in 'integrating party politicians into a common approach' in their investigations into partisan sensitive issues. To many of the other contributors the roots of bipartisanship in the new committees already have a stunted appearance. Yet how are these roots to be nurtured in a House in which power is concentrated and centralised in the conjunction of party and executive leadership roles? If attitudinal change is the answer: from whence is this change to come? A question which circles back to the criticism of Norton's chapter!

Alternatively, explicit recognition of the party divide within the Commons could be acknowledged and the new committees restructured accordingly. In 1978 a study group of the NEC of the Labour party, chaired by Eric Heffer, supported the idea of departmental select committees but argued that 'since we see no future in consensus government by all-party committees these investigatory committees would . . . be staffed and advised by specialists and on party political lines' (Statements to Annual Conference 1978: 8). The group's intention was, through the medium of select committees, to 'disperse power in Parliament and out of it to the political parties, and to those groups and individuals who support political parties'. Yet in view of this emphasis upon parties, and the desire to maintain the strength of the executive, it is difficult to envisage how party MPs, charged with helping the 'executive to push its policies through against opposition in Parliament', could reasonably be expected 'to check the executive' as the study group wished. This tension is most acute in those proposals made in relation to legislation. The group's statement that 'the task of the minister is to get his Bill through with as little damage to the Government and himself as possible and to do so with reasonable speed' (1978: 6) is clearly in the mainstream of adversary thought. But this philosophy does not fit well with the proposals for powerful all-party legislative committees in which 'Members would discuss the issues and amend the legislation before them' (1978: 7). Yet on what criteria would these amendments be carried if government bills adequately reflected the majority party's manifesto proposals? Even if governments acted contrary to their election commitments the experience of post-war majority governments demonstrates, despite Norton's limited claims to the contrary, that partisan loyalty is usually sufficient to ensure the successful passage of governent bills. Indeed, within George and Evans' chapter is the telling statement of Terry Davis that the value of the Special Standing Committee experiment was limited to technical and 'non-political' bills: 'if political principles were involved, and if he were in government, he said he would rather see the bill go through without any amendments at committee stage'. Encapsulated within this statement is the major political problem confronting 'internal' reformers; George and Evans resolve this problem only by ignoring it.

An Aside: Tony Benn on Parliamentary Reform

The confusion over how the Commons is conceived – whether as a collective representative whole, or fissured by party and hence a sectional tool of governments – finds reflection in the thoughts of Tony Benn on parliamentary reform. As an example of this confusion, as well as of the linkage between ideological precepts and the advocacy of reform identified on page 7, Benn's thoughts are worthy of examination. To David Judge, Benn's confusion over the conception of the Commons is in marked contrast to his percipient analysis of the parliamentary system in general. In common with social democrats Benn believes that Parliament is capable of becoming 'the agent that will alter the structure of society'. Moreover, this change 'will be done peacefully by electing a government with a majority in the House of Commons, which can then use the statute book and the machinery of the state to bring about that transformation by consent' (Benn 1982b: 9). Benn does, however, recognise and identify the institutional and contextual constraints which presently frustrate this objective. The power of capital, both national and international; the power of the mass media; and the power of international organisations, such as the EEC and NATO, provide a 'formidable array of opposition' to socialist governments. But it is the institutional entrenchment of opposition in Britain that has preoccupied Benn in recent times. In his words: 'unless we can extend democracy by major institutional reform in Britain, the interests of the people may be halted, by-passed, diverted and defeated by all those other institutions of power which are still without any effective democratic validation' (Benn 1982b: 12). Hence his argument for the abolition of the House of Lords, the transference of royal constitutional prerogative powers to the Speaker of the House of Commons, withdrawal from the EEC, open government, civil service reform and a constitutional premiership responsible directly to party backbenchers and the wider party. With the enactment of these reforms Benn envisages the parliamentary realisation of the party theory of representation (see Judge 1981a: 35–40). In future the PLP and its leadership would be committed by their election pledges to a radical programme; once in office the government would be accountable to its activists, and with the removal of the aforementioned institutional obstacles, it would act as an incisive weapon with which to dismember the inequities of capitalist society. In which case Benn sees a '*Labour* House of Commons . . . as the liberator unlocking the cells in which people live' (1982a: 70, emphasis added). There is here an explicit recognition of strong party government in the House. Indeed, so clear is this commitment that Benn is opposed to PR on the grounds that it would 'effectively paralys[e] the parliamentary process and elected governments' through institutionalising coalition governments.

Yet having set out the case for strong, single party government, to the extent that the Commons becomes literally a *Labour* House; once inside the chamber Benn's analysis becomes clouded by corporate notions of the House. Indeed, there is a fundamental contradiction between the hopes for a Labour House and his statement that 'this would not diminish the power of the *House of Commons as a whole*

over a government . . .' as a 'majority of MPs would still have the power
to overthrow a government if they wished' (1982c: 40, emphasis
added). But why would Labour MPs in search of socialism join with
non-socialist MPs to overthrow a mandated Labour government? This
problem becomes particularly acute in Benn's claim that stronger
parliamentary control over the executive highlights the 'need to
develop select committees to probe into the heart of Whitehall policy-
making' (1982c: 66). Such committees would boldly claim on behalf of
the *Commons* and the electorate greater knowledge and control of
executive decisions. Unless the House does so 'it will slowly shrink
back to the role of ex-post-facto auditor of decisions already taken'
(Benn 1980: 132). But if this is a general right, a right of all backbenchers, then does Benn also accept the right of the House representing 'the people' to criticise, expose and control the policies of a
Labour government which have been derived from Labour party
conference proposals, election manifestos and in turn sanctioned
through the ballot box by 'the people'? On what basis would government backbenchers seek to expose the policies of their government?
Are Labour governments to be frustrated in their drive towards
socialism by opposition parties in the Commons which are unsympathetic to their objectives? Will Labour governments, which in all
probability will be elected by a minority of electors under the first-past-
the-post system, accept the House's collective identification with the
interests of 'the people' – including a majority unsympathetic to
socialist objectives? The answer to the last two questions undoubtedly
is: no. Yet only if Benn assumes a consensus *for* socialism within the
House and within the electorate generally does his vision of collective
parliamentary control over a future socialist government make sense.

Benn's proclamation that 'I am an old parliamentarian' (*The
Guardian*, 3 January 1983) reveals the source of his dilemma. On the
one hand he is wedded to the notion of parliamentary sovereignty
whereby Labour governments can eventually wield power through the
Commons. On the other hand this partisan image of the House is
counterpoised by the 'old parliamentarian' view of the Commons as the
corporation of the nation wherein its members enjoy equal rights and
status: a residue in fact from the *consensual* proceedings of the 18th
century House. Yet without consensus this image is shattered. The
difficulty for Benn is that he recognises that 'what we are now seeing . . .
is a return to polarisation' (*The Guardian*, 3 January 1983). A
polarisation which is manifested both in extra-parliamentary movements and intra-parliamentary partisan conflicts. The prospects of the
Labour party developing a new socialist consensus out of the present
polarisation are obviously open to conjecture. But its attempts to do so
arguably will deepen the political polarisation and guarantee that a

future radical Labour government will encounter strengthened partisan and sectional opposition within the House. In these circumstances the contradiction will become ever more apparent between the view of the Commons as a collective representation of the people and the perspective of it as the sustainer of committed party government.

The House of Lords

Donald Shell's rejection of plans to abolish the House of Lords centres around his conception of Parliament as a collective watchdog of the actions of government. Unlike Tony Benn, however, he identifies the partisan dilemma at the heart of parliamentary reform in his question: 'at what point does the concern for strong government become a denial of parliamentary government?'. Shell's own answer is that that point is reached with the abolition of the Lords with no compensatory reform of the Commons. Yet several contributors believe that Shell, in arguing the case for reform rather than abolition of the Lords, runs up against the classic dilemma of the upper chamber identified by Abbe Sieyes that 'if the Lords agree with the Commons it is superfluous, if it disagrees it is obnoxious'. To argue that the role of the upper chamber is complementary to that of the Commons simply points to the need to reform the latter. As Stuart Walkland comments: 'the trouble with the British parliamentary system is not the House of Lords but the House of Commons. Get the latter right as a representative agency and the problems of a second chamber become technical only'. Other contributors disagree that the issue of Lords' reform is reducible to a technical matter. The very interdependence of its functions, its power and its composition makes the reform of the Lords a complex political matter.

Throughout his chapter Shell is aware of the intricacies of the political relationships between the two chambers, especially the potential rivalry which might result between a reformed and reconstituted Lords and the House of Commons. He seeks to resolve this problem by stipulating that the Commons does indeed need a rival, but accepts that the Lords should remain a junior rival. The main weakness of this argument is that a reconstituted upper chamber, whether directly elected or composed of nominated representatives from either regional bodies or organised interests, would have a source of authority and a claim to its own legitimacy independent of that of the Commons. This danger is tacitly recognised in Shell's question: 'is it desirable to entrench within Parliament the *de facto* power such groups as the CBI, the TUC, and the professional bodies already possess?' Unfortunately Shell does not provide the answer. David Coombes (1982: 146), on the other hand, in his recent work *Representative Government and Economic Power* maintains that the 'inclusion within a reformed House of Lords of a substantial number of members appointed to represent the main social and economic interests would serve to give industrial spokesmen a much more direct and public opportunity to express their views on relevant policies and measures. . . . It would be one sensible way of approaching the functions of a reformed second chamber.' But Coombes then proceeds to trample the sense out of this statement by acknowledging the difficulties entailed in the selection of representatives, the possibilities for this selection process to become intermeshed with party politics and the problems of conflating functional representation with the existing constitutional role of the Lords. Yet, even in those reformist schemes where the second chamber simply acts as an advisory and deliberative body (see Webb and Webb 1920; Churchill 1930) there is an evident contradiction between the claims of superiority on behalf of the amateur, territorially elected lower chamber and the actual capacity of a functionally based 'sub-Parliament' to dominate legislative outputs.

If the incorporation of functional representation into the Lords appears to create as many problems as it solves for reformers, then what other options are available? Always bearing in mind Donald Shell's desire to maintain the existing powers of the Lords as a revising chamber, his argument in favour of an elected membership 'on a properly proportional system from regional sized constituencies', attracts several critical comments. It is difficult to see why such representatives would not be able to claim equal, if not more, legitimacy in the eyes of their electorates than MPs. Even if elections were staggered and at lengthy fixed periods it remains unclear why representatives in the upper House 'could not claim the same popular legitimacy as the Commons' as Shell suggests. The experience of the United States Senate reveals that in many ways it is more prestigious than the House of Representatives. The length of tenure in office, the attention of the state media and the wider electoral base of Senators all enable them to develop and call upon their own legitimate sources of power. Correspondingly, in West Germany, where members of the Bundesrat are not directly elected, their 'indirect' election and responsibility to their own *Laender* electorates, still serves as a countervailing source of legitimacy in their dealings with the Bundestag. Nonetheless, Shell maintains that schemes for either directly or indirectly elected regional representation in a reformed British second chamber have a 'clear rationale'. This rationale only becomes apparent however with the creation of a regional tier of government.

Devolution
Michael Keating's advocacy of elected assemblies for the nations and regions of the United Kingdom allows for the provision of a 'second

chamber ensuring the representation of the nations and regions at the centre and the protection of their constitutional position'. Whether such a system be called federalism is unimportant to Keating. Whether such a system be needed at all appears to be unimportant to most of the other contributors – if the relative absence of critical comments on chapter 6 is anything to go by. But the failure to respond to Keating's challenge is important in itself. Richard Rose's (1982: 214) observation appears to apply equally to the authors represented in this book: 'The bulk of Westminster politicians are Engish and indifferent Unionists. They are indifferent not because they dislike Union but because they do not think about it, and therefore have no emotional commitment for or against Union as do politicians in Scotland, Wales and Northern Ireland.' Michael Rush does, however, question Keating's lack of concern over whether a devolved system would be called federalism as, by definition, federalism is a *legal* division of responsibilities, and as such can produce the problem of institutionalising and reinforcing regional differences as revealed in Canada. Of those other contributors who comment on Keating's proposals, their criticisms focus upon the interrelated issues of parliamentary sovereignty and the equality of civil rights in the UK, as well as the notion of 'territorial politics' itself.

In chapter 6 Keating makes a distinction between those parliamentary systems founded upon *popular* sovereignty and those, like the UK, founded upon the principle of *parliamentary* sovereignty. Other than for administrative lawyers and political philosophers this distinction has had little practical meaning. Marshall and Moodie (1971: 16) explain that 'exercising political sovereignty is not what the electorate does as distinct from Parliament, but what everybody (including Parliament) does in his or their political capacity'. Similarly parliamentary sovereignty is not what Parliament has as distinct from the electorate, if it is conceded that the function of legislating is conferred upon representatives by the electorate. If anything therefore Keating endows the concept of sovereignty with too positive and definite a meaning in his argument that it has reduced 'the status of the citizen *vis-à-vis* the state' and has simultaneously failed to guarantee civil rights. Such failures are more visibly the product of political forces rather than constitutional maladies and limitations. Crick's (1968: 24) words should perhaps be heeded that 'it is necessary to put this abstract concept in its place since it does obscure . . . the real restraints there are on any British Government. These restraints are, of course, all political'. If the citizen and his rights have been threatened by the state then this is the result of political action rather than constitutional inaction.

A related criticism is that Keating's linkage of the erosion of civil liberties to the actions of a unitary and sovereign Parliament implies first, that centralisation has failed to maintain these liberties in the past and second, by deduction, that some form of decentralisation will better serve individual and collective liberties in the future. Yet, devolution is no guarantee in itself of the defence of civil liberties; as Catholics in Northern Ireland between 1922 and 1972 will testify. Nor does federalism, complete with the incorporation of the notion of popular sovereignty within a written constitution, necessarily guarantee civil liberties. Negroes in the southern states of the US long recognised the hollow ring of the 14th amendment that 'no state shall . . . deny to any person within its jurisdiction the equal protection of the laws'. Equal rights were denied to blacks both by the practices of state governments and in some cases segregation was written into and institutionalised in state laws. Indeed, when the federal government and the Supreme Court sought to enforce the provisions of the 14th amendment the states were able to challenge and frustrate the promotion of civil rights through recourse to constitutional principles. American experience therefore simply reinforces the point that political practice, rather than constitutional theory, is the crucial factor in the maintenance of civil rights.

The third problem with Keating's analysis, for David Judge at least, is the concept of 'territorial politics' itself. To talk of the UK as a multi-national state and one that is territorially differentiated obviously means that there is a territorial *dimension* to UK politics. A dimension which might be overlooked in constitutional theory but which the practice of UK government has been unable to ignore. But this dimension simply overlays and helps to structure political activity generated by underpinning economic and social divisions. In what sense is it meaningful to talk of unemployment, for example, as a territorial issue? If anything in the 1980s unemployment has been increasing the similarities between the nations within the UK (see Rose 1982: 216). How are the common economic difficulties, cultural patterns and religious rivalries within the cities of Glasgow and Liverpool best ascribed to the politics of 'territory'? Would these parallels dramatically change if Glasgow become part of a federal state of Scotland? Indeed, throughout the devolution debate of the 1970s there was an undercurrent of concern in Scotland that the creation of a Scottish Assembly would exacerbate, rather than solve, social divisions within the territory of Scotland. 'Scottish' problems could rapidly crystallise into religious disagreements between Catholics and Protestants, or economic disputes between the declining industrial west-central belt and the rural, sparsely populated Highlands. Whether these disputes are themselves 'territorially', or economically or socially determined is open to debate. If they are part of territorial politics then this concept extends well beyond the regional and national units specified by Keating down through localities, communities, even to households. If this is the case then the choice of area for 'sub-national' government outside of Scotland, Wales and Northern Ireland becomes problematic; a fact acknowledged in successive failures to delimit 'regional' areas as the potential basis for devolved assemblies within England.

Another question which occupied the minds of many Scottish people during the protracted debate on devolution was why would an Assembly in Edinburgh be any more of an efficient or effective allocator of resources than Westminster? Equally concerned by this issue is Philip Norton who believes that 'devolved government of the type proposed by Keating would threaten governmental effectiveness through sharing power and through facilitating economic disparity between regions'. Indeed, at one stage of his argument Keating acknowledges the force of this criticism in the recognition that it is difficult to adapt federalism to the needs of the modern state as governments' responsibilities for economic management 'have led them directly, or through attempts to control expenditure, into all areas of policy; and the welfare state demands equal provision of services irrespective of location'. In which case the advocacy of federalism may be more soundly based upon the grounds of participation and democratic accountability rather than upon effectiveness or the sustaining of civil rights. Even then a few contributors suggest that there 'is little apparent need felt for such change'; one further observes that he had it 'on good authority that even within the SDP there is little support for regional government'.

Why Reform?

It would have been pleasurable to report that the editor's own contribution to this book had escaped criticism. However, the adage that people who live in glass houses should not throw stones is as true for editors as it is for anyone else. Thus just as David Judge has difficulty in accepting Michael Keating's notion of territorial politics so Keating found the neo-Marxist interpretation 'less than totally convincing and in some places redundant. In particular . . . this model was unable to cope with the territorial issues raised in chapter 6'. He cannot accept that issues of nationalism and religion can be subsumed within the class/economic model outlined in chapter 1. In particular Keating disputes the relevance of explanations of the rise of the SNP in terms of an economic development gap between the Scottish peripheral economy and the English economy. Generally, he believes that theory has got the better of explication in Judge's chapter. In this respect chapter 1 suffers from too high a level of theory which the historical examples cannot substantiate. One example that both Keating and Norton identify in this context is the claim made on page 17 that the

1867 Reform Act 'can be seen as an attempt to forge an alliance between skilled workers and the Conservative aristocratic base against commercial and industrial capital'. As Philip Norton argues, 'That is a seemingly plausible *post hoc* interpretation. But I am not sure it can be well substantiated by an examination of the contemporary evidence. Disraeli, in romantic mood, may have seen it like that, and the effects of the Act may have had the galvanising effect referred to, but can one prove that there was a *conscious* act to forge such an alliance?' Generally, Norton believes that 'the problem inherent in any Marxist analysis is one of falsification. It might sound plausible but it can neither be proven nor falsified'. Moreover, he can only detect a quasi-Marxist rather than a neo-Marxist analysis. Shed of its 'Marxist trappings' Norton finds little in Judge's conclusion with which he disagrees. Similarly, Stuart Walkland would have appreciated the removal of 'Marxist jargon' from chapter 1. Although not necessarily disagreeing with that chapter's analysis he counsels the editor that 'it is possible to make the same points as you do in clear English. I suggest you read James Madison's contribution to *The Federal Papers* – the proceedings of the 1787 constitutional conference in the USA which provided that country with its 1789 constitution. There the economic basis of politics is set out elegantly, many years before Marx wrote.' *Touché*!

Conclusion

So where does this leave us? At the end of this book and at the beginning of a new phase in the debate on parliamentary reform. All of the contributors have lived in glass houses in this book; cheerfully they have thrown academic stones at each other and manfully, and woman-fully, have suffered a few broken panes in their own arguments. The reformers may now retire to their own glass houses to undertake some glazial reinforcements and to fire some weightier bricks for the next round in the discussion. In the final analysis how successful their reinforcements are seen to be, or for that matter, the direction in which they choose to throw their analytical bricks in the future will be determined by their political perspectives. One thing is certain, those analysts who shelter within the glass walls of the idea that parliamentary reform is solely a technical matter concerned only with procedural reform should look out for a hailstorm of bricks. Parliamentary reform is a political matter.

References

ALDERMAN, G. 1978, *British Elections: myth and reality*, London, Batsford.

BAGEHOT, W. 1867, *The English Constitution*, (1963 edn), Glasgow, Fontana.

BEER, S.H. 1969, *Modern British Politics* (2nd edn), London, Faber & Faber.

BEER, S.H. 1982a, 'The struggle to create a new political consensus', *New Society*, 16th September.

BEER, S.H. 1982b, *Britain Against Itself: the political contradictions of collectivism*, London, Faber.

BELL, S. 1981, *How to Abolish the Lords*, London, Fabian Tract 476.

BENN, T. 1980, *Arguments for Socialism*, Harmondsworth, Penguin Books.

BENN, T. 1982a, *Parliament, People and Power*, London, Verso.

BENN, T. 1982b, 'Power, parliament and the people', *New Socialist*, September/October 1982, pp. 9–15.

BENN, T. 1982c, *Arguments for Democracy*, Harmondsworth, Penguin Books.

BENNET, C. 1982, 'The mental health bill', *The House Magazine*, vol. 7, pp. 4–5.

BERRINGTON, H.B. 1968, 'Partisanship and dissidence in the 19th century House of Commons', *Parliamentary Affairs*, vol. 21, pp. 338–373.

BERRINGTON, H.B. 1975, 'Electoral reform and national government', in S.E. FINER (ed), *Adversary Politics and Electoral Reform*, London, Anthony Wigram, pp. 269–92.

BIRCH, A.H. 1964, *Representative and Responsible Government*, London, Allen & Unwin.

BIRKE, A.M. 1981, 'Das konstruktive misstrauensvotum in den verfassungshandlungen der laender und des bundes', *Zeitschrift fuer Parlamentsfragen*, 8th year, pp. 78–92.

BLAKE, R. 1966, *Disraeli*, London, Eyre & Spottiswoode.

BLONDEL, J. 1975, *Voters, Parties and Leaders* (rev. edn), Harmondsworth, Penguin Books.

BOGDANOR, V. 1979, *Devolution*, Oxford, OUP.

BOGDANOR, V. 1981, *People and the Party System: the referendum and electoral reform in British politics*, Cambridge, CUP.

BOOTH, A. 1982, 'Corporatism, capitalism and depression in 20th century Britain', *British Journal of Sociology*, vol. 33, pp. 200–223.

BOW GROUP 1977, *Secundus Inter Pares*, London, Conservative Party.

BRAND, J. 1978, *The National Movement in Scotland*, London, Routledge & Kegan Paul.

BUNDESTAG 1976, 'Beratungen und empfehlungen zur verfassungsreform', *Parlament und Regierung*, vol. 1.

BURKETT, T. 1975, *Parties and Elections in West Germany: the search for stability*, London, C. Hurst & Co.

BUTT, R. 1969, *The Power of Parliament* (2nd edn), London, Constable.

CAMPBELL, C. 1978, *The Canadian Senate: a lobby from within*, Toronto, Macmillan.

CANNON, J. 1972, *Parliamentary Reform 1640–1832*, Cambridge, CUP.

CATER, D. 1965, *Power in Washington*, London, Collins.

CAWSON, A. 1978, 'Pluralism, corporatism and the role of the state', *Government and Opposition*, vol. 13, pp. 178–198.

CHANGING GEAR 1981, *Proposals from a Group of Conservative MPs*, London, Macmillan.

CHURCHILL, W.L.S. 1930, 'Parliamentary government and the economic problem', *Romanes Lecture*, Oxford.

CHRISTIAN, W. and CAMPBELL, C. 1974, *Political Parties and Ideologies in Canada*, Toronto, McGraw.

CLARK, J.C.D. 1980, 'A general theory of party opposition and government, 1688–1832', *The Historical Journal*, vol. 23, pp. 295–325.

CLOSE, D.H. 1977, 'The collapse of resistance to democracy: conservatives, adult suffrage, and second chamber reform, 1911–1928', *The Historical Journal*, vol. 20, pp. 893–918.

CMND 9038 1917, *Report of the conference on the second chamber: chairman Viscount Bryce*.

CMND 8323 1981, *The role of the Comptroller and Auditor General*.

COATES, D. 1979, *Labour in Power? A study of the Labour government 1974–1979*, London, Longman.

COATES, D. 1982, 'Britain in the 1970s: economic crisis and the resurgence of radicalism', in A. COX (ed), *Politics, Policy and the European Recession*, London, Macmillan, pp. 141–66.

CONSERVATIVE CENTRAL OFFICE 1979, *The Conservative Manifesto*, London, Conservative Party.

COOMBES, D. 1982, *Representative Government and Economic Power*, London, Heinemann Educational Books.

CRICK, B. 1965, 'The prospects for parliamentary reform', *Political Quarterly*, vol. 36, pp. 336–46.

CRICK, B. 1968, *The Reform of Parliament* (2nd edn), London, Weidenfeld & Nicolson.

CRICK, B. 1970, 'Parliament in the British political system', in A. KORNBERG and L.D. MUSOLF (eds), *Legislatures in Developmental Perspective*, North Carolina, Duke University Press, pp. 33–54.

CROSLAND, A. 1956, *The Future of Socialism*, London, Jonathan Cape.

CROSSMAN, R.H.S. 1975, *The Diaries of a Cabinet Minister*, vol. 1, London, Hamish Hamilton/Jonathan Cape.

CROSSMAN, R.H.S. 1976, *The Diaries of a Cabinet Minister*, vol. 2, London, Hamish Hamilton/Jonathan Cape.

CROSSMAN, R.H.S. 1977, *The Diaries of a Cabinet Minister*, vol. 3, London, Hamish Hamilton/Jonathan Cape.

CROWTHER-HUNT, LORD and PEACOCK, A.T. 1973, Memorandum of Dissent, *Cmnd 5460–1*, Royal Commission on the Constitution 1969–73.

CUNNINGHAM, G. 1980, 'Book review', *The Parliamentarian*, vol. 61, pp. 192–3.

DAVIDSON, R.H., KOVENOCK, D., O'LEARY, M. 1966, *Congress in Crisis: politics and congressional reform*, Belmont, Wadsworth.

DAVIES, A. 1980, *Reformed Select Committees: the first year*, London, Outer Circle Policy Unit.

DAWSON, W.F. 1962, *Procedure in the Canadian House of Commons*, Toronto, University of Toronto Press.

DRUCKER, H. 1979, *Doctrine and Ethos in the Labour Party*, London, George Allen & Unwin.

EDINGER, L. 1975, *Politics in Germany*, Boston, Little Brown.

ELCOCK, H. 1978, 'Regional government in action: the members of two regional health authorities', *Public Administration*, vol. 56, pp. 379–398.

EPSTEIN, L.D. 1980, 'What happened to the British party model?', *American Political Science Review*, vol. 74, pp. 9–22.

FAIR, J.D. 1980, *British Interparty Conferences: A study of the procedure of conciliation in British politics 1867–1921*, Oxford, Clarendon Press, OUP.

FENNO, R.F. 1966, *The Power of the Purse: appropriations politics in Congress*, Boston, Little Brown.

FENNO, R.F. 1973, *Congressmen in Committees*, Boston, Little Brown.

FINER, S.E. 1970, *Comparative Government*, Harmondsworth, Penguin Books.

FLEGMANN, V. 1980, *Called to Account: the Public Accounts Committee of the House of Commons*, London, Gower.

FRASER, P. 1960, 'The growth of ministerial control in the 19th century House of Commons', *English Historical Review*, vol. 75, pp. 444–463.

GAMBLE, A. 1974, *The Conservative Nation*, London, Routledge & Kegan Paul.

GAMBLE, A. 1981, *Britain in Decline: economic policy, political strategy and the British state*, London, Macmillan.

GAMBLE, A. 1982, 'Continuity and discontinuity in British economic policy 1960–80', Annual Conference of the Political Studies Association, Kent University.

GARRETT, J. 1980, *Managing the Civil Service*, London, Heinemann.

GASH, N. 1953, *Politics in the Age of Peel: A study in the technique of parliamentary representation 1830–1850*, London, Longmans Green.

GASH, N. 1978, 'The British party system and the closed society', in A. SELDON (ed.), *The Coming Confrontation: will the open society survive to 1989?*, London, IEA.

GEORGE, B. and PIERAGOSTINI, K. 1981, 'The making of British defence policy: a new role for the House of Commons?', American Political Science Association Conference, New York.

GILMOUR, I. 1969, *The Body Politic*, London, Hutchinson.

GOUGH, I. 1979, *The Political Economy of the Welfare State*, London, Macmillan.

GOLAY, J.F. 1965, *The Founding of the Federal Republic of Germany* (2nd edn), Chicago, Mayflower Reprints.

GRANT, A.R. 1982, *The American Political Process* (2nd edn), London, Heinemann Educational Books.

GRANT, W. and MARSH, D. 1977, *The Confederation of British Industry*, London, Hodder and Stoughton.

GRIFFITH, J.A.G. 1974, *Parliamentary Scrutiny of Government Bills*, London, George Allen & Unwin.

GRIFFITH, J.A.G. 1981, 'Standing committees in the House of Commons', in S.A WALKLAND and M. RYLE (eds), *The Commons Today*, Glasgow, Fontana, pp. 118–136.

HAILSHAM, LORD. 1976, *Elective Dictatorship*, London, BBC.

HAILSHAM, LORD. 1978, *The Dilemma of Democracy*, Glasgow, Collins.

HANSARD SOCIETY FOR PARLIAMENTARY GOVERNMENT 1967, *Parliamentary Reform 1933–1960* (2nd edn), London, Cassell.

HARVEY, J. and BATHER, L. 1965, *The British Constitution*, London, Macmillan.

HAYWOOD, S. and ELCOCK, H. 1982, 'Regional health authorities: regional government or central agencies?' in B. HOGWOOD and M. KEATING (eds), *Regional Government in England*, Oxford, OUP, pp. 119–142.

HC 161 1931, *Special report from the select committee on procedure on public business, session 1931.*

HC 463 1973, *Second report from the select committee on European Community secondary legislation, session 1972/3.*

HC 535 1977, *Eleventh report from the expenditure committee: the civil service, session 1976/7.*

HC 588 1978, *First report from the select committee on procedure, session 1977/8.*

HC 42 1980, *First report from the foreign affairs committee; British North America Acts: the role of Parliament, session 1980/1.*

HC 36 1981, *First special report from the defence committee, strategic nuclear weapons policy, session 1980/1.*

HC 118 1981, *First report from the select committee on procedure (supply), session 1980/1.*

HC 163 1981, *Third report from the treasury and civil service committee: monetary policy, session 1980/1*.

HC 366 1981, *Second report from the environment committee: enquiry into the sale of council houses, session 1980/1*.

HC 385 1981, *The House of Commons Commission third annual report, session 1980/1*.

HC 40 1982, *First report from the environment committee; the private rented housing sector, session 1981/1*.

HC 92 1982, *First report from the liaison committee: the select committee system, session 1982/3*.

HEALD, D. 1980, 'Territorial equity and public finances', *Studies in Public Policy* 75, Glasgow, University of Strathclyde.

HECHTER, M. 1975, *Internal Colonialism*, London, Routledge & Kegan Paul.

HEFFER, E. 1978, on 'Talking Politics', BBC Radio 4 broadcast 28th October.

HILLS, J. 1981, 'Britain', in LOVENDUSKI, J. and HILLS, J. (eds), *The Politics of the Second Electorate: women and public participation*, London, Routledge & Kegan Paul, pp. 8–32.

HOBSBAWM, E.J. 1968, *Industry and Empire: an economic history since 1750*, London, Weidenfeld & Nicolson.

HOGWOOD, B. and KEATING, M. (eds) 1982, *Regional Government in England*, Oxford, OUP.

HOME, LORD. 1978, *Report of the Review Committee on the Second Chamber*, London, Conservative Political Centre.

HOOD PHILLIPS, O. 1978, *Constitutional and Administrative Law* (6th edn), London, Sweet & Maxwell.

HUEBNER, E., OBERREUTER, H. and RAUSCH, H. 1969, *Der Bundestag von innen gesehen*, Munich, Munclever Verlag.

JENKINS, R. 1954, *Mr. Balfour's Poodle* (1968 edn), London, Collins.

JENNINGS, I. 1934, *Parliamentary Reform*, London, Gollancz.

JESSOP, B. 1978, 'Capitalism and democracy: the best possible political shell?', in LITTLEJOHN, G. et al, *Power and the State*, London, Croom Helm, pp. 10–51.

JESSOP, B. 1980, 'The transformation of the state in post-war Britain', in R. SCASE (ed), *The State in Western Europe*, London, Croom Helm, pp. 23–94.

JESSOP, B. 1982, *The Capitalist State: Marxist theories and methods*, London, Martin Robertson.

JEWELL, M.E. and PATTERSON, S.C. 1977, *The Legislative Process in the United States* (3rd edn), New York, Random House.

JOHNSON, N. 1973, *Government in the Federal Republic of Germany: the executive at work*, Oxford, OUP.

JOHNSON, N. 1977, *In Search of the Constitution*, Oxford, Pergamon.

JOHNSON, N. 1979, 'Select committees and legislation', in S.A. WALKLAND (ed), *The House of Commons in the 20th Century*, Oxford, Clarendon Press, OUP, pp. 426–475.

JONES, C.O. 1981, 'Can our parties survive our politics?', in N. ORNSTEIN (ed), *The Role of the Legislature in Western Democracies*, Washington DC, American Enterprise Institute, pp. 20–36.

JONES, J.B. and KEATING, M. 1979, 'The British Labour party as a centralising force', *Studies in Public Policy* 32, Glasgow, University of Strathclyde.

JORDAN, G. 1979, 'The committee stage of the Scotland and Wales bill', *The Waverley Papers: Occasional Paper 1*, Edinburgh, University of Edinburgh.

JUDGE, D. 1981a, *Backbench Specialisation in the House of Commons*, London, Heinemann Educational Books.

JUDGE, D. 1981b, 'Specialists and generalists in British central government: a political debate', *Public Adminstration*, vol. 59, pp. 1–14.

KAVANAGH, D. 1976, 'The deferential English: a comparative critique', in R. ROSE (ed), *Studies in British Politics* (3rd edn), London, Macmillan, pp. 58–83.

KEATING, M. 1975, *The Role of the Scottish M.P.*, unpublished Ph.D. thesis, CNAA.

KEATING, M. 1978, 'Parliamentary behaviour as a test of Scottish integration in the UK', *Legislative Studies Quarterly*, vol. 3, pp. 409–30.

KEATING, M. 1982a, 'Area, power and intergovernmental relations in the UK: some problems of analysis within the liberal-democratic tradition', *Journal of Area Studies*, vol. 6, pp. 23–7.

KEATING, M. 1982b, 'Devolution and the politics of constitution-making', *Bulletin of Scottish Politics*, vol. 3.

KEATING, M. and BLEIMAN, D. 1979, *Labour and Scottish Nationalism*, London, Macmillan.

KEATING, M. and LINDLEY, P. 1981, 'Devolution: The Scotland and Wales bills', *Public Administration Bulletin* 37, pp. 37–54.

KEATING, M. and MIDWINTER, A. 1981, 'The Scottish Office in the United Kingdom policy network', *Studies in Public Policy* 96, Glasgow, University of Strathclyde.

KEATING, M. and RHODES, M. 1979, 'Is there a regional level of government in England?', *Studies in Public Policy* 49, Glasgow, University of Strathclyde.

KEATING, M. and RHODES, M. 1981, 'Politics or technocracy? The regional water authorities', *Political Quarterly*, vol. 52, pp. 487–90.

KING, A. 1974, *British Members of Parliament: a self-portrait*, London, Macmillan.

KING, A. 1976, 'The problems of overload', in A. KING (ed), *Why is Britain Becoming Harder to Govern?*, London, BBC, pp. 8–30.

KING, A. 1981, 'How to strengthen legislatures – assuming that we want to', in N. ORNSTEIN (ed), *The Role of the Legislature in Western Democracies*, Washington DC, American Enterprise Institute, pp. 77–89.

KIRCHHEIMER, O. 1968, 'Germany: the vanishing opposition', in R.A. DAHL (ed), *Political Oppositions in Western Democracies*, Yale, Yale University Press, pp. 127–57.

KITZINGER, U. 1973, *Diplomacy and Persuasion*, London, Thames & Hudson.

LABOUR CO-ORDINATING COMMITTEE 1982, *Labour and Mass Politics: rethinking our strategy*, London.

LABOUR PARTY 1973, *Scotland and the UK*, Glasgow, Labour Party Publications.

LASKI, H.J. 1938, *Parliamentary Government in England*, London, George Allen & Unwin.

LEES, J.D. and SHAW, M.T. (eds), 1979, *Committees in Legislatures: a comparative analysis*, Durham, N.C., Duke University Press.

LE MAY, G.H.L. 1979, *The Victorian Constitution: conventions, usages and contingencies*, London, Duckworth.

LENIN, V.I. 1917, *The State and Revolution* (1949 edn), Moscow, Progress Publishers.

LIBERAL PARTY, Reform of Government Panel 1980, *A New Constitutional Settlement*, London, Liberal Publications Department.

LOEWENBERG, G. and PATTERSON, S.C. 1979, *Comparing Legislatures*, Boston, Little Brown.

LOWE, D. 1981, 'Legislative oversight and the House of Commons new committee system', American Political Science Association Conference, New York.

LOWELL, A.L. 1924, *The Government of England*, vol. 2, New York, Macmillan.

MACKENZIE, K. 1950, *The English Parliament*, Harmondsworth, Penguin Books.

MACKINTOSH, J.P. 1968a, *The British Cabinet* (2nd edn), London, Methuen.

MACKINTOSH, J.P. 1968b, *The Devolution of Power*, Harmondsworth, Penguin Books.

MACKINTOSH, J.P. 1974, *The Government and Politics of Britain* (3rd edn), London, Hutchinson.

MACNEIL, N. 1963, *Forge of Democracy: The House of Representatives*, New York, McKay.

MACPHERSON, C.B. 1966, *The Real World of Democracy* (1972 edn), Oxford, OUP.

MACPHERSON, C.B. 1977, *The Life and Times of Liberal Democracy*, Oxford, OUP.

MCCORD, N. 1967, 'Some difficulties of parliamentary reform', *The Historical Journal*, vol. 4, pp. 376–390.

MARSHALL, G. and MOODIE, G.C. 1971, *Some Problems of the Constitution*, London, Hutchinson.

MARQUAND, D. 1981, 'Discussion' in N.J. ORNSTEIN (ed), *The Role of the Legislature in Western Democracies*, Washington DC., American Enterprise Institute.

MARX, K. and ENGELS, F. 1848, *The Communist Manifesto* (1967 edn), Harmondsworth, Penguin Books.

MAY, E. 1976, *Treatise on the Law, Privileges, Proceedings and Usage of Parliament* (19th edn), London, Butterworth.

MERKL, P. 1959, 'Executive-legislative federalism in West Germany', *American Political Science Review*, vol. 53, pp. 732–41.

MEZEY, M. 1979, *Comparative Legislatures*, North Carolina, Duke University Press.

MIDDLEMAS, K. 1979, *Politics in Industrial Society*, London, Andre Deutsch.

MILIBAND, R. 1969, *The State in Capitalist Society*, London, Weidenfeld & Nicolson.

MILIBAND, R. 1977, *Marxism and Politics*, Oxford, OUP.

MILIBAND, R. 1982, *Capitalist Democracy in Britain*, Oxford, OUP.

MILLER, W.L. 1981, *The End of British Politics?*, Oxford, Clarendon Press, OUP.

MOODIE, G.C. 1964, *The Government of Great Britain*, London, Methuen.

MOORE, B. 1966, *Social Origins of Dictatorship and Democracy* (1973 edn), Harmondsworth, Penguin Books.

MORGAN, J. 1975, *The House of Lords and the Labour Government 1964–70*, Oxford, Clarendon Press, OUP.

MORGAN, K.O. 1981, *Wales: Rebirth of a Nation*, Oxford, OUP.

MULLER, S. 1968, 'Federalism and the party system in Canada', in J.P. MEEKISON (ed), *Canadian Federalism: Myth or Reality*, Toronto, Methuen, pp. 119–32.

NAIRN, T. 1982, *The Break-Up of Britain: crisis and neo-nationalism* (2nd edn), London, New Left Books.

NEWMAN, O. 1981, *The Challenge of Corporatism*, London, Macmillan.

NORMANTON, E.L. 1966, *The Accountability and Audit of Government*, Manchester, Manchester University Press.

NORTHFIELD, LORD. 1978, 'Reforming Procedure in the Lords', in D. BUTLER and A. HALSEY (eds), *Policy and Politics*, London, Macmillan.

NORTON, P. 1976, 'Intra-party dissent in the House of Commons: a case study. The immigration rules 1972', *Parliamentary Affairs*, vol. 29, pp. 404–20.

NORTON, P. 1978a, *Conservative Dissidents*, London, Temple Smith.

NORTON, P. 1978b, 'Government defeats in the House of Commons: myth and reality', *Public Law*, Winter, pp. 360–78.

NORTON, P. 1978c, Party organisation in the House of Commons', *Parliamentary Affairs*, vol. 31, pp. 406–23.

NORTON, P. 1978d, 'Government defeats in the House of Commons; three restraints overcome', *The Parliamentarian*, vol. 59, pp. 231–38.

NORTON, P. 1979, 'The organisation of parliamentary parties', in S.A. WALKLAND (ed), *The House of Commons in the 20th Century*, Oxford, OUP, pp. 7–68.

NORTON, P. 1980, *Dissension in the House of Commons 1974–79*, Oxford, OUP.

NORTON, P. 1981a, *The Commons in Perspective*, Oxford, Martin Robertson.

NORTON, P. 1981b, 'The US Congress in comparative perspective: the British Parliament', American Political Science Association Conference, New York.

NORTON, P. 1982, *The Constitution in Flux*, Oxford, Martin Robertson.

NORTON, P. and AUGHEY, A. 1981, *Conservatives and Conservatism*, London, Temple Smith.

NOTESTEIN, W. 1924, 'The winning of the initiative by the House of Commons', *Proceedings of the British Academy*, vol. 11, pp. 125–175.

OPPENHEIMER, P. 1970, 'Muddling through: the economy 1951–64', in V. BOGDANOR and R. SKIDELSKY (eds), *The Age of Affluence*, London, Macmillan.

OWEN, D. 1981, *Face the Future*, Oxford, OUP.

PANITCH, L. 1979, 'Socialists and the Labour party: a reappraisal', in R. MILIBAND and J. SAVILLE (eds), *The Socialist Register 1979*, London, Merlin, pp. 51–74.

PANITCH, L. 1980, 'Recent theorizations of corporatism: reflections on a growth industry', *British Journal of Sociology*, vol. 31, pp. 159–187.

PARRIS, H. 1960, 'The 19th century revolution in government: a reappraisal reappraised', *The Historical Journal*, pp. 17–37.

PATTERSON, S.C. 1973, 'Review article: the British House of Commons as a focus for political research', *British Journal of Political Science*, vol. 3, pp. 363–81.

PITKIN, H. 1967, *The Concept of Representation*, Berkeley, University of California Press.

PORTER, J. 1965, *The Vertical Mosaic*, Toronto, University of Toronto Press.

POULANTZAS, N. 1968, *Political Power and Social Classes* (1973 edn), London, New Left Books.

POULANTZAS, N. 1975, *The Crisis of the Dictatorships* (1976 edn), London, New Left Books.

POULANTZAS, N. 1976, 'The Capitalist State: a reply to Miliband and Laclau', *New Left Review*, vol. 95, pp. 63–83.

PREAMBLE TO THE BRITISH NORTH AMERICA ACT 1867, in R.J. VAN LOON and M.S. WHITTINGTON 1976, *The Canadian Political System* (2nd edn), Toronto, McGraw-Hill.

PROCTOR, W.A. 1979, 'The House of Commons select committee on procedure 1976–9', *The Table*, vol. 47.

PUNNETT, R.M. 1980, *British Government and Politics* (4th edn), London, Heinemann Educational Books.

RAUSCH, H. 1980, *Politische Kultur in der Bundesrepublik Deutschland*, Berlin, Colloquium Verlag.

RAUSCH, H. 1981, 'Parlamentsreform in der Bundesrepublik Deutschland. Die diskussion im Uberblick', in Oberreuter (ed), *Parlamentsreform*, Passau, Passavia Universitaets Verlag, pp. 143–57.

REDLICH, J. 1908, *The Procedure of the House of Commons: a study of its history and present form*, London, Constable.

ROBINSON, A. 1978, *Parliament and Public Spending: the expenditure committee of the House of Commons*, London, Heinemann Educational Books.

ROBINSON, A. 1981, 'The House of Commons and public expenditure', in S.A. WALKLAND and M. RYLE (eds), *The Commons Today*, Glasgow, Fontana, pp. 154–74.

ROSE, R. 1979, 'Ungovernability: is there fire behind the smoke?', *Political Studies*, vol. 27, pp. 351–70.

ROSE, R. 1980, *Do Parties Make a Difference?*, London, Macmillan.

ROSE, R. 1982, *Understanding the United Kingdom: The territorial dimension in government*, Harlow, Longman.

RUSH, M. 1974a, 'The development of the committee system in the Canadian House of Commons: diagnosis and revitalisation', *The Parliamentarian*, vol. 55, pp. 88–94.

RUSH, M. 1974b, 'The development of the committee system in the Canadian House of Commons: reassessment and reform', *The Parliamentarian*, vol. 55, pp. 149–58.

RUSH, M. 1979, 'Committees in the Canadian House of Commons', in J.D. LEES and M. SHAW (eds), *Committees in Legislatures*, Durham, N.C., Duke University Press, pp. 191–241.

RUSH, M. 1982, 'Parliamentary committees and parliamentary government: the British and Canadian experience', *Journal of Commonwealth and Comparative Politics*, vol. 20, pp. 138–54.

RUSH, M. and SHAW, M. 1974, *The House of Commons: Services and Facilities*, London, George Allen & Unwin.

SANKEY, LORD. 1930, Edwards and others v. the Attorney General for Canada, *A.C. 124 (PC)*, Ottawa.

SCHAEFER, F. 1975, *Der Bundestag* (2nd edn), Opladen, Westdeutscher Verlag.

SCHMITTER, P. and LEHMBRUCH, G. 1979, *Trends Towards Corporatist Intermediation*, London, Sage.

SCHEUTTEMEYER, S. 1978, 'Funktionsverluste des Bundestages durch die europaelsche integration?', *Zeitschrift fuer Parlamentsfragen*, Year 9.

SCHWARZ, J.E. 1980, 'Exploring a new role in policy-making: the British House of Commons in the 1970s', *American Political Science Review*, vol. 74, pp. 23–37.

SCOTTISH CONSTITUTIONAL COMMITTEE 1970, *Scotland's Government*, Edinburgh, Conservative Political Centre.

SEDGEMORE, B. 1980, *The Secret Constitution*, London, Hodder & Stoughton.

SHANKS, M. 1961, *The Stagnant Society*, Harmondsworth, Penguin Books.

SHAW, M. 1981, 'Congress in the 1970s: a decade of reform', *Parliamentary Affairs*, vol. 34, pp. 272–90.

SHONFIELD, A. 1965, *Modern Capitalism*, Oxford, OUP.

SHORT, J. 1982, 'Public expenditure in the English regions', in B. HOGWOOD and M. KEATING (eds), *Regional Government in England*, Oxford, OUP, pp. 191–216.

SOCIAL DEMOCRATIC PARTY 1982, *Decentralising Government*, London, Decentralisation of Government Policy Group.

SOCIETY OF CONSERVATIVE LAWYERS 1978, *Report by the Constitutional Reform Committee*, London, Macmillan.

SMITH, G. 1979, *Democracy in West Germany*, London, Heinemann Educational Books.

SMITH, T. 1979, *The Politics of the Corporate Economy*, London, Martin Robertson.

STATEMENTS TO ANNUAL CONFERENCE BY THE NATIONAL EXECUTIVE COMMITTEE 1978, London, Labour Party.

STEFFANI, W. 1973, 'Parlamentarische demokratie zur problematik von effizienz, transparenz und partizipation' in W. STEFFANI (ed), *Parlamentarismus Ohne Transparenz* (2nd edn), Kritik Bd. 3, Opladen, Westdeutscher Verlag.

STEWART, J.B. 1977, *The Canadian House of Commons*, Montreal, McGill-Queen's University Press.

THAYSEN, U. 1972, *Parlamentsreform in Theorie und Praxis*, Opladen, Westdeutscher Verlag.

THAYSEN, U. 1976, *Parlamentarisches Regierungssystem in der Bundesrepublik Deutschland*, Opladen, Westdeutscher Verlag.

THERBORN, G. 1977, 'The role of capital and the rise of democracy', *New Left Review*, vol. 103, pp. 3–41.

THOLFSEN, T.R. 1973, 'The transition to democracy in victorian England', in P. STANSKY (ed), *The Victorian Revolution: government and society in Victoria's Britain*, New York, New Viewpoints, pp. 169–198.

THOMAS, G. 1982, 'The first Hansard society lecture: the changing face of parliamentary democracy', *Parliamentary Affairs*, vol. 35, pp. 348–355.

THOMPSON, E.P. 1968, *The Making of the Engish Working Class* (rev. edn), Harmondsworth, Penguin Books.

TREASURY 1980, *Needs Assessment Study*, London, HMSO.

URRY, J. 1981, *The Anatomy of Capitalist Societies: The Economy, Civil Society and the State*, London, Macmillan.

WALKLAND, S.A. 1963, 'A liberal comment on recent proposals for parliamentary reform', *Parliamentary Affairs*, vol. 16, pp. 338–41.

WALKLAND, S.A. 1968, *The Legislative Process in Great Britain*, London, George Allen & Unwin.

WALKLAND, S.A. 1979a, *The House of Commons in the 20th Century*, Oxford, Clarendon Press, OUP.

WALKLAND, S.A. 1979b, 'Committees in the British House of Commons' in J.D. LEES and M.T. SHAW (eds), *Committees in Legislatures: a comparative analysis*, Durham, N.C., Duke University Press, pp. 242–87.

WEBB, S. and WEBB, B. 1920, *A Constitution for the Socialist Commonwealth of Great Britain*, (reprinted 1975), Cambridge, CUP.

WHEARE, K.C. 1968, *Legislatures*, Oxford, OUP.

WINKLER, J.T. 1976, 'Corporatism', *European Journal of Sociology*, vol. 18, pp. 100–136.

WOODHOUSE, C.M. 1976, 'Mutiny on the benches', *Times Literary Supplement*, 12th March.

WRIGHT, D. 1978, *Understanding Intergovernmental Relations*, London, Duxbury.

WRIGHT, D.G. 1970, *Democracy and Reform 1815–1885*, Harlow, Longman.

Index